Further Praise for *Race Experts*

"After a talk I once gave suggesting new practical paths that the Civil Rights movement might take, a black student told me disappointedly that she had expected that I would lend her guidance in 'forming an identity.' *Race Experts* crisply uncovers the source of this student's expectation. Elisabeth Lasch-Quinn deftly shows how the original Civil Rights leaders' quest for concrete community uplift has been hijacked by attempts to police and cleanse the thought processes of individuals. Anyone seeking truly to understand the theatrics of Jesse Jackson, the black-white score gap in education, the new career of 'diversity counselor,' the rise and fall of the Black Panthers, or many other often perplexing aspects of America's racial landscape cannot afford to let this book pass them by."

—JOHN MCWHORTER, AUTHOR OF *LOSING THE RACE*

"Richly textured and thoroughly readable, *Race Experts* boldly explores the dense thicket of contemporary racial confusions about self-identity and color consciousness. How refreshing it is to find a work so crammed with common sense on a topic that too often has prompted scholarly muddle-headedness and theoretical overkill. Joining the trenchant work of Orlando Patterson and Daryl Scott, *Race Experts* should draw wide acclaim."

—BERTRAM WYATT-BROWN, AUTHOR OF *THE SHAPING OF SOUTHERN CULTURE*

"In this insightful and troubling book, Lasch-Quinn explores the subtle and not so subtle ways in which the reification of race is perpetuated, despite the absence of biological evidence for the existence of race itself and even in the name of fighting racism."

—DAVID NOBLE, AUTHOR OF *AMERICA BY DESIGN*

"*Race Experts* is an important book, which should be read by every corporate leader, every educator, and every parent. Lasch-Quinn explains carefully and quietly how the idealistic goals of the civil rights movement have been displaced by misguided 'therapies' that promote racial divisiveness and narcissism, which harm all of us."

—DIANE RAVITCH

ALSO BY ELISABETH LASCH-QUINN

Black Neighbors: Race and the Limits of Reform in the American Settlement House Movement, 1890–1945

How Racial Etiquette,
Sensitivity Training, and
New Age Therapy Hijacked the
Civil Rights Revolution

ELISABETH LASCH-QUINN

W · W · NORTON & COMPANY
NEW YORK · LONDON

Copyright © 2001 Elisabeth Lasch-Quinn

Since this page cannot legibly accommodate all the copyright notices, pages 255–56 constitute an extension of the copyright page.

For information about permission to reproduce selections from this book, write to Permissions, W.W. Norton & Company, Inc., 500 Fifth Avenue, New York, NY 10110

The text of this book is composed in Perpetua, with the display set in Orator
Desktop composition by Gina Webster
Manufacturing by The Maple-Vail Book Manufacturing Group

Book design by Rubina Yeh
Library of Congress Cataloging-in-Publication Data

Lasch-Quinn, Elisabeth.
Race experts : how racial etiquette, sensitivity training, and new age therapy hijacked the civil rights revolution / Elisabeth Lasch-Quinn
p.   cm.
Includes bibliographical references and index.
ISBN 0-393-04873-X
1. African Americans—Civil rights—History—20th century. 2. Civil rights movements—United States—History—20th century. 3. Multiculturalism—United States. 4. Diversity in the workplace—United States. 5. Multicultural education—United States. 6. Cross-cultural counseling—United States. 7. Interpersonal relations—United States. 8. Etiquette—United States. 9. United States—Race relations. 10. United States—Race relations—Psychological aspects. I. Title.

E185.615.L292001
305.8'00973—dc21   2001030913

W.W. Norton & Company, Inc.
500 Fifth Avenue, New York, N.Y. 10110
www.wwnorton.com

W.W. Norton & Company Ltd.
Castle House, 75/76 Wells Street, London W1T 3QT

1   2   3   4   5   6   7   8   9   0

FOR RAY

"The face of all the world is changed, I think,
Since first I heard the footsteps of thy soul."

—Elizabeth Barrett Browning,
Sonnets from the Portuguese

CONTENTS

ACKNOWLEDGMENTS

I am profoundly grateful to all those who showed their interest and support as I wrote this book.

Grants from the Schlesinger Library at Radcliffe College, the Appleby-Mosher Fund at Syracuse University, and the Rockefeller Archives Center, and yearlong fellowships at the Whitney Humanities Center at Yale University and the Woodrow Wilson International Center for Scholars in Washington, D.C., helped tremendously. The Maxwell School at Syracuse University provided moral and material support. Yeshayah Goldfarb and James Eichsteadt supplied extraordinary research assistance, and I was blessed with a superb typist, Fran Bockus. Parts of this book appeared in *Salmagundi,* the *New Republic,* and the *Journal of Social History,* which allowed me to reprint them in changed form here. I am grateful to Robert and Peggy Boyers, Leon Wieseltier, Peter N. Stearns, and to the editors at Norton, for their heartening interest in my work, as well as to Joyce Seltzer, Lewis Bateman, and Stephen Wrinn. Bruce Laurie and Jean Bethke Elshtain gave generous support. Phillip Richards, Rochelle Gurstein, James Eichsteadt, Jeannette Hopkins, Nell Lasch, and Ray Lasch-Quinn read the manuscript in its entirety and their responses were invaluable.

As always, special gratitude goes to close friends and family members, especially my mother and the memory of my father.

My two daughters, Isabel and Honoré, have given my work new meaning. I write for them—out of my dreams for them. The ways my husband, Ray Lasch-

Quinn, helped bring this book to fruition are too many to name. It is the joy of our daily existence that inspires me to write at all. For this, I am grateful beyond measure.

"Something has gone terribly wrong with the way we view and talk about 'race' in America," wrote the Harvard sociologist Orlando Patterson in his 1997 book, *The Ordeal of Integration*. "For the truth is that we no longer make sense on the subject of 'race.' We have talked ourselves into a hole full of rhetorical quicksand. Our attempts to clarify merely confound, and language itself has become a trap." The reason for this confusion, Patterson said, is that "so much 'race' speech has become ritualized and rhetorical." [1]

Turning to the period from the 1960s to the present, this book traces the origins and emergence of a new lens through which Americans increasingly came to see racial matters. Surprisingly, it turns out that our new rituals and rhetoric about race cannot be understood apart from the culture of therapy. The therapeutic sensibility, which reinterprets all of social and political life in terms of its relevance for individual "growth," emotional well-being, and gratification, has become deeply implicated in the way we view race. In order to extricate our best hopes from the confusion that has grown up around them like choking weeds, we need to understand this historical development.

The overlapping of the wane of the civil rights movement and the psychotherapy boom represented a fateful, and more than coincidental, conjunction. Many attempts have been made to explain just what happened to the ideals, direction, and mass coalition of the early civil rights movement, which tore down barriers to full citizenship for blacks and promised to revitalize American democracy in the process. Some blame the eclipse of the earlier interracial vision by black power militancy; others fault government repression of the radical activists, the intransigence of southern bigotry, liberal stonewalling, or the later rolling back of governmental support for civil rights in the Reagan years. While all of these factors played a role, the convergence of the therapeutic crusade and the shift in the 1960s from civil rights universalism to the black identity movement, however, offers a different explanation. The civil rights movement rested on such a powerful set of moral and political premises that it managed to succeed to an astounding degree despite these obstacles. It brought an entire way of life—racial segregation and oppression—to an end, together with the legal apparatus that legitimated it. But the movement's run-in with the therapeutic sensibility helped prevent it from achieving the most ambitious of its ends: a democratic nation able to transcend racial and other cleavages; a revived civic culture; and a truly humane social order.

Out of the maelstrom of the 1960s rose an army of race experts whose ministrations unintentionally helped prolong old racial tensions and foster new misunderstandings and anxieties. The interpretations of our racial situation offered by these experts stand in the way of our adjustment to an integrated America. Understandably enlivened by the real revolution that civil rights brought to this country, and by the implications of that revolution for a radical reconstruction of social and political life, self-proclaimed experts sought to continue the revolution to its logical conclusion. Persuaded by 1960s rhetoric and social science theorizing, they believed that the new frontier of revolution was the mind, particularly individuals' "attitudes." Certain of their view that the revolution had yet to be carried out, they underestimated the extent to which the civil rights movement had culminated in an altogether new commitment to egalitarianism. Rather than moving efforts to fulfill the possibilities of a truly integrated, democratic nation to a new level, this commitment itself came under scrutiny and suspicion. Convinced of the entrenched bigotry of middle America and of their role in its exposure and enlightenment, experts carved out niches for themselves in established fields, like teaching, social work, and psychiatry, and created altogether new professional roles, such as those of interracial etiquette advisers and diversity trainers. Those who aimed their attention at whites sought to combat racial oppression by rooting out the benighted mental habits of racism, as manifested in stereotypes and incorrect behavior. Those who aimed their attention at blacks sought to combat so-called internalized oppression by rooting out the benighted mental habits of racial inferiority, as manifested in low self-esteem and identification with mainstream, "white" norms.

The race experts moved in to fill a void created by the collapse of the civil rights coalition and the loss of the clarity of the early movement, capitalizing on a long-term trend in American culture toward reliance on experts for guidance in all aspects of public and personal life. Social engineers turned to sensitivity training, an approach toward changing individual attitudes through small-group activity. Sensitivity training's pioneers thought the training group, or T-group, as it was nicknamed, was a technique that could allow for a conscious confrontation of racial attitudes in order to transcend them. Initially posing as a scientific innovation under the rubric of the profession of human relations, a branch of social psychiatry, the sensitivity training workshop later transformed into the encounter group, the embodiment of the human potential movement.

The epitome of the self-obsession and self-referentialism of what Tom Wolfe called the Me Decade, sensitivity training's main innovation was "feedback": the instantaneous, radically honest verbalization of one's criticism or appreciation of others in the group. The encounter group, also a product of the 1950s and 1960s cultural offensive against formality, convention, and emotional repression, was more than a workshop; it was a way of being in the world that would supposedly lead to peak experiences, heightened group awareness through total emotional disclosure, and "transcendence" of the mundane, numbing world. Although the encounter group vogue waned by the 1980s, the cult of personal growth persisted, and the encounter mode came to pervade mainstream American life. Now it stands as the dominant demeanor of American social life and even cultural expression, continually pushing matters best left private into the public arena, influencing the terms and tenor of our collective life and culture, and ironically edging out the kind of open and disinterested discussion we need on issues of genuine public concern. Despite its ostensible commitment to baring all emotion and thought, the encounter mode has its own rituals and forms that actually constrain certain kinds of expression, perhaps the kinds we as a public need the most.

The great agony is that the civil rights movement offered a genuine alternative to the stultifying and hypocritical social world that the 1960s counterculture rightly questioned. The civil rights movement reminded Americans of their commitment to true egalitarianism, posited a universal standard of conduct, and placed in the forefront of public interest the quality of democratic civic life. It rested on historical truths about America's pluralism and its racial crimes. It rested on moral truths about harmony and justice.

The civil rights movement did bring a revolution to American life, but the forces of reaction—though often striking a liberal or radical pose—gave a new lease on life to race-conscious behavior not entirely unlike the double racial standard that ruled under white supremacy. Racial identity theory, oppression pedagogy, interracial etiquette, ethnotherapy—these are only a few examples of the new ministrations of the self-appointed liberation experts. That we have allowed the civil rights revolution to be hijacked by these social engineers is one of our best-kept secrets and one of our greatest tragedies. The issue of affirmative action occasioned much debate throughout the 1990s, as many liberals and conservatives treated the issue of race as though it were some kind of political football, paying no attention to the real nuances and concerns on either side of the issue. Meanwhile, nearly unnoticed, a whole army of diversity experts has penetrated mainstream America equipped with half-baked, contradictory, quasi-scientific pseudo-truths that promise to liberate whites from their alleged racism and blacks from their assumed bondage of low self-esteem.

The triumph of the race experts in many ways embodies the "harangue-flagellation ritual" writ large. A routine of black assertion and white submission came to the fore in the mid-1960s, when it was briefly attacked for its disingenuousness and its departure from civil rights universalism. This ritual cast blacks in the role of repressed, angry victims and whites in the role of oppressors who need to expiate their guilt. Strikingly familiar to present-day Americans, it is one ritual by which racial issues often get raised and explored. It is also one reason racial issues often stay unresolved. And it is a ritual played out and renewed through the mushrooming diversity training programs in workplaces, educational institutions, counseling rooms, and numerous other social arenas.

Guided by the imperatives of this ritual, race experts posit a world of their making. Despite all the evidence that suggests that American racial attitudes have undergone a genuine "sea change," in Patterson's phrase, these experts are deeply invested in programs and careers dedicated to the social engineering of attitudes. If the multicultural educators, counselors, trainers, and consultants allowed themselves to believe the newspapers and polls, they would have only the attitudes of a few die-hard bigots to engineer. This is not to trivialize or downplay the appearance of such attitudes when they do surface, but to suggest that the structures and mentality of white supremacy—those of mainstream America under slavery and segregation—are no longer the primary problem we face regarding race. Focusing on the engineering of all whites' attitudes distracts us from the tasks of vigilance against expressions of ethnic chauvinism and bigotry from any person or group, attention to the concrete realities of inequality still in need of redress, development of a more updated perspective on our new complexities and challenges concerning race, and concentration on our other vital common concerns. The world of the diversity engineers is a world in which virulent white racism and white supremacist attitudes still reign unchallenged, a world of victims and victimizers, a world in perpetual recovery, a world of endless slights. Here racist crimes and social faux pas are one and the same—all inspired by a monolithic, unabated white racial hatred. All whites must confess to their inherent racism, or they are, in the words of the recovery movement, "in denial."

The dominance of the therapeutic mentality has allowed New Age therapies that once rightly existed on the fringe of society to insinuate themselves into the mainstream. Far-fetched notions about the capacity of self-obsessed wallowing in emotional outpouring to heal not only the individual but all the ills of the world are incorporated into the diversity training programs to which our co-workers, children, and teachers are exposed. These approaches reinvoke the old guilty white and angry black roles that narrow emotional expression rather than broadening it as promised. And these approaches pose as a challenge to the status quo but end up guaranteeing that the moment of emotional catharsis will never end.

The popularization and dissemination in culture of the therapeutic sensibility is not to be confused with the valiant efforts of those counselors in many walks of life today who assist individuals in their times of trouble or with the real insight that can be gained from psychological interpretations of culture. Nor should the race experts examined in this book be mistaken for those intellectuals, journalists, religious figures, and others who devote their lives to serious study of public issues and add real wisdom to our common storehouse.

The race experts and these thinkers are quite distinct. The former group is notable for its tendency to simplify and codify matters concerning race beyond all correspondence with the nuances of experience and perspective, while the latter group is known for its insistence that complexities and differences of opinion cannot fit the strictures of the received orthodoxies the former promotes. The former group takes as its starting point that correct attitudes on race are self-evident able injustice, the basis for claiming legitimate redress recedes. The therapeutic sensibility works against our making this vital distinction, instead leaving us mired in a generalized sense of complaint and outrage that never seems to subside.

The experts who steer the movement toward "cultural reeducation" seem oblivious to the totalitarian connotations of the phrase. If anything, their attempts at wholesale manipulation of feeling and their tendency to find racism in every action and phrase add to our difficulties. Hypersensitivity makes for thinner and thinner skins. In the hands of the diversity trainers, it makes us sensitive to all the wrong things at all the wrong times. Without a doubt, democratic social life requires the legitimate authority of an etiquette that should not have to be enforced by law but that is crucial to shoring up laws against discrimination and injustice. Sensitivity itself is an inadequate and cynical substitution for civility and democracy—both of which presuppose some form of equal treatment and universal standard of conduct. Anything less gives racial thinking a new lease on life.

This book joins other efforts to begin to understand how we got into this "quicksand." Perhaps in looking at whence we came, we will get another chance to find our way out. One thing is for sure: the experts are not going to help us.

and all that is needed is the right technique for instilling them in the minds of the populace, which it assumes to be universally ill informed and backward looking. Members of the latter group, in their role as informed citizens, can provide a powerful counterweight to the force of professional expertise gone awry.

The 1990s saw a kind of renaissance in the writing about race and brought to the fore a number of bold and fresh perspectives. Compelling arguments were made for a reconsideration of where we are on race now that a generation has passed since the civil rights movement. On the one hand, we can celebrate the incredible advances in citizenship rights, the expansion of the black middle class, and remarkable achievements in many realms. On the other hand, as th economist Glenn Loury reminds us, our struggle against remainir inequities is by no means complete.[2] Problems persist, ranging fro racial profiling and housing discrimination to differential rates wages, unemployment, infant mortality, and life expectancy. But Loury and others suggest, a full acknowledgment of the problems still plague us regarding race must go further and explore the racial differences continue to be inscribed in American life.

Sailing against political winds, a small number of observers warn us about new difficulties to be overcome, from what Pat and others argue is a self-defeating, even oppositional outlook some African Americans to a kind of white liberal condescensi racial thinking that the journalist Jim Sleeper asserts is similar aging to the cause of an integrated democracy. Across the spectrum, writers argue for a recovery of our moral bearings ing a sense of individual responsibility, obligation, and sacrifi greater good. Disagreeing on many matters, they insist that a more careful accounting of what problems we have over what problems remain.[3]

Our rituals and rhetoric erect serious roadblocks in the accomplishing this crucial task. When we lose our abilit when we are crying wolf and when our cries are based on

RACE EXPERTS

CHAPTER ONE

The New Racial Etiquette:
The Ritual of Racial Reprimand

In *The Content of Our Character,* Shelby Steele describes what he calls a new "public choreography of black and white" under integration. He recalls a dinner party on a "warm, windless California evening," where a racially mixed group mellowed out over a pleasant meal, drinks, and trusting self-disclosure. Then a jarring note rang out. A black engineer turned the conversation to the issue of race with "accusation in his voice." He spoke of his irritation that his daughter was only one of three black children at her school: "I didn't realize my ambition to get ahead would pull me into a world where my daughter would lose touch with her blackness." The effect of this assertion was stunned silence, but the man persisted in his truculent demeanor. Awkward and at a loss for what to say, the guests soon left. This is Steele's autopsy of the party: "death induced by an abrupt and lethal injection of the American race issue."[1]

Steele interprets this scene as a reenactment of the "harangue-flagellation" ritual well known at the end of the 1960s and early 1970s, when the civil rights movement had shifted to the more militant notions of black power and black identity. He forsakes and chastises such behavior now—despite occasionally getting a faint "itch" for it—but at the time he, too, enjoyed the "cheap thrills" to be gained from intentionally provocative behavior or incendiary talk about race, particularly in interracial settings. In those days, "it was such great fun to pinion some professor or housewife, or, best of all, a large group of remorseful whites, with the knowledge of both their racism and their denial of it."[2]

In Steele's account, such behavior was simply a means of pulling rank—"a power play"—by inducing white guilt. But there is nothing simple about it today. It has instead become part of a larger and even more troublesome attitude that Steele associates with the insecurities and the crises of confidence in the black middle class's adaptation to integration. In recent decades, racial anxiety has been transformed into an unanxious racialism, as many blacks seek a way of holding on to race rather than risk being judged by universal measures of character or achievement.[3]

Whether or not one agrees with Steele's explanation, it would be difficult for a conscientious observer of contemporary American culture to deny that the "harangue-flagellation" ritual and other such scripts have become "part of the texture of integration."[4] To be sure, we can also laugh at such scenes, as popular culture makes abundantly clear, and the premature death of a mellow night of California self-disclosure may not be such a bad thing. Yet not all the rituals of race under integration are so benign. Nor are the consequences of those rituals insignificant. They can seep into our thinking and set the terms in which an event or behavior is understood. They influence everything from how the problems of the black family can be discussed to the images of black men that appear in the media. These rituals affect, and sometimes severely compromise the effectiveness of, movements to improve race relations and living conditions for African Americans and others.

Indeed, an exploration of racial rituals broadly conceived—our unwritten expectations, our taboos, our notions of proper etiquette—helps to pinpoint the ways in which we have failed thus far in some of the most important tests of integration. In arenas like sports, entertainment, and the military, there is often much to suggest that we are serious about accepting and embracing the racially mixed nature of the American citizenry. In places like counties, neighbor-hoods, and schools, however, we often see the legacy of our problems in continued racial separation. If the commitment to integration and equality is to triumph permanently over the inherited mental and spa-tial structures that keep us apart, we must reconsider the terms on which our integrated social life rests to be certain we are creating a foundation sturdy enough to support long-lasting change.

BLACK ASSERTION, WHITE SUBMISSION

Black assertiveness or expressiveness and white submission, restraint, or acquiescence have been honed into styles of self-presentation so familiar in American life under integration that the mere reference to this dynam-ic is guaranteed to produce at bare minimum a tremor of recognition, if not outright hilarity. One of the most memorable scenes in any 1990s American film, not just those involving race, was the "show me the money" scene in the film *Jerry Maguire*. In this scene, a black football star, played by Cuba Gooding Jr., harangues his white sports agent, played by today's highest-paid Hollywood actor, Tom Cruise, and Cruise's charac-ter responds with total submission. The scene gives a perfect—if extreme—illustration of the harangue-flagellation ritual that has become a familiar aspect of the cultural landscape of integrated America.

Before the scene opens, Cruise's character, Jerry Maguire, under-goes a late-night epiphany about his profession, deciding that he has lost touch with the real essence of sports—the love of the game—in his pursuit of the largest sums of money he can command for his clients. In a frenzy of inspiration, he types up a memo and deposits copies in the mailboxes of all of his co-workers, who don false, but temporary, expressions of admiration for his virtue. Soon afterward, the young upstart company boss, whom Maguire initially trained, takes him out to lunch and fires him on the spot. Maguire storms out of the restaurant and rushes back to his office to call each of his clients.

He aims to win as many clients away from the company as possible so that he can go into business for himself. While he talks to his clients, viewers see Maguire's boss talking on the phone with the same people, succeeding in nearly every case to keep them with the company.[5]

One of Maguire's clients, though, does not hang up on him. This is the football star, Rod Tidwell, played by Cuba Gooding. What ensues is a highly entertaining, and now renowned, scene in which Tidwell keeps Maguire on the phone during the pivotal period in which Maguire loses valuable clients each minute he fails to answer their calls. Tidwell slows down the intense tempo of the film and makes Maguire (and us) concentrate solely on him and his family's situation. He makes Maguire jump through hoop after hoop with only a remote possibility that he will remain Maguire's client. The hoops get more and more absurd, until Tidwell has Maguire repeating after him his family's motto, "Show me the money!" Starting off quietly, Maguire repeats the phrase until he is shouting at the top of his lungs. Completely visible in his glassed-in office, and now audible, Maguire's surrender to Tidwell's outrageous demands draws the attention of the entire company. As the conversation reaches a climax, with Tidwell smiling and strutting around his house to loud music and Maguire yelling each phrase Tidwell wants him to, Tidwell asks, "Do you love this black man?" *"I love the black man!"* shouts Maguire. "I *love* black people!" says Tidwell. *"I love black people!"* shouts Maguire. *"Who's your mother fucker?!"* shouts Tidwell. *"YOU'RE MY MOTHER FUCKER!!!"* shouts Maguire. *"What you gonna do, Jerry?"* asks Tidwell. *"SHOW ME THE MONEY!!!"* screams Maguire. "Congratulations, you're still my agent," Tidwell says, with a cocky grunt, cutting off the music and abruptly hanging up the phone.[6]

The resonance of scenes like these has everything to do with the rise, since the 1960s, of a new confusion about the appropriate way to behave in interracial settings and an attempt to address that confusion through an etiquette of race. Certainly this extreme assertiveness by blacks and total submission by whites is not the rule in everyday

American life. This dramatization is extreme by any measure—a hyperbolic treatment aimed at comic results. At least part of its humor has to do with the way it evokes and subverts the inhumane code of behavior under slavery and Jim Crow, white supremacy and enforced black submission. However, it also plays on the audience's awareness of a more recent interracial dynamic that emerged in some parts of the culture under integration. It is a syndrome of white liberal guilt and black self-assertion that became prominent in the mid- to late 1960s, as the civil rights coalition lost its cohesiveness and direction, and has since become a stock theme in our popular culture.

Although we can laugh at it in movies, this new interracial complex deserves serious attention. It simplifies the remaining problems we face that have to do with race, not least by perpetuating the false dichotomy of white and black in the first place. A great deal of energy has gone into the endeavor to establish what common sense should have long ago: that beyond a notion of shared genetic pools that explains general similarities within ethnic groups, race has little concrete existence, particularly in the stark sense of black and white.[7] People of mixed race, like the golf champion Tiger Woods, have made it clear that, even as a cultural construction, race often has little salience for those of mixed parentage.[8] The recent debate over whether racial categories should continue to be used in the U.S. census brought into question the future of the black-white racial distinction.

The harangue-flagellation ritual is just one of a larger set of stock roles Americans have come to expect. The journalist and Northwestern University political science professor Adolph Reed Jr. wrote in reference to Tiger Woods, for instance, that the notion that black athletes should be held to higher standards because of their obligations as spokespersons and role models was "unreasonable and unfair." Still, Steele's harangue-flagellation ritual whereby blacks ostensibly take the upper hand does seem to characterize, if not explain, the behavior of some leaders in the public eye and the public's willingness to give them a hearing. The Reverend Al Sharpton is but one example of someone who falls in line with this ritual by play-ing the race card at every opportunity.[9]

FROM RACIAL PROTOCOL TO CIVIL RIGHTS AND BACK AGAIN

The ritual portrayed so strikingly by Cruise and Gooding zeros in on the way in which Americans—faced with the sudden overthrow of the social code of segregation—failed to translate the universalism of the civil rights movement into a guide for behavior under integration. Cultural changes beyond the civil rights movement helped put in question our sense of the proper underpinnings for the treatment of other citizens (mutualism, respect, integrity, fairness, dignity, the golden rule) about which the civil rights movement was so certain. The 1960s also witnessed the counterculture's questioning of all authority and pretense, the revolt against formality and etiquette as relics of elitism, and the increasingly uncivil social relations and self-obsession of advanced consumer capitalism. In this context, the very real question of how a society with deeply differential, racialized codes of behavior would adapt to integration and equality was solved only partially and uneasily. New codes of interracial etiquette sought to reverse the old patterns of racial deference by itemizing endless numbers of new rules, an endeavor that produced unintended conse-quences for American race relations.

Attempting to address the conundrum of race under integration in significant part through etiquette, Americans became deeply mired in a set of assumptions and practices from which it was increasingly dif-ficult to extricate themselves. The new interracial etiquette gurus stepped eagerly to the fore, giving their own theories and advice, nearly always helping to undermine faith in the possibilities for a uni-versal code of behavior. They often based their ideas on the existence of separate basic black and white identities that mandated different behavior, treatment, and social roles. Even more important, they helped ensure that the civil rights movement would be reoriented away from the realm of politics, civic, and business life, where it began and where the worst inequalities remain. Casting interracial problems as issues of etiquette put a premium on superficial symbols of good intentions and good motivations as well as on style and appearance rather than on the substance of change.

There is some irony in the persistence of such themes in a society that just one generation ago underwent the civil rights revolution. That movement not only tore down the legalized caste system that relegated blacks to a separate and inferior social status and attacked informal discrimination; it also delivered a frontal assault on the entire cultural apparatus that buttressed and rationalized Jim Crow and de facto segregation with its rigidly differential treatment and protocol. Building on important precedents of earlier agitation, the movement exposed the heinous race-sex complex that undergirded the rigid southern social etiquette of white supremacy, under which a misplaced glance seemed to many whites to constitute a violation tantamount to rape, drawing swift retribution from a lynch mob. At the same time, the civil rights movement questioned the North's extralegal conceptions of turf ownership that made unwitting trespass, even by a child at play, explode into recrimination, retribution, and riot.

The civil rights era activists and later scholars made it common knowledge just how much race relations had become ritualized under the violent reign of slavery and segregation and just how brutal a stranglehold the etiquette of race managed to maintain on everyday social life. The civil rights crusade sought to confront the nation's crimes against humanity by rooting out the double standards ingrained in every aspect of daily life: separate and inferior schools and public facilities; lies and myths about black inferiority perpetuated under the banner of hard science and social science; unshakable rules for behavior that maintained a rigid social hierarchy. The totality of white victimization of blacks had expressed itself not only in economic and

7

political arrangements but also in elaborate social codes, which black parents were forced to teach their children for sheer survival. Generation after generation was thus socialized anew into the inherently unfair, dehumanizing world that was once America.[10]

It was precisely the moral objections to this way of life raised by Martin Luther King Jr. and other civil rights leaders that resonated to a vast number of Americans and ensured drastic change. King appealed constantly to universal rights and dignity as well as unity and interdependence when he called on Americans "to make real the promises of democracy." These promises were embodied, he said, in "the magnificent words of the Constitution and the Declaration of Independence," which announced that "all men, yes, black men as well as white men, would be guaranteed the unalienable rights of life, liberty and the pursuit of happiness." King's "I Have a Dream Speech" at the March on Washington in 1963 invoked the nation's "sacred obligation" to "rise up and live out the true meaning of its creed—we hold these truths to be self-evident, that all men are created equal." His legendary words made the implications of this universalism concrete, comprehensible, and compelling: "I have a dream my four little children will one day live in a nation where they will not be judged by the color of their skin but by the content of their character."[11] The unrelentingly moral logic that caused King to emphasize character, with its connotations of self-discipline and obligation to the common good, had everything to do with the movement's success in attacking the brutal hypocrisy and racial double standard of segregation.

What has not received sustained analysis is what happened to racial etiquette in the era of integration. While civil rights brought tremendous improvements in conditions for African Americans and many others, the new racial protocol that emerged in the late 1960s helped steer it off track. Although the new etiquette hardly causes all remaining problems regarding race, it constrains how these problems can be faced and reflects our larger difficulties, tensions, and uncertainties about the very foundations of our collective life.

A classic film articulated race relations in the language of the etiquette of integration and began to explore the possibilities of the emerging new model of black assertiveness and white submission. *Guess Who's Coming to Dinner,* released in 1967, depicted a young, ingenuous white woman (played by Katharine Houghton) who shocks her well-to-do but liberal parents by bringing home unannounced the man she has met and wants to marry, played by Sidney Poitier.[12]

This film explores the humor and tension inherent in the confrontation of the woman's parents (played by Spencer Tracy and Katharine Hepburn) with their own hypocritical reservations about the prospect of their precious only daughter marrying a black man. More complexity develops when the man's parents also have trouble accepting the match. The bulk of the dramatic tension results from the excruciating politeness among the characters, especially the members of the older generation. The women, endowed with a superior, almost spiritual sense of common humanity, have far less trouble accepting the interracial couple, ostensibly because of their romantic view of marriage, but one suspects the ulterior motive of wanting to keep the social event running smoothly. The fathers are concerned, on the surface in any case, with the practical difficulties the pair would inevitably encounter, as is even the fiancé. One of the lessons of the movie is that the treatment of all according to the same standard of respect should triumph over specific expectations held by a particular community.

The film stood in between the old racial etiquette of segregation and the new social demands of integration. The old etiquette is represented by all the forces aligned against the young couple, including the family's black maid, who makes it known she does not approve of people getting out of their proper places.

But there was a foreshadowing of a new etiquette. While the interracial scenes are characterized by extreme politeness, the scenes of Poitier's character alone with his fiancée show him uninhibited and flirtatious. But the best example of changing rules of deference is the speech he delivers to the parents of the young woman. In a strident tone, he informs them that, unbeknownst to his eager would-be bride, he will break off the engagement if the parents cannot promise to give unwavering support of their marriage. His reasoning is that the new couple will face so many obstacles that he is not willing to take on any "new problems." The young woman's father, played by Spencer Tracy, replies that he respects that decision, but resents its being communicated in the form of an ultimatum. Poitier's character has the last word: it is not an ultimatum, because his fiancée's parents have the power to call the whole thing off. Of course, this would crush her and perhaps sever their tie with their daughter. But the more striking message, to the viewer, is that the woman means a great deal to the young man but is not worth everything. Love can conquer most, but not all—not the prospect of continued disrespect from the white parents. In the highly palatable form of Poitier's engaging and confident masculinity, mainstream America was gently initiated into a new style of black assertion. Quietly firm in his demand for respect, Poitier's character adhered to impeccable standards of politeness and civility and even conviviality. The lesson is that there should be a single standard of good behavior all around.

The Masochistic Pleasures of Racial Liberalism

Three years later, another work humorously explored the prevailing etiquette between the races, but here the flashes of assertiveness in Poitier's character give way to a much more demonstrative black style for public interracial encounters, a style that reflected the shift in the black movement from civil rights to vocal black power militancy. Whereas *Guess Who's Coming to Dinner* questioned the superficiality of a racial liberalism still resting on the premise of social segregation, Tom Wolfe's satirical commentary *Radical Chic and Mau-mauing the Flak Catchers* pierced through the artificiality of an interracial fund-raising party thrown for the Black Panthers by the white liberal elite of New York City. *Radical Chic* ridiculed a new racial order in which interracial harmony was now purchased with abject white submission.

Unveiling the white elite's self-interested motives for supporting the black cause, Wolfe illustrates its obsession with an etiquette based on white sensitivity to the dictates of the blacks who seem to be most authentically black—the Panthers. The host and hostess, Lenny Bernstein and his wife, Felicia, prove themselves to be "geniuses" for figuring out how to solve the problem of servants for the Black Panther fund-raiser: they hired white South Americans in place of their "Negro butler and maid, Claude and Maude":

> Plenty of people have tried to think it out. They try to picture the Panthers or whoever walking in bristling with electric hair and Cuban shades and leather pieces and the rest of it, and they try to picture Claude and Maude with the black uniforms coming up and saying, "Would you care for a drink, sir?" They close their eyes and try to picture it *some way,* but there *is* no way. One simply cannot see that moment. So the current wave of Radical Chic has touched off the most desperate search for white servants.[13]

Wolfe's treatment of white liberals exposes their less than admirable motives for embracing the routine of black assertiveness and white submission. Their adherence to the new etiquette serves their own fragile egos and image consciousness. The important thing is to be correct according to their inner, wealthy, radical circle; correctness in this radical etiquette is what proves that one is authentic, genuine, the real thing. The test of authenticity ironically seems to be distance from their own circumscribed and artificial existence. Establishing authenticity thus entails a rejection of this repressed world for one without rules, the world of Norman Mailer's "White Negro," the white hipster enthralled by blacks' seeming ability to live "in the perpetual climax of the present."[14] Wolfe writes that it is "*nos-*

talgie de la boue, or romanticizing of primitive souls," which "was one
of the things that brought Radical Chic to the fore in New York Society":
"*Nostalgie de la boue* is a nineteenth-century French term that means, lit-
erally, 'nostalgia for the mud.'" The nouveaux riches, eager to distinguish themselves from the "hated 'middle class,'" either "take on the
trappings of aristocracy, such as grand architecture, servants, parterre
boxes, and high protocol," or "indulge in the gauche thrill of taking on
certain styles of the lower orders," or both.[15] Any genuine fellow feeling or egalitarianism is eclipsed by a superficial show of authenticity, a
form of total self-absorption that nevertheless hinges on certification
by others, and has its own elaborate rituals and protocol.

According to the etiquette of this new constellation of social relations, a mere gesture, such as the black power symbol—a raised fist
denoting exclusive fraternity, danger, and unyielding strength—
inspires envy among whites. Because to be black becomes a badge of
authenticity and authenticity is tied with rejection of a world strait-
jacketed by interdictions, blacks' behavior gains admiration when it is
at its most self-righteously self-assertive, however outlandish, whereas whites can score points only through submission to that authentic
expressiveness. That whites need to submit—they must take their
turn—is a larger lesson reinforced by many of the prescriptions for
interracial conduct that proliferated from the 1960s on.

The 1993 film *Six Degrees of Separation* (from the Broadway play by
John Guare) depicts the rise and fall of a young black man who gains
entry into the social world of the New York white liberal elite by mas-
tering its diction and etiquette. With great aplomb, the film's main
character, Paul "Poitier" (played by Will Smith), claiming to be the son
of the actor Sidney Poitier, endears himself to the parents of several
boarding school friends, armed with inside information received in
return for sexual favors for one of their homosexual classmates. In
scenes reminiscent of *My Fair Lady* (the 1964 film based on the stage
musical, which in turn drew on Shaw's *Pygmalion*), Paul practices
articulating "bottle of beer" instead of slurring it in street dialect, and

learns customs such as sending small jars of fancy jams and jellies as a token of gratitude.[16]

These skills serve Paul well as he worms his way into the hearts of the wealthy, whose money-grubbing, status-obsessed lives and alienation from their own spoiled children readied them for the catharsis brought about by friendship with the adoring, attractive young black man. While his presence allows them to unburden themselves of all varieties of guilt and makes them feel young and radical (or at least countercultural) again, Paul positions himself to take advantage of the accoutrements of their wealth by using their apartment for sexual adventures and stealing expensive possessions.

The manner in which Paul Poitier enters the liberal elite's social world, through a mastery of its etiquette—including its racial complex—had resonance by the 1990s precisely because the ritual of white liberal guilt and overcompensation had become such a stock feature of the American cultural landscape. In the case of Six Degrees, Paul Poitier plays the race card with a finesse that disarms his rich white victims. Paul's only mistake is his failure to realize that this tack can take him only so far. Liberal guilt runs deep but exists within a framework of elite prerogative that runs deeper still. Violation of the rules of high society, an essential underpinning of which is the privacy of property, ends up destroying the very illusion of belonging that Paul manages to create through a mastery of its etiquette.

INTERRACIAL ANXIETY

A high level of anxiety over interracial etiquette understandably accompanied the prospect of full integration, which symbolized a true revolution in mainstream social arrangements. The attempt by some to assuage this anxiety through a new etiquette of race led to a frenzied attempt to lay out specific pressure points and to itemize particularly sensitive areas of social intercourse. Further nervousness followed not just gross violations of the new interdictions but at times mere mention of or allusion to them. Each one became part of a kind of social script, according to which it is now hardly even necessary to speak the full name of a particular plank in the etiquette platform. A shorthand reference or allusion will often do. Examples include the notorious phrase "these people" to refer to African Americans or any other minority group; any slip—however remote—referring to the powers or prowess of animals in conjunction with black athleticism; and any references to the shortcomings of the black family. These and others constitute a new list of taboos that was developed under integration. On the surface, ruling gauche or crude old stereotypical formulations out of polite discourse seems appropriate. How could any well-intentioned, enlightened person think otherwise? The problem has less to do with the motivations, which are for the most part good ones, than with the character and broader consequences of their prescriptions, as well as the tack taken to get them across. Minor or idiosyncratic irritants get mixed in with clear racial slurs, doing away with any sense of the importance or method of differentiating between them. This unspoken, invisible list of sensitivities that all enlightened whites are expected to master evokes the same kind of racially differentiated codes that suffused the segregation era, even while it turns them on their head.

One of the effects of this new racial etiquette is to give members of different social or ethnic groups the sense that interaction with members of other groups is automatically a minefield. When not discouraging contact altogether, this trepidation can stunt the little communication that does exist. The upshot—the stilted atmosphere of many interracial encounters—has attracted much recent attention, again often through humor.

Lore Segal's 1985 novel, *Her First American,* explores the dynamics of interracial etiquette with a keen eye for the intricacies of human personality and interactions—dynamics still apparent today. In the novel, we encounter the relationship between Ilka Weissnix, a young

Jewish refugee from Nazi Germany, and a black intellectual named Carter Bayoux, a brooding heavy drinker who is significantly older than twenty-one-year-old Ilka.

The story is set in the early 1950s, so the civil rights movement has not yet transformed American race relations. Weissnix, either disarmingly naïve or deliberately obtuse, seems to have no knowledge of the American racial taboos or the de facto social guidelines governing black-white relations. Making matters more complicated still, the novel's New York City milieu is largely that of the bohemian, intellectual subculture, which was, at least in part, integrated. This means that, while Segal is ostensibly exploring the racial dynamics under segregation, her observations capture some of the tensions that characterized American society later on. In the decades more directly preceding Segal's writing of the book, the 1960s and 1970s, integration made the norms or dynamics already encountered in the interracial radical subculture of an earlier era more mainstream. The genre thus gives her a way, whether intended or not, to explore indirectly the intricacies of the racial dynamics of integration.

Much of the book's plot involves an elaborate dance between Carter Bayoux, who is never quite sure what Ilka knows about race and what she feels about him either as a black man or as a man, and Ilka, who is nearly impossible to read on these matters and whose halting English compounds the problem. For her part, Ilka desperately seeks to find her sea legs in a social world whose racial dimension in particular is unrelentingly new to her. Even Carter's racial identity seems to elude her, despite his pronounced features, which would have been easily recognizable to most Americans.

In a key scene, Carter baits Ilka over the issue of racial identification—how members of one group refer to members of another—in a combined attempt to learn something about her and provoke any kind of reaction on the topic of race. They have just attended a wedding reception in a friend's apartment and walked through drizzling rain to a luncheonette, where they begin to converse over coffee. Carter brings up Hemingway's *The Sun Also Rises,* and Ilka gleefully cries that she has read it. Carter comments that "the Jew—rich, good-looking, a good athlete"—has "no sense of protocol," which triggers an amusing discussion of racism and racial protocol:

> "Are you anti-Semitish?" Ilka surprised herself by asking.
>
> "Of course," said Carter Bayoux. "Aren't you?"
>
> "I am a Jew," said Ilka.
>
> "Then you know more Jews you cannot stand, no? Just as I'm anti more Negroes. A matter of one's opportunity."
>
> He *is* a Negro! Ilka thought. Or does that mean he isn't . . .?
>
> "You think *I* am anti-Negroes?" Ilka marveled.
>
> "Of course. Give you a test. You're at the wedding and the skinny fellow with the nose asks you, 'Who's that out in the kitchen?' Are you going to tell him, 'It's the Negro guzzling Chivas Regal'?"
>
> "No! Of course not!" said Ilka, and thought, So he *is* a Negro.
>
> "Of course not!" Carter said. "Or would you say, 'It's the Jew in the kitchen'?"
>
> He's *Jewish*? Ilka thought. "No, I don't say that!" she said.
>
> "No," Carter said, "you don't say that. You say, 'It's that guy in the tweed jacket drinking himself into a coma.' But, say, I'm an Englishman drinking myself in a coma—you'd say, 'It's that English chap in the kitchen,' wouldn't you?"
>
> "But that is different," said Ilka.
>
> *"Yes?"* said Carter, and Ilka laughed and blushed, embarrassed and bedazzled in the full light of his brown stare on which he held her impaled.[17]

Segal's deft hand both gently mocks Carter's self-obsessed hypersensitivity by giving him the tabula rasa of the immigrant Ilka as a foil, and pierces through Ilka's claims of total ignorance as a defense against differential attitudes. While we cannot see either one as the noble victor, we can surely see the folly of the differential conduct Carter tries to expose.

Even though Segal treats this scene as emblematic of the absurdities of interracial social life, tarnished as they were by layer upon layer of misunderstanding and sensitivity, a growing body of etiquette advice increasingly sought to resolve such everyday anxieties by spelling out the proper rules for behavior. Though the etiquette guides did not always agree on specifics, they nearly always tried to confront the anxieties of interracial interactions under integration with the same overarching message that interracial encounters required a new set of social rules and the overthrow of outmoded notions of general civility. Etiquette for interracial settings needed to be unique, tailored to fit the cultural differences blacks allegedly brought to such settings. A universal code of conduct would not suffice, usually because it failed to recognize the imperatives of black expressiveness.

The New Racial Double Standard

In the aftermath of the civil rights movement, the new etiquette experts shared two assumptions: that interracial interactions demanded a special set of guidelines and that blacks and whites needed different treatment. Moreover, these advisers cast white behavior toward blacks, in particular, as beyond the ken of the average citizen and requiring special expertise. The themes of authenticity, emotional expression, and assertiveness ran through the advice literature. In 1971, for example, an actual etiquette guide entitled *How to Get Along with Black People: A Handbook for White Folks, and Some Black Folks Too,* by Sheila Rush and Chris Clark, chastened whites who, in proximity with blacks, misguidedly thought they could be part of a less circumscribed world by socializing and identifying with blacks. In a foreword by Bill Cosby, the reader encounters a scenario in which a white man has a black colleague over for dinner. The evening's development mirrors the scene of "social death" described by Shelby Steele:

> We [my wife and I] invite them [him and his wife] in and I introduce my wife, who looks very white to me now, I tell them 'I dig' and my wife says she's 'hip' but somehow, between the pre-dinner cocktails and sitting at the table, they leave. For the life of me, I cannot figure out why.[18]

The book goes on to delineate rules for whites on how to conduct themselves properly around blacks, implying that the reasons for the black couple's rejection of the white couple's hospitality was poor interracial etiquette. The book lists faux pas in conversation, such as "He's just the *nicest* person," "He would make it no matter what his color was," and (now especially familiar) "One of my closest friends when I was a child was a little colored girl."[19] These and what the authors call other "liberalisms" come under attack. As for interracial relationships, readers get the impression that these are rarely advised. If both parties find it necessary to pursue the romance, they should "discuss racial problems or incidents openly and candidly but avoid agonizing over them. A sense of humor helps." In addition,

> whites should exercise restraint in seeking to "find out about blacks." While the black partner might appreciate an interest in good food or music preferences, zealous researching into the folk ways of blacks is resented.
>
> White women in particular should be careful not to dispute, contradict, or challenge the black partner *publicly*. They [*sic*] just don't like it, especially coming from a white woman.
>
> Very few blacks, male or female, enjoy public displays of affection.[20]

Whites should also avoid black expressions, like "soul-brother," "man," "right-on," "dig," "getting it together," "tell it like it is," and "doing your own thing."[21] When deciding what to call blacks—colored, Negro,

black, or Afro-American—whites should make the decision according to an "integration index" that typecasts blacks according to their likelihood to endorse integration on the basis of their age, birthplace, skin color, and education.[22] This advice both unveiled the cool style projected by some blacks as a highly self-conscious insouciance and claimed possession of that style. Blacks could say "dig" and be authentic. Whites who adopted this language were imposters. But if whites insisted on hanging around blacks, they needed to know strict rules for keeping their impulses in line.

Cultural Etiquette, by Amoja Three-Rivers, published twenty years later, in 1991, echoed many of the sentiments of *How to Get Along with Black People* but took them to even greater extremes. In *Cultural Etiquette,* enthusiastically excerpted in *Ms.* magazine[23] later in the year it came out, a differential standard had become a guiding principle for propriety under the guise of intercultural tolerance and "healing." At times this became a kind of double standard, according to which the belittling or stereotyping of whites was acceptable, even in a tract condemning such caricaturing of blacks. The pamphlet reduces etiquette to a rigid set of rules seemingly detached from any standard of mutual respect. This separation of etiquette from such a standard creates a need for the elaboration of more and more etiquette rules.

Cultural Etiquette is an odd mixture of strict commandments and strained definitions whose aim seems to be to claim possession of emotional territory for African Americans. Attacking the stereotype of blacks as having "rhythm," the author ends up hinting that they do, not by nature exactly, but because they are more in touch with nature:

> Everyone has "natural rhythm." It is our human birthright. If you don't have perceptual or neuromuscular impairment, and yet you feel unable to perceive or respond to rhythms in any relevant, satisfying or graceful way, then perhaps you may want to examine the personal, cultural and historical paths that led to this unfortunate deficiency. Not having rhythm is not natural.[24]

Clearly, the implication is that whites are less natural, less expressive, than blacks—even if the condition is only temporary and "cultural," and theoretically can be remedied with the right instruction.

The larger message of this etiquette advice is that whites need to restrain their impulses and accept black expressions as having nothing to do with whites. Such expressions are the prerogatives of blacks, and any desire to make contact is governed by a strict set of hands-off rules.

Besides this strange possessiveness of the terrain of expression, *Cultural Etiquette* exhibits a propensity running through this etiquette literature to inflate the importance of behavior all out of proportion to common sense or reality. Touching other people's drums is forbidden, since these objects "have strong spirits." One wonders whether the author was aware of the amusing Freudian undertones here: "Never touch another person's instruments without asking permission and do not take it personally if they [*sic*] say 'no.'" It is not proper to persevere "in the hopes that the instrument's owner will eventually change her mind." "She might," if she so desires, but only "after she gets to know you better."[25] The touching of hair is also prohibited. The reader receives a definition of dreadlocks, and the information that "it is not a style" but "a cultural, spiritual and philosophical expression" or "an expression of solidarity with other African peoples." Defensive and possessive, the author chides, "Although straight-haired people can dread, it is an expression that uniquely lends itself to the hair of African people." And, just in case you were thinking about it, "No, you may not touch it, don't ask."[26]

In a chapter entitled "Just Don't Do This, OK?" Three-Rivers lists a number of interdictions. One should not "equate bad, depressing or negative things with darkness," such as a "black mood," "a dark day," "a black heart." One should neither "assume that it is o.k. to ask people of color about their racial background" nor encroach on "the personal space of a person of color or a Jewish person" if one is not already on intimate and equal terms. Perhaps most helpful is this advice:

"Please don't go around expecting you can be part of another ethnic group now because you feel you were part of that group in a former life."[27]

Like its subtitle, *A Guide for the Well-Intentioned, Cultural Etiquette*'s commandments seem geared to readers who consider themselves to be liberal and sympathetic to, or perhaps even honorary members of the group, or "wanna-bes." And some of the pieces of advice make more sense than others, such as the suggestion that, in discussing a "racist remark," a mere allusion is better than actual repetition. Of course, even this suggestion is not the universal preference of African Americans. The comedian Dick Gregory, for instance, believes one must confront and destroy such language head-on by repeating it and thus wresting it away from the racist context of its original use.[28]

The urge to draw boundaries or assert one's presence is one understandable legacy of the racial caste system extant in the United States until as recently as the mid-twentieth century, the vestiges of which are still present in some places. But basic respect for other people's sense of personal space needs eventually to transcend race or it may be seen as idiosyncratic, trivial, and one-sided. The pose struck by books like *Cultural Etiquette* to be the mouthpiece of all "people of color" lacks credibility and risks painting the whole project of racial civility as either chauvinistic or ridiculous. The decision to enforce sensitivity by endlessly elaborating racially encoded rules of etiquette also evokes those innumerable daily expectations and taboos that once buttressed segregation, which makes it an unfortunate and ultimately disastrous approach.

To "Act Colored": The Effusive Black Style

Not all advice on interracial contact aims, of course, to mitigate the pain inflicted by "well-intentioned" whites. Karla Holloway writes about behavior, particularly of blacks, in the more academic treatise *Codes of Conduct: Race, Ethics, and the Color of Our Character,* published in 1995. Just as *How to Get Along with Black People* and *Cultural Etiquette* warned whites not to mistake an effusive black style for a relaxation of social guidelines, *Codes of Conduct* chastised blacks who failed to project an uninhibited sensibility. In this line of thought, expressiveness emerges as highly self-conscious, codified, and guided by an etiquette of its own. Commenting on everything from court cases to novels and films, Holloway sets up a code of conduct by which she judges other blacks. She scolds Whoopi Goldberg for compromising her "passionate self-embrace" by carrying on an interracial romance with Ted Danson and supporting his appearance at a Friar's Club roast for her at which he appeared in black face and joked about her sexual appetites. Though Goldberg said she had approved of Danson's jokes as humor, Holloway commands, "B(l)ack talk has to be a consistent and passionate articulation."[29] Maya Angelou also comes under attack for speaking her poem "On the Pulse of the Morning" at the first presidential inauguration of Bill Clinton. Since Angelou had customarily delivered her poems with much expression and gesticulation, she disappointed many blacks, according to Holloway, for breaking a kind of "African American cultural code":[30]

> When Angelou did not step or gesture, when she did not move at all around the small space of the inaugural platform, and especially, when she did not modulate or *culturate* her voice, African Americans like me felt quite keenly the loss of those cultural codes that could have marked the moment.[31]

Similarly, Anita Hill garners disapproval for her self-control. Holloway would have preferred her to "turn it out," a term that means to unleash the anger and frustration appropriate to a demeaning situation—to "act colored."[32] Holloway quotes the feminist scholar bell hooks's assertion that, instead of integrity, Hill's behavior exemplified to many just "another example of black female stoicism in the face of sexist/racist abuse." If Hill had allowed herself to become passionate, the hearings would have been "less an assault on the psyches of black females watching," according to hooks.[33]

Holloway admits that she hesitates to endorse behavior such as "turning it out," on the grounds that it might reinforce the very stereotypes blacks have fought for so many years to counteract. When one member of her book club, the Friday Night Women, asked the others if they had ever had to turn it out, "the tenor of the night's discussion changed," she wrote, "as we alternately shared the hilarity of the moments when we just decided to go on and 'act colored' as some of us called it, and we also relived the pain of us all having had that same experience [sic]":

> In one sense, turning it out or acting colored means that we give up trying to respond to a situation as if both we and they (white people and/or men) are operating within the same codes of conduct. It can mean handing over to our adversary our version of the stereotype that motivates their disrespect to us. . . .

"Turning it out" involves losing control, unleashing anger, acting obstinate and unreasonable—all of the things unfairly constituting longstanding stereotypes of black female behavior—exactly those limited preconceptions underlying the insult that triggered "turning it out" in the first place. The result, Holloway admits, is that "no one wins." "But usually we feel better," she adds.[34]

BLACK RAGE

The notion of special prerogatives for blacks' behavior was buttressed by the more formal invective of the late twentieth century. As popularized through the etiquette guides, this invective contributed, ironically, to a narrowing of the emotional possibilities under integration. In the course of the 1960s, the range of emotional experiences made possible by the collapse of older interdictions against black self-expression was curtailed. Black assertiveness was increasingly funneled into either black rage or black self-affirmation. A new genre of quasi-confessional racial harangue, in which blacks let flow a range of emotions and admissions concerning the American racial scene helped redefine assertion as rage. This stylized genre was validated by the antiauthoritarian climate of the age, in which personal testimony enjoyed newfound respect for its emotional immediacy and, again, its supposed authenticity. The confessional harangue tended to lack logical organization, taking on the loose form associated with journal writing or even resorting to stream-of-consciousness ramblings or self-disclosure.

In *The Fire Next Time,* for instance, James Baldwin largely eschewed his usual complicated insights into the human condition for an angry stream-of-consciousness polemic against what had already, by the time he wrote it in 1963, been widely acknowledged by most Americans as the undeniable outrage of racial oppression. His tirade contained a threat that if whites did not end the evil of racism, retribution would come in the form of "the fire next time." Continued "intransigence and ignorance" by whites would lead to "a vengeance that does not really depend on, and cannot really be executed by, any person or organization, and that cannot be prevented by any police force or army: historical vengeance, a cosmic vengeance."[35] Blacks needed to exact this vengeance "at no matter what risk—eviction, imprisonment, torture, death."[36] Though the book begins with a letter from Baldwin to his nephew, he clearly intends his book as a warning to whites. He asserts that "everything white Americans think they believe in must now be reexamined" and threatens a solidified black force for revolutionary change: "What one would not like to see again is the consolidation of peoples on the basis of their color. But as long as we in the West place on color the value that we do, we make it impossible for the great unwashed to consolidate themselves according to any other principle."[37]

The Fire Next Time undoubtedly reached a white audience as well as a black one, helping it to earn rave reviews from all the major publications and become a best-seller. In an interview with the scholar William Banks, the writer Ishmael Reed saw the intentions of Baldwin's book as those of a whole genre of black writing aimed as much at whites as at blacks:

> I see some of these books that come out, and I know to whom they are directed. You can always tell when the narrator becomes an anthropologist and starts explaining black folkways in their books. . . . That's a sign. It's a tip-off because blacks know them already. Who are they writing for? I think Baldwin plays the role, a guide. He will take time out to get a footnote to explain to the white reader what's going on . . . because his audience is a white-middle class audience. There are always going to be millions of liberals who read in this country, and that's his audience. Of course, Baldwin isn't the only one who does this.[38]

Obviously, blacks' rage over racial injustice had a history as long as their systematic racial exploitation on American soil. One can hardly question its legitimacy. From Daniel Walker's openly threatening "Appeal" to Richard Wright's implicit warning in *Native Son,* published in 1945, the expression of black rage had a major role in mobilizing the armies of change. But as the civil rights movement gained momentum and achieved stunning successes in the late 1950s and early 1960s, expressions of rage gained unprecedented exposure and new meaning. Though often compelling—even justifiable—such expressions soon became a mode or style with a life of its own. While presented as a kind of authentic black voice or rising consciousness of oppression, the expressions of rage drew their significance from a real or presumed interracial audience, as Ishmael Reed's comment about Baldwin's audience suggests.

The Black Panther Eldridge Cleaver's *Soul on Ice* was one of a number of works that rested on the new legitimacy of unrestrained emotional venting. Its popularity indicated Americans' growing penchant for extremity in African American expression. The book explores, in part, the course Cleaver took from serving time in 1954 for possession of marijuana, when, in his telling, his consciousness of racial oppression was forged, to his transformation into a rapist, and then his incarceration in Folsom prison. Cleaver by no means approves of the path he took in life, but the overriding message of his book is that distorted race relations in the United States created the conditions in which he could come to view the rape of white women as "an insurrectionary act." The line between excuse and explanation is a tricky one, made even murkier in a genre whose very essence seems a combination of emotional purging and invective. His account of the political intent of his rapes ends movingly when he admits, "I was wrong. . . . I had gone astray." But Cleaver's analysis fails to explore factors other than white racism in his reprehensible behavior and thus is unable to broach the question of why most black men do not rape white women. And his recounting of his initial motivation continues to carry an implied threat:

> It delighted me that I was defying and trampling upon the white man's law, upon his system of values, and that I was defiling his women—and this point, I believe, was the most satisfying to me because I was very resentful over the historical fact of how the white man has used the black woman. I felt I was getting revenge.[39]

Cleaver quotes now infamous lines from LeRoi Jones's *Dead Lecturer,* "Rape the white girls. Rape / their fathers. Cut the mothers' throats,"[40] and proceeds,

I have lived those lines and I know that if I had not been apprehended I would have slit some white throats. There are, of course, many young blacks out there right now who are slitting white throats and raping the white girl. They are not doing this because they read LeRoi Jones' poetry, as some of his critics seem to believe. Rather, LeRoi is expressing the funky facts of life.[41]

The "funky facts of life" that led to the attitude encapsulated in LeRoi's lines are those that led Cleaver to become possessed by evil urges. The reason he took up writing, he says, was to save himself by unraveling "the snarled web" of his motivations: "I understood that what had happened to me had also happened to countless other blacks and it would happen to many, many more."[42]

Throughout the book, Cleaver expresses intense feelings for his white lawyer, Beverly Axelrod, and even sees their relationship as part of the larger crumbling of barriers between blacks and whites. "We are mere parts" of a "complex movement," he writes. "We represent historical forces and it is really these forces that are coalescing and moving toward each other." Yet, by the end of the book, Cleaver's cure for the sickness that he claims drove him to his career as a rapist is to forsake the allure of the white female as the ultimate object of beauty and desire. Instead, he will revolt against racial oppression by uniting with black women. Addressing "Queen—Mother—Daughter of Africa / . . . My Eternal Love," he casts this union as an expressly sexual one: "Let me drink from the river of your love at its source, let the lines of force of your love seize my soul by its core and heal the wound of my Castration, let my convex exile end its haunted Odyssey in your concave essence which receives that it may give."[43] The answer to past racist wrongs seems to Cleaver to be sexual union between blacks— for only through sexual union will black men and black women begin to heal the wounds of racism.

Sex, in fact, takes on a crucial role here, because only liberation from the cerebral ways of whites, according to Cleaver, can offer any escape from the chains of slavery. According to a typology he constructs to illustrate the social structures of racial discrimination, white men retain power over blacks by casting themselves as the "omnipotent Administrator" and black men as the "Supermasculine menial." While his point is that whites have used this dichotomy to their advantage by maintaining power and control in society, he ends up accepting the image of blacks as more physical. Cleaver finds the greatest hope of the 1960s to be white youths who attempted to celebrate the body as he thinks blacks do. Ultimately, expressiveness becomes an end in itself, which to Cleaver means sexual expression above all. The only better world Cleaver can envision is one in which sex takes on the role of historical healer.

Before mainstream white popular culture embraced black expressiveness in the 1950s and 1960s, particularly in the form of music or dances like the twist, America was cold and sexless, according to Cleaver. He elevates emotional expression to launch a compelling attack on the rationalization of modern life: "the increasingly mechanized, automated, cybernated environment . . . —a cold, bodiless world of wheels, smooth plastic surfaces, tubes, pushbuttons, transistors, computers, jet propulsion, rockets to the moon, atomic energy."[44] Yet, by seeing this rationalization purely as a racial matter, a legacy of racial segregation, he falls short of offering a compelling alternative. Instead, he prescribes a reunion of America's "Mind with its Body, to save its soul,"[45] which would draw on blacks' supposed affinity with nature: "It is in this connection that the blacks, personifying the Body and thereby in closer communion with their biological roots than other Americans, provide the saving link, the bridge between man's biology and man's machines."[46] His acceptance of the depiction of blacks as more sexual—he embraces Mailer's "White Negro" and attacks Baldwin's "violent repudiation" of Mailer's piece as a sign of Baldwin's "hatred of blacks"[47]—ironically works against his very effort to do away with the image of the "Supermasculine" menial black man. Using black hypersexuality as a model to be extended to the rest of society, he equates freedom from sexual and psychic repression with social equality.

> People are feverishly, and at great psychic and social expense, seeking *fundamental and irrevocable liberation*—and, what is more important, *are succeeding in escaping*—from the big white lies that compose the monolithic myth of White Supremacy/Black Inferiority, in a desperate attempt on the part of a new generation of white Americans to enter into the cosmopolitan egalitarian spirit of the twentieth century.[48]

Cleaver's treatise presented a model of black expressiveness and uninhibitedness that others would repeat throughout the century. Many later observers lacked Cleaver's passion and perception but shared a notion his writings helped put into common currency: the idea that rage, or at least unapologetic self-assertion, was the legitimate—perhaps the only legitimate—response blacks should have to the racial situation in America. These writers treated blacks' situation as the result of a monolithic, unchanging original sin that explained and justified the attenuation of rage, despite any ostensible gains for civil rights. Their works often shared other qualities of Cleaver's harangue: they attributed heightened expressiveness to blacks as a group; adopted a stream-of-consciousness mode or another form of personal disclosure; and criticized blacks who failed to adopt this model of uninhibited self-disclosure or self-expression as traitorous, self-hating, or somehow not black at all.

STYLIZED RAGE

Ralph Wiley's *Why Black People Tend to Shout: Cold Facts and Wry Views from a Black Man's World,* published in 1991, shared all of these tendencies. Wiley, however, was either too far removed from the cauldron that made Cleaver's analysis boil, too impatient, or just unable to offer any real analysis. Instead, he briefly treated each item in an erratic list of subjects. By the time he came to it, the harangue-confessional could be seen as a predictable script à la Cleaver on the black rage theme.

Wiley's treatise spews forth its venom on major events and minor idiosyncrasies with equal force, giving the very impression of uncontrolled expression that the book's main purpose is to justify. Wiley focuses on the reasons "black people tend to shout," subtly dismissing any questions about whether such a generalization is accurate in the first place. "Black people tend to shout in churches, movie theaters, and anywhere else they feel the need to shout," he says, "because when joy, pain, anger, confusion and frustration, ego and thought, mix it up, the way they do inside black people, the uproar is too big to hold inside. The feeling must be aired."[49] After establishing the unique condition of universal black expressiveness, Wiley invokes the entire legacy of racial oppression as a still-extant force, drawing an implicit comparison between the egregious wrongs of slavery and the incidents he relates throughout the book. Blacks revel in the very "luxury" of being able to express themselves openly, given all the cruelty they as a people have endured.[50]

From this opening, which calls up the worst horrors of a truly horrific day, Wiley leads us to lesser questions such as the one treated in a section called "What Black People Won't Eat." Issue after issue comes up in a way that appears random until one realizes that the book is intended as a kind of etiquette manual for whites. And scene after scene gains brief treatment but lacks any clear argument or resolution, until one realizes that Wiley's central endeavor is to list all of the matters he can which might anger blacks. His goal seems to be to make whites aware of all possible areas of sensitivity. The food passage is illustrative. Wiley jokes that a sure way to provoke a black person is to try to introduce the idea of eating something that strikes him or her as unpalatable. The imagined scenario goes like this:

"Try some of this."

"What is it?"

"Meat."

"What kind of meat?"

"Lamb, I think."

"I don't eat lamb."

"But it's good."

"I said I don't eat lamb."

"Have you ever had lamb?"

"No."

"Then how do you know you don't like it?"

"I didn't say I don't like it. I said I don't eat it. I like my dog, but I wouldn't eat her either. Got any steak?"

Further probing could result in receiving a blow, Wiley concludes. What is the moral of the story? "Never assume."[51]

In another section, reminiscent of Cleaver's dismissal of Baldwin as self-hating, Wiley attacks Julian Bond, the civil rights veteran and now NAACP chairman, for not confronting more vigorously David Duke, the Louisiana politician who was a former Ku Klux Klansman and founder of the National Association for the Advancement of White People. Sure, Julian's aim was to bring into the open Duke's racism by questioning Duke's past actions and words. But Bond fell far short of the attack Wiley thinks he himself would have made.

Wiley says he could have unmasked Duke by asking only one key question. After six sentences and four questions, Wiley finally delivers his clincher. If Duke could achieve what Wiley says is Duke's ideal society—nearly all white but with a small number of blacks to do the menial and mental labor—then, Wiley hypothetically asks Duke, "What would you do? What would you create?" "You'd have Mr. Duke there, because he is apparently short on talent," Wiley concludes, apparently assuming that the cause of racism is a lack of real creativity or ability.[52] That Bond did not pose this question, Wiley suggests, shows that he is only black "under certain lights." "Julian is black, according to the rules of the deciders" but since he did not think to ask Wiley's question, Wiley does not "know what to make of him anymore."[53]

The Same Treatment

A whole body of etiquette advice and stream-of-consciousness confessional literature thus openly encourages a double standard of heightened sensitivity for whites and uninhibited confrontation or expression for true blacks, and more academic works add their seal of approval. Such works reinforce our sense that different etiquette rules and different standards for behavior are proper and legitimate, either because of the cultural differences between blacks and whites or because of the historical treatment of blacks in this country.

This history of racial discrimination and exploitation cannot be denied, nor should it ever be. Yet not everyone, not even every etiquette adviser, accepts historical treatment of blacks as a mandate for a double standard of conduct. An otherwise rather innocuous etiquette book aimed at a black audience, *Basic Black: Home Training for Modern Times,* published in 1996, is notable for its departure from the racially tinged etiquette games discussed earlier. This book firmly advises its readers to adhere to a single, overarching standard of good conduct. Despite the unique demands of the black experience in America—and partly *because* of it—blacks need to practice what used to be called "home training." The authors Karen Grigsby Bates and Karen Elyse Hudson define "home training" as traditional African American understandings of good manners or politeness as rooted in "the education, instruction, or discipline of a person in accepted mores or values," reflecting "proper rearing" and denoting "correct breeding."[54]

Basic Black goes on to make an unyielding case for a single standard of conduct, which the authors stress has to do with more than simply arcane etiquette rules; it involves, rather, a whole posture toward social life that rests on a deep sense of civility and mutual respect. Good manners, Bates and Hudson argue, "transcend social status, race, and gender." While they manifest themselves in particular etiquette rules, they embody a larger principle of respect for others: "All major religions have a simple phrase that distills what good manners are: doing unto others as you would like others to do unto you. This Golden Rule applies to friendships, workplace relationships, romances, and family interaction—virtually all human relationships."[55]

The authors discourage particular tendencies they see as counterproductive. An example they give is the use of "chronic" excuses for lateness under the inner rationalization that one's people live according to a slower pace. Instead, it is vital to adhere to an overarching standard of respectful behavior.

> "Act your age, not your color" used to be how some folks reminded others that the world expected lesser standards of us because of our race. When we behaved poorly, we were "acting like . . ." well, *you know*. And when we behaved well, we were considered a "credit to our race." Both phrases assumed that black people were one big population, one lumpen stereotype. Good behavior, like manners, transcends race, gender, and even age. Reflecting well on oneself should be the rule of thumb.[56]

Specifically treating the issue of the "different cultures and ethnicities" that help make the United States "such a vibrant country," Bates and Hudson refuse to get caught up in elaborating a separate code of conduct for different social situations depending on their racial or ethnic composition. Acknowledging that behavior considered proper by one cultural group could be taboo in another, they nevertheless suggest that an overarching set of guidelines can negotiate such differences smoothly in the American context. When in doubt of the customs of a particular group, they state simply, "It's always a good idea to ask." For example, "Mai Lee, when we go to your sister's wedding next Saturday, how should we dress?" "Robin, do women have to have their heads covered to visit your mosque?"

Overly detailed itemizing of different etiquette rules for interracial settings betrays cynicism about the potential for and willingness of individuals from different backgrounds to learn (and want to learn) about one another in social intercourse. Bates and Hudson instead harbor a basic hopefulness that causes them to be able to say with quiet assurance, "The key . . . is to be as sensitive to another culture's traditions as we would want others to be to ours."[57] Absent is the ritual thrashing of dominant, middle-class norms—those often assumed to be specifically those of whites—everywhere apparent in the words of those involved in the ritual of white submission and black assertiveness.

These advisers are not the only ones to emphasize the need for a universal standard of respect. Social critics who argue that we are in the midst of a larger crisis of civility show that this crisis has occurred in part because we are unclear about the principles undergirding our relations with others. From the etiquette adviser and astute social commentator Judith Martin (alias Miss Manners) to the Yale law professor Stephen Carter, those who see a large-scale "rudeness crisis" as a significant part of the contemporary landscape point to etiquette as a vital part of democratic life, but insist on the need to recover our sense of the moral underpinnings of such an etiquette to help us govern social life according to the dictates of egalitarianism. The historian Rochelle Gurstein goes even further to warn us that an overemphasis on mere politeness arose in the nineteenth century as a replacement for civic virtue as the new commercialism gave priority to individual freedom over "public spiritedness." Other social critics, including the political philosopher Jean Bethke Elshtain, have linked the decline in civility to our waning sense of the collective good and the coarsening of public life that results in the absence of any distinction between private and public interests.[58] Restoration of basic civility would require recapturing a sense of collective purpose beyond individual self-interest, which in turn would entail resisting the ways that social relations have been molded according to the dictates of the economic sphere. It would also rely on a renewal of open democratic debate and deliberation, lest the imperatives of civility be corrupted for the sake of crushing dissent.

SELF-CONSCIOUS INFORMALITY: THE ECONOMIC IMPERATIVE

The new racial etiquette makes it appear that white self-control is mandated by the racial past and that black expressiveness is authentic release from that past. But the proliferation of expert advice spelling out the need for different roles for blacks and whites unveils the embrace of supposedly spontaneous, unleashed emotionalism as highly stylized, conscious, and preconceived. The received wisdom is that life has become increasingly informal as strict social hierarchies have been dismantled over the last century. But some historians of twentieth-century American emotional life have pointed out that in some ways demands on self-control have increased. The new fluidity of social life, coming with increased opportunities for social mobility and democratization movements, and new corporate work climates actually called for new kinds of emotional control. While particular traditions of self-discipline and sublimation tied to the work ethic may have eroded, new codes of behavior have arisen.

Turning to the nineteenth and twentieth centuries, the historians John Kasson and Cas Wouters build on what the sociologist Norbert Elias has revealed to be a long-term trend toward greater emotional control as the modern liberal nation-state relied on self-discipline more than outright force to maintain order.[59] The ideas of these scholars shed light on the late twentieth-century reemergence of the etiquette anxiety seen in the movies and etiquette guides cited earlier. Kasson argues that the rise of bourgeois refinement over the course of the nineteenth century resulted from urbanization, the advancement of capitalism, and heightened geographical and social mobility. These conditions caused middle-class Americans to create public identities that served their economic and social interests. Twentieth-century consumerism only heightened the degree to which individuals sought to control their emotions in order to compete in the marketplace by gaining "cultural capital" through the projection of particular images. The etiquette of refinement paralleled a new segmentation of the self, which resulted from the imperative of rehearsing theatrical parts for public consumption. The basis for any solidity of the self eroded in a climate in which facades, possessions, and other external signs of worth dominated daily life.[60]

Other scholars have similarly charted the heightening of expectations for self-control in modern life, sometimes drawing on a more explicit connection with economic motivations. In their study of the history of anger, Carol Zisowitz Stearns and Peter Stearns cite everything from social fluidity, democratization, and population growth to the rise of investment capitalism as factors in the increasingly stringent requirements for the repression of anger. But a large part of their book *Anger: The Struggle for Emotional Control in America's History* involves a discussion of the rise of the human relations programs in early twentieth-century American industries through which managers sought to deflect emotion from the job site to the personal realm, suggesting that a primary imperative for the shift in emotional style was economic. Management had a direct interest in restricting outbursts and through an onslaught of programs, such as counseling services and sensitivity training, directed employees' behavior "toward a style more suitable for corporate and service sector behavior."[61]

The sociologist Arlie Hochschild's *The Managed Heart* also emphasizes the role of the service industries in demanding so much emotional exertion from certain employees that they become alienated from their own feelings. The whole apparatus of training programs and advice intruded between their impulses and their actual expressions. Both *Anger* and *The Managed Heart* point to the twentieth-century work world's demand for emotional control. This perspective raises the question of the connection between the fascination with etiquette in the late twentieth century and the imperatives of the economic sphere. With the rise of the black middle class since the civil rights movement as well as with the globalization of the economy, businesses stood increasingly to lose from the alienation of blacks as customers and even, on occasion, as workers. Economic imperatives, of course, were tangled with legal ones, which managers could neglect in an increasingly litigious society only at their peril. The need to court those of different backgrounds with ultra-sensitive etiquette is, in some cases, directly related to the impulse to constrict emotions for the sake of better business and more controllable workplaces and market transactions. Hochschild speaks of the workplace requirement for flight attendants, for example, to suppress their genuine emotions and to force other ones to surface. *The Lucas Guide,* an organ that ranked the quality of service on airlines, delivered high praise in one case in these terms: "The atmosphere was that of a civilized party—with the passengers, in response, behaving like civilized guests."[62]

The economic utility of etiquette is declared up front in some contemporary etiquette guides, which frankly posit that failure to master the new diversity etiquette will hurt business. A 1996 guide entitled *Multicultural Manners* tells readers how they might use the book:

> If you work in marketing, for example, and are looking for ways to expand your customer base among ethnic groups, you might check the index heading of a particular group and read the listed entries to find out what would or would not be congruent with their values and customers. This might help you reach your target market more effectively.

> Because people often realize their mistakes too late, sometimes

Multicultural Manners will be consulted after the fact, to find out what went wrong. Let's say you sell real estate, and you've had difficulty in closing sales with Chinese clients. You could look under "Chinese" and discover a *"Feng Shui"* entry that would unlock the mystery and explain the reluctance of your customers to purchase certain houses or commercial properties. You would discover ancient Chinese beliefs that influence contemporary purchasing decisions. That would give you clues as to how to salvage future sales.[63]

In his attempt to make sense out of the California dinner party he describes so beautifully, Shelby Steele interprets the "harangue-flagellation ritual" as being a result of a historical shift away from the moral basis of early civil rights agitation and a by-product of the psychological tensions of racial integration. First, the civil rights movement, in his eyes, made such huge strides precisely because it sought to sever any tie between race and power. Its underlying moral principle was that "in this society, race must not be a source of advantage or disadvantage for anyone,"[64] and the movement rested on the assumption that whites had at least the capacity to act morally on this (and every other) score. The black power movement instead revived the use of race as an avenue to power, thus "affirming the very union of race and power it was born to redress."[65]

The problem with this ritualistic power play is not only that it perpetuates divisiveness and the differential codes of behavior we should be rid of by now but also that it is at root a charade—a replacement for a real change in the allotment of social authority or redistribution of wealth or power. In many ways, whites have given in to the assertions of blacks in the realm of expression because such assertions can be entertaining and cathartic, as we saw in the seductions of Cuba Gooding's rhythmic dance and calls. But this charade of expiation exacts no price. When we still face many real challenges resulting from this nation's racial crimes, this ritual represents a classic diversion. It sidetracks us from the genuine civil rights vision of democratic universalism and substitutes role reversal for egalitarianism. And whenever we allow our sights to move off our egalitarian ideal, our best hopes for a multiracial, democratic community flounder.

Only by seeing this racial drama in the context of larger cultural changes can we grasp how it presents a diversion from the key issues of our day. As we will see, the diversity etiquette all too well fits the economic imperative for smooth relations at work in the pursuit of productivity and business dealings as well as smooth relations with consumers in the pursuit of profit. This set of roles demands a level of self-control, but what is crucial is the particular type of control that is demanded. As set forth, the rules necessitate a funneling of emotion into acceptable terms of expression. While sometimes jarring and divisive, emotional expressiveness on the part of some blacks or, alternatively, obsequiousness on the part of whites does not really threaten the fundamental structures of work or society. Black expressiveness provides an outlet but not a cure, and white submission channels racial feeling but does not cause it to subside. While all societies have forms of self-control, etiquette, and sublimation, the particular contours these follow reveal a great deal about the culture involved. Social scripts can serve to contain dissent and difference, even social scripts based on difference.

Shelby Steele speaks of the "delinquent's delight" he took in provoking whites on race issues. It was part of "the adolescent impulse to sneer at convention." Although Steele managed to put this role behind him, as a culture we have not. Unlike Steele, who denies himself the transitory boost the ritual could give him when his self-esteem "ebbs" in integrated settings, a whole host of etiquette gurus support our decision to give in to our most theatrical impulses.[66]

CHAPTER TWO

Radical Chic and the Rise of a
Politics of Therapy

One of the main rationales for the notion that integration demanded a differential or racialized code of behavior came from the tenets of the therapeutic culture, which pervaded American life at the same time that the civil rights movement achieved its landmark legislation in the mid-1960s. This turned out to be a fateful coinciding of events. The premium on individual identity, emotional satisfaction and expression, and an immediate, superficial sense of well-being were the staples of the therapeutic sensibility that increasingly held Americans in thrall. Although openly disdainful of much of mainstream culture, the militant turn taken by 1960s dissent ironically helped pave the way for a triumph of a politics of therapy.

"BLACK POWER AND HONKY BAITING"

In his essay "Civil Rights Blues," the cultural critic Stanley Crouch conveyed his impression of a conference he attended in Jackson, Mississippi, marking the fifteenth anniversary of Freedom Summer. Largely because of the participation of southerners, he wrote, the conference "countered the pompously disillusioned and narcissistic constipation" of the political scene at the time. Crouch noted a certain seriousness of purpose among the southerners, who differed from "many of the shills of northern radical movements" who "seem almost always to be seeking some form of therapy, if not the romance of anarchy."[1]

Crouch found two things disconcerting about the Jackson conference: the chasm that seemed to exist between the conference, hosted by Tougaloo College, and the surrounding black community and the angry debate over the issue of whites in the civil rights movement. The community felt "ambivalent" about and even "betrayed" by the outcome of the civil rights movement, since it had given the people the political rights but not economic means to participate fully in American life. Meanwhile, the conference participants reviewed what had become a major issue of contention in the mid-1960s in the twilight of the nonviolent movement: interracial organizing. When the white civil rights lawyer Allard Lowenstein stood to speak, one woman (who was white herself) whispered to the black man sitting next to her, "Why is *he* speaking? All he knows about the movement is that he tried to destroy it!"[2]

Crouch reflected on the moment when such sentiments first came to the fore, arguing that the expulsion of whites from the movement and the breaking of alliances with other groups was "the beginning of the end . . . for most reasonable politics in the black community." He faulted black nationalists for adopting the "swagger and style" of the hero of Hollywood westerns who resorted to violence to accomplish his ends; this posturing was irrelevant to the southern civil rights movement—which Crouch thought really was revolutionary—except insofar as it sapped its spirit. The black power movement's intense preoccupation with the place of whites, as it shifted its base of operations from the South to the North, indicated how it had lost touch with those it claimed to represent as well as its allies. In Crouch's view, this shift "was one of the greatest tragedies of African-American history."[3]

Crouch's piece, perhaps because of its necessarily abbreviated length as a newspaper column, explained this tragedy primarily as a loss of valuable alliances. The breakdown of interracialism in the civil rights movement certainly brought serious tactical problems, but interracialism had its own difficulties, particularly in the realm of ideology. The historians Harold Cruse and Christopher Lasch, at the time, suggested that the inability of white New Leftists to develop an original political analysis based on American conditions debilitated the black movement, laying the groundwork for a turn to mere therapy as a replacement for real change.[4] Cruse wrote that "the Afro-American Nationalists cannot come to terms with themselves as American products, created out of American conditions and ingredients, requiring, in the final analysis, an American solution."[5]

Lasch's essay "Black Power: Cultural Nationalism as Politics" observed that, while the black power movement's great promise was its suggestion that the creation of distinctive collectivist institutions could lay the grounding for political and economic power and for "moral rehabilitation," it faltered primarily in failing to free itself of the "worst features" of the New Left: its self-destructiveness, its "romantic anarchism," its preference for rhetoric and gesture over practical politics, its distrust of the older generation, its "sense of powerlessness and despair," and its lack of "political analysis." What analysis it offered, based on a simplified version of imported revolutionary ideology, did not apply to the situation of black Americans. Lasch thought that Marxism, for instance, at least in the way the New Left drew on it, did not directly address the American experience, since blacks were not in the same situation then as white workers but instead constituted a "marginal lower class" by virtue of being largely shut out of the labor market. The left, he thought, threatened to divert the black movement's emphasis away from collective self-help to a nonexistent class-based movement for radical social change, which was a misplaced dream, not a practical plan.[6] Crouch alluded to this importation of white leftists' influence when he criticized the limited political vision of "black nationalists or thugs shaped into transparent Marxists."[7]

THE RISE OF THE THERAPEUTIC

Crouch's lament made a vital connection between the movement's increasing preoccupation with itself, particularly with the question of white participation, and its growing distance from the people it claimed to represent. In 1970, referring to the black movement, the political philosopher Michael Walzer addressed this distance in his analysis of "the obligations of activists, given the claim they commonly make: to speak or act on behalf of oppressed men and women." Regardless of whether they belong to the group they seek to help, their obligations are threefold: "Activists must pay attention to and be guided by the consciousness of the oppressed (even if they hope to change that consciousness); . . . they must not despise concrete improvements in the condition of the oppressed (even if such improvements make their own work harder); . . . [and] they must act so as to open up (or keep open) the possibilities of democratic action." Like a number of other social critics at the time, Walzer argued that the shift to revolutionary rhetoric in the black movement marked a betrayal of this ethical code. In fact, unlike the earlier movement, the new militancy failed to capture the imagination of the huge numbers of poor blacks who had courageously supported the civil rights movement, suggesting that it was indeed cut off from the "consciousness of the oppressed."[8]

While it offered a brief glimmer of hope for an alternative both to the economic and social impoverishment of the black ghetto and to limited conceptions of integrationism—hope for a fresh mixture of both traditional patterns of community strength and new intentions for full citizenship—black power's increasing focus on the issue of white participation signaled a growing preoccupation in the country with identity as an end in itself, and with a particularly therapeutic rendering of identity at that. Crouch alluded to the northern radicals' search for "some form of therapy"; Lasch called black nationalism "a radical cultural therapy for the ghetto"; Cruse criticized the "Back-to-Africa mood" of many black nationalists as "a romance of the mind and a balm for the psyche which has a bolstering effect on black self-esteem."[9]

In *The Triumph of the Therapeutic*, the sociologist Philip Rieff argued that a long-term cultural shift had changed the entire basis of modern society and personality as the therapeutic sensibility replaced religion as the dominant way of understanding the world. Faith and revelation had given way to analysis and psychotherapy as the windows to truth about the human condition, eroding any sense of moral authority external to the individual.

Rieff cast traditional culture as the inheritance of "permissions and restraints," which were expressed and understood in ideals and "distinctions between right actions and wrong." The repression of certain impulses for the sake of communal living constituted sublimation, in Freud's term, but this self-sacrifice on the part of individuals translated into cultural activity, "directing the self outward, toward those communal purposes in which alone the self can be realized and satisfied." Faith involves, in part, the internalization of moral authority that takes place as children are socialized, helping to constitute an authority over their behavior "from which they cannot detach themselves except at the terrible cost of guilt." Rieff thought the emergent therapeutic culture was an "anti-culture" based on an "ethic of release," which fostered individualism and preoccupation with the self. Falling by the wayside was the earlier belief that communal commitments provided salvation from the unbridled self and that culture provided relief from the pressure of impulses by limiting them to "fixed wants" and disciplining their expression. Whereas the religious world view erected "creedal hedges . . . around impulses of independence or autonomy from communal purpose," the therapeutic one removed all such boundaries. By Rieff's logic, the new focus on "a manipulatable sense of well-being" as an end in itself not only atomized individuals but also foreclosed fulfillment of the profound human need for meaning and common purpose.[10]

Rieff held that the early civil rights movement had the potential to challenge the emergent psychological perspective that seemed to be overtaking all realms of social life. Not only did the civil rights movement promise to change the status and conditions of life for blacks, but it had the potential to renew the entire "moral demand system in the white American culture."[11]

Because society itself had changed irrevocably, however, Rieff speculated that it was more likely that, instead of changing culture itself, blacks would adapt to the mainstream order. And because the religious and therapeutic frameworks of understanding were so completely at odds, he thought that this adaptation was probably necessary. The religious origins of the civil rights movement would need to be shed in order for blacks to be integrated into the new, secular order: "The national good demands that they be educated up to the post-religious level of the whites as quickly as possible, if further civil disorder is to be avoided." Rieff saw the new direction taken by the movement in the mid-1960s as likely to help seal the triumph of the new therapeutic sensibility.[12] Indeed, the portion of the black power movement that concentrated on image and identity shifted the locus of activity from the nation to the individual, sidestepping the most critical arena—the community. The therapeutic notion of identity called for unlimited self-expression as a goal, instead of a collective rehabilitation aimed at the formation of a morally viable community.

Like Rieff, the sociologist Richard Sennett pointed to the rise of an "ideology of intimacy" that came to govern social life. The personalizing of relations in public betokened a growing inability to distinguish between the public and the private realms and to value each for its distinctive character and demands. A meaningful public realm, with its impersonal "manners, conventions, and ritual gestures," was increasingly edged out by the new "self-absorption" of what the literary critic Lionel Trilling called the "boundaryless" self. Drawing on Trilling, Sennett stressed the vital point that, while a new premium was placed on individual "authenticity," or the "direct exposure to another of a person's own attempts to feel," the actual content and import of that expression was compromised: "The more a person concentrates on feeling genuinely, rather than on the objective content of what is felt, the more subjectivity becomes an end in itself, the less expressive he can be."[13]

Sennett, like Rieff, thought that "greater psychic absorption" was directly linked to "lessened social participation" since the more individuals laid bare their entire emotional interior under the "aegis of authenticity," the more they lost the "habits of sociability" and the code of civility that underpinned social relations in public and allowed them to express their public selves in a measured and meaningful way. In the meantime, not only did intimate life get more shallow as it was conceived increasingly in terms of fleeting emotional or psychological states, but social relations themselves, invested with misguided expectations, became more isolated, atomized, and "fratridical."[14] This elaboration of the problems with the seemingly benign notion of individual authenticity helps us make sense of aspects of the rhetoric about race in the 1960s by placing them in the context of the broader culture. The therapeutic approach to the world clearly clashed with the religious and moral grounding of the early civil rights movement.

In a letter to a friend in 1968, Virginia Durr, a southerner engaged in interracial organizing since the 1930s, mentioned that some of her fellow activists believed that the movement's new emphasis on black identity as the basis for worldwide revolution and as a mandate for violence "was psychological": it rested on the idea that blacks "had to be encouraged to let out their hatred and bitterness as a sort of catharsis before they could be cleansed."[15] A month later she wrote,

> I do get so angry and really frightened of these Northern white radicals or liberals who say "Hatred is a good catharsis"—"Let the Blacks

beat the Whites over the head for a change" and while they don't actually say they approve of sniping, they don't seem to condemn it. . . .
I think they are using the Negro movement as their own catharsis and
letting the Negroes bear the brunt of the brutality and it makes me
mad as Hell.[16]

Durr's reference to the manipulation of blacks by whites for their
own psychic relief eerily echoed the accusations that the Freedom
Summer voting rights project of four years earlier had recruited
northern white students for the sake of media attention, disregarding
the dangers they would face. Both displayed an instrumentalism that
was foreign to the doctrine of individual dignity, self-worth, and mutual respect at the core of the movement. That the stakes were so high—
at times involving imprisonment, beatings, and even death—made the
later reorientation of the movement toward separatism that much
more tragic. People like Durr considered it remarkable that many
white radicals supported black militants, even when the militants
asserted that they viewed all whites as enemies. This was a particularly disheartening phenomenon to some of those who had fought for a
generation, often at great peril, against white supremacy, racial
hatred, anti-Semitism, and enforced segregation.

Payback Time

It was only in the context of the rising black identity movement that
the issue of white participation in the black movement could gain such
salience. A ritual of exclusion became commonplace as a kind of pay-
back for blacks' exclusion from the white world during years of discrimination. Perhaps the most dramatic incident concerning white
participation in the changing civil rights movement was the decision
of the Student Nonviolent Coordinating Committee (SNCC), the
organization mainly of college student activists founded in 1960 to

battle segregation and discrimination with tactics like sit-ins and voter registration drives, to take a vote on whether whites should be expelled from the organization. At a retreat at a New York estate on December 1, 1966, tensions over the role of whites came to a head. After hours of debate, a vote was taken at two in the morning, long after many workers had given up on resolving the issue and gone to bed. The final vote was 19 in favor, 18 opposed, 24 abstentions (including the handful of whites remaining by then), with about 40 other staff members not taking part in the vote.[17] Ironically, most whites had already left the organization of their own accord. The civil rights movement's shift in focus from the rural South to northern ghettos and from nonviolent direct action to community organizing were given as reasons why whites were no longer needed to work among blacks. In addition, as Stokely Carmichael and Charles Hamilton argued in their treatise *Black Power,* many came to believe that leadership of the black movement should naturally go only to blacks.[18] Many whites accepted these terms and followed the suggestion that they fight racism in white communities or otherwise provide support but not actively participate in or lead the movement.

Certainly for some of the younger, militant, new black activists, the exclusion of whites from the movement was a way of aggressively asserting black identity—asserting control over what it meant to be black. Ironically, some black activists declared that the most damaging case against whites in the movement was that they sought blackness as a kind of therapy, and yet, many black advocates of identity assertion as a political end in itself—a vaguely defined task, at best—increasingly used therapeutic terms. Some of their critics within the black movement feared an overly personal and psychological interpretation of black power. Martin Luther King Jr., Bayard Rustin, and many NAACP leaders, for instance, thought this emphasis on identity directly threatened social and economic goals. For those who considered themselves to be the vanguard of revolutionary struggle, the stress on identity both allowed for and called for proof of authenticity.

Belonging to the middle class or refusing to adopt the new revolutionary rhetoric could cause black activists to fail the test of having a genuine black identity. Cruse wrote, "There is a purification process going on constantly within nationalist ranks, each faction vying with each other over standards of purity, blackness, and anti-whiteness or pro-African traditionalism."[19] Of course, disqualification worked most easily in the case of whites, for race alone was sufficient evidence of inadequacy for the task of revolutionizing the black condition.

One contemporary sociological study sought to capture the psychological process by which whites allegedly came to understand that they were unfit for membership in the changing black struggle. In particular, it accused whites of possessing ulterior motives for wanting to participate in the civil rights movement. The Harvard University sociologist Charles J. Levy's *Voluntary Servitude: Whites in the Negro Movement,* published in 1968, was based on his experiences as a member of a civil rights organization and as an instructor in a nearly all-black college in the South. In it he described the psychological stages through which he thought white participants in the movement progressed. Although quirky, the study helps show just how far afield of the earlier movement's focus on full citizenship and community building the discussion had run. It also illustrates the extent to which the search for identity and feeling good about individual identity through a sort of social release or therapy had become a preoccupation.

At the outset, Levy characterized his book as "an attempt to understand what happens when members of a dominant group seek membership in a dominated group; when, in addition, the admission requirements set by the dominated group are at least as insurmountable as those imposed on its members for entrance into the dominant group." Levy meant that blacks, given their historical treatment by whites, refused to trust white activists: "For trust," wrote Levy, "is perhaps the one thing that members of a dominated group can withhold."[20]

To Levy, all interactions between blacks and whites were predicated on the mistrust all blacks harbored for all whites. He thought that whites yearned desperately for the trust of blacks and that whites entering the civil rights movement sought a sense of belonging and even forgiveness, which they soon realized was unattainable. Levy laid out a scheme of four emotional stages over the course of which whites encountered blacks' deep reservoir of suspicion: contentment, indignation, awkwardness, and dismay.[21]

According to Levy, after becoming involved in a civil rights group, whites were protected by a variety of "shields" that prohibited them from grasping the full extent of blacks' mistrust. Temporary involvement in the movement, for instance, and the initial formality of social relations kept interracial interactions on a superficial level so that whites tended to mistake deference for trust and friendship. As whites and blacks began to associate more closely, however, numerous new misunderstandings developed. The deep psychological need on the part of whites to be trusted and accepted by blacks rendered them abjectly dependent upon blacks. These activists, or "movement whites," as many called them at the time, trusted blacks without reserve and assumed the feeling was mutual.[22]

Thinking they had found acceptance and identity, certain white people rejected their old identity in order to search for one with more meaning. They found the answer in "'passing' as a Negro." As the civil rights movement became widely publicized and popular in the early 1960s, particularly among youth, and "shifted from a lost to a won cause," it drew many people who felt disenchanted with the dominant culture. Their "alienation now provides a sense of belonging," Levy wrote, and "a seamless bond with the Negro, expressed through a trust relationship, still appears to the white as the most convincing proof of alienation." In order to forge this "seamless bond," whites rejected their own past and sought a new identity in "Blackness." "The rejection [of the White world] is used by the White as a basis for acceptance; he offers it to the Negro and himself as certification of his disengagement from Whiteness," Levy argued. In the less analytical terms of one white civil rights worker, "A lot of people are in the

Movement because they're alienated from White society, and Black is what's happening, and they want to identify with Black. The White community is what they're running away from—there's no sex appeal."[23]

As blacks in the movement felt more at ease around white participants, and as time eroded some of mutual reserve, however, whites reacted with indignation when they suddenly experienced a "partial recognition of the mistrust, and a total recognition of its legitimacy." They believed that such mistrust must be misguided when directed at their own case; they merely needed to prove that their own contribution to the movement was heartfelt.[24] Entering a phase characterized mainly by awkwardness, whites subsequently searched for "an exemption from Whiteness," by overworking, deferring to blacks on all matters, or focusing on the sources of their own alienation from mainstream bourgeois America.

Interracial sex, according to Levy, could be the epitome of exemption seeking. Some white women thought that "making themselves sexually available to Negroes" would earn them acceptance, but instead found themselves rejected by black women. Levy also suggested that whites who tried hardest to work through these interracial dynamics, those most committed to the movement, ended up becoming the target for blacks' accumulated anger toward racist whites.[25]

Levy argued that attempts to gain exemptions from black mistrust only backfired, breeding further suspicion, since blacks simultaneously needed to justify their own mistrust of whites by seeking evidence everywhere, especially in the motives and behavior of those whites most willing to take risks for the movement. At this point, whites realized they lacked the basic requirements for membership in the in-group, but, rather than rebelling, they acceded to blacks' right of self-determination and found they could not even disagree with blacks' judgments of them as whites. They could not defend themselves without becoming "defensive."

The motive for white involvement in civil rights then became a central preoccupation on both sides. A typical dialogue, according to Levy, proceeded as follows: a black worker asked a white worker why he or she was in the movement and received this answer: "I'm certainly not in it to help the Negro, because I'm not paternalistic. I'm in it to help me." Rather than dismissing charges of paternalism, this answer confirmed preconceptions about white self-interest, desires for "self-advancement," or beliefs in "self-divinity." And in fact, whites next turned on themselves and found their own motives unsatisfactory. They faced a "demolition of fantasies" as they realized that a true "trust relationship" with blacks was impossible. During this last stage of "dismay," whites felt shocked, rejected, and lost, and thus disengaged themselves from civil rights activism altogether. They decided that they had "been undermining the Movement."[26]

CRITICISM OF THE WHITE LIBERAL

Whether or not Levy's perceptions applied to most activists, they do capture the growing obsession with the role of whites and the employment of terms of racial identity to explain both white and black behavior in the movement. Levy's interpretation of the interracial tensions in the civil rights movement as grounded in psychological drives was part of a larger set of criticisms of white liberal behavior and attitudes. In the 1960s, liberals increasingly came under attack, as in Loren Miller's "Farewell to Liberals: A Negro View," published in the *Nation* in 1962. Miller expressed frustration with the willingness of liberals to compromise with customs and traditions that prevented blacks from achieving equality.

What is interesting is that much of the earlier criticism faulted white liberals for failing to treat blacks exactly the way they treated other whites—for failing to fulfill the imperatives of early civil rights universalism in both daily interactions and public life. The journalist

Louis Lomax, defending white participation in the civil rights movement, discussed how whites could damage the black cause by becoming "knee-jerk liberals," who ostensibly held liberal views but failed to put them into action in their own lives; they "become blinded by their liberality and thus find it impossible to say something critical about an individual who happens to be a Negro, when, indeed, something critical needs to be said."[27] In "Delusions of the White Liberal," the sociologist Kenneth Clark attacked liberals' tendency to try to dissolve the "deep feelings of guilt about Negroes" by "exaggerated warmth," "sentimentality," and "condescension." Because of the history of white oppression of blacks, whites wrongly sought a return to a psychological state of "original innocence":

> No one should expect purity of himself or others. Any genuine relationship between Negro and white must face honestly all of the ambivalence both feel for each other. Each must identify with the other without sentiment. The white must resist the tendency to attribute all virtue to the underdog; he must respond insofar as he is able with a pure kind of empathy that is raceless, that accepts and understands the frailties and anxieties and weaknesses that all men share, the common predicament of mankind.[28]

Clark and Lomax pierced through the disingenuous behavior of many liberals, exposing a kind of rhetoric of authenticity that feebly paralleled that of some black militants. Clark's embrace of "a pure kind of empathy" while attacking precisely the search for "purity"— revealed how shaky the foundation for this criticism could be. His phrasing—"genuine," "honestly," "without sentiment"—hinted at the possibility of relationships free of complexity and outside of history. He simultaneously argued compellingly that the ability to tolerate nuance, ambivalence, and weakness needed to be part of any universalistic approach. His view was symptomatic of a political climate at a crossroads between civics and therapeutics. Fixated on purity or authority, even critics of liberal condescension or overcompensation seemed unable at the time to get beyond them completely. Politics were becoming personal, and few seemed able to stop that from happening.

In 1967, the journalist Andrew Kopkind wrote in the *New Republic,* "What galls SNCC people most is the way white radicals seem to have treated SNCC as a kind of psychotherapy, as a way to work out problems of alienation and boredom and personal inadequacy." Some critics saw student activists as driven by other psychological instincts, such as those unleashed in adolescent rebellion against their parents, and argued that whites in general and not just liberals were suspect. Still others directly confronted these charges, marshaling statistics and interviews on activists' backgrounds to prove that their motivations were not personal. In *CORE and the Strategy of Non-Violence,* published in 1968, Inge Powell Bell argued that the idea that white activists turned to the movement as a rebellion against their parents was not borne out by her research into their motivations.[29] And the sociologist Alphonso Pinkney, in *The Committed: White Activists in the Civil Rights Movement,* offered the common defense that a vast difference existed between the white liberal and radical. Citing the definition of the "Genuine Liberal" in *The Authoritarian Personality* by T. W. Adorno and others as someone with "moral courage," individuality, and "the vigor of identification with the underdog," Pinkney wrote that "the white civil rights radical" was "free of racial prejudice toward Negroes." Unlike that of liberals, "their commitment is total and genuine. . . . Sometimes, although not always, their identification is so complete that they think of themselves as Negroes."[30] Writing in 1968, Pinkney insisted that whites were as welcome as ever in the civil rights movement, as long as they agreed to take supporting roles and organize white communities against racism. He dismissed the accusation that white activists were "acting out their inner psychic needs stemming from early childhood" as rooted in the American tendency to eye "those who seek to speed up the process of change . . . with suspicion."[31]

This debate over white motivations for civil rights activism illustrates the extent to which race had become tied to the psychological rehabilitation of blacks and whites alike and to the attendant waning of a sense that racial justice was a public matter of importance to every citizen. Norman Mailer's famously controversial essay "The White Negro," published in 1957, had pointed to what he considered the psychological needs behind many whites' interest in immersing themselves in the world of blacks. In his essay, subtitled "Superficial Reflections on the Hipster," Mailer portrayed the hipster as a "psychopath" who sees blacks as a model, since they have lived "on the margin between totalitarianism and democracy for two centuries." Because of the constant threat of violence, Mailer believed, a black man "could rarely afford the sophisticated inhibitions of civilization, and so he kept for his survival the art of the primitive. He lived in the enormous present, he subsisted for his Saturday night kicks, relinquishing the pleasures of the mind for the more obligatory pleasures of the body."[32]

In Mailer's account, blacks' supposed lack of inhibitions appealed to the white rebel: "Giving expression to the buried infant in himself, he can lessen the tension of those infantile desires and so free himself to remake a bit of his nervous system. Like the neurotic, he is looking for the opportunity to grow up a second time, but the psychopath knows instinctively that to express a forbidden impulse actively is far more beneficial to him than merely to confess the desire in the safety of a doctor's room."[33] Mailer continued this description of the hipster as a sort of self-analyst: "He exists for those charged situations where his senses are so alive that he can be aware actively (as the analysand is aware passively) of what his habits are, and how he can change them." The requisite therapy entailed "the divorce of man from his values, the liberation of the self from the Super-Ego of society." Blacks supposedly held the key to this self-administered therapeutic, since "psychopathy is most prevalent with the Negro" because of the self-hatred caused by prejudice. In response to racism, blacks developed the language and behavior of the hipster, a whole code of life in which truth "is no more nor less than what one feels at each instant in the perpetual climax of the present." The high point in life was to "swing": "For to swing is to communicate, is to convey the rhythms of one's own being to a lover, a friend, or an audience, and—equally necessary— be able to feel the rhythms of their response."[34]

THE IMAGE WAR

Some of the white activists interviewed by Charles Levy echoed Mailer's clichéd idealization of blacks' libidinal freedom as well as his idea that association with blacks could fulfill a need for psychological release. "A White in the Movement notes that Negroes have 'the healthiest life in the world,' whereas 'White minds are always cracking up; the hospitals are full of them. You can't get along very long without love—without your body, Freud says.' A White who was once deeply involved in the Movement, continues to see the world in terms of: 'White is rigidity; Negro is freedom,'" Levy wrote.[35]

These whites were obviously not alone in connecting blacks with hypersexuality. Eldridge Cleaver argued that the myth of exaggerated black masculinity perpetuated racism by legitimizing white fear and repression of the supposedly unrestrained instincts of blacks through segregation, institutionalization, and policing. Black men themselves, Cleaver thought, helped perpetuate the stereotype of hypermasculinity and prowess out of the very real need to establish an identity in the dehumanizing context of the violent and racially stratified American city.[36]

The myth of hypermasculinity encouraged black men to live up to their image, as conveyed by the wider culture, in order to reject the arbitrary authority of whites. By embracing this imposed definition of their very identity, however, black men participated in their own subjugation. In Cleaver's view, their show of machismo through violence ended up buttressing the portrait drawn under slavery by white slave-holders of blacks as uncivilized and unthinking brutes. This image simultaneously exaggerated black men's masculinity and denied their humanity. On the other hand, white men's monopoly on intelligence made them seem not only quintessentially human but also the best fit for powerful roles.

While rejecting the purported sexual superiority of black men, Cleaver acquiesced in the reorientation of the civil rights struggle to the realm of image. He concluded that black men, unable to determine their own self-image through regular social intercourse and development, were in the midst of an identity crisis, the only solution for which was to bring the myths out into the open. Although he was right to detect the ways in which racial myths bolstered existing social relations, his solution indicated how far away the discussion had moved from ways to address the social conditions blacks faced on account of racism. The way to thaw the frozen soul, in the end, seemed to be through personal self-analysis aimed at enhancing one's self-image.

What was most limited about this increasingly widespread view was the way in which identity, reconfigured in the end to mean self-image, became the crucial terrain of struggle. Both blacks and whites, in this new ethos, were in the midst of an identity crisis. Black self-depreciation, despair, and even self-hatred resulting from American social conditions were certainly crucial subjects, but the lack of ideas for addressing those conditions obscured the real connection between the psychological and the material and focused attention on the effect and not on the structures of racial stratification.

One of the most virulent antiwhite (but also strangely antiblack) documents in this debate referred to black liberation as a distinctly psychological enterprise. For the authors of *We Want Black Power,* a leaflet published by the Chicago office of SNCC in 1967, regaining control over "blackness" was essential for psychic stability: "We have got to begin to say and understand with complete assuredness what black is. Black is an inner pride that the white man's language hampers us from expressing. Black is being a complete fanatic, who white society considers insane." Like Mailer's psychopath, the person in touch with his or her deepest inner feelings, however wild and irrational, was judged the most vital. Yet, for these SNCC activists, being black was not enough to establish this identity; the "bourgeois Negro," who "has been force-fed the white man's propaganda . . . cannot think for himself because he is a shell of a man full of contradictions he cannot resolve. He is not to be trusted under any circumstances until he has proved himself to be 'cured'." Turning Mailer's phrase on its head, the document cast these "white Negroes" as "Uncle Toms": these traitors' "black skin is a lie and their guilt the shame of all black men. We must ostracize them and if necessary exterminate them." Whites, too, clearly had no part in the movement, for, as the document went on, "We must fill ourselves with hate for all white things."[37]

This document, to say the least, represented a complete reversal of the early interracial vision of SNCC and the social, political, and economic goals of the civil rights movement more generally. The NAACP went further and called it antiwhite propaganda: "It is a reverse Mississippi, a reverse Hitler, a reverse Ku Klux Klan. . . . It is the wicked fanaticism which has swelled our tears, broken our bodies, squeezed our hearts and taken the blood of our black and white loved ones. It shall not now poison our forward march." In some ways, though, the document is connected to certain whites' romanticization of blacks. The Conference for a New Politics in 1967, for instance, epitomized the tendency among liberals and radicals to romanticize any black voice as the authentic representation of all black people, possessing inherent legitimacy. The conference was characterized by the capitulation of whites and liberals to even the most outrageous and unfair demands of the most extreme black separatist groups in attendance. An editorial in the *Crisis* explained that "certain masochistic liberals have sought to placate the angry voices by endorsing whatever outlandish proposals they advance including hate 'whitey' slogans and archaic segregation nostrums."[38] Even Charles Hamilton, coauthor of *Black Power,* which threatened Americans with violent retaliation if they did not accept the tract's principles, called for a "black-white rapprochement" based on "mutual self-interest, not from the feelings of guilt and altruism that were evident at the National Conference of New Politics Convention in Chicago in August."[39]

Interestingly, the Black Panthers also attacked SNCC's attitude toward whites. Even though the Panthers were an all-black organization, they accepted the assistance of anyone who believed in their programs, as long as there were "no strings attached." Since the Panthers' aim was a socialist revolution, anyone willing to participate in an overthrow of the "oppressor," "simply by resisting"—not by belonging or participating—was welcome. The Panthers faulted SNCC for fearing whites, and for failing to differentiate between liberal whites and white revolutionaries who "accept our program in full." "We are the real slaves!" Huey Newton said. "Therefore we should decide what measures and what tools and what programs to use to become liberated. Many of the young white revolutionaries realize this and I see no reason not to have a coalition with them." True to the dictates of the ritual of white submission and black assertion, Newton allowed whites to participate on an inferior basis, since they lacked the authenticity of the truly oppressed, the "real slaves." Huey Newton criticized SNCC and other "cultural nationalists" for focusing on identity, as though that could bring freedom: "Culture itself will not liberate us. We're going to need some stronger stuff." Yet his own posturing and undisciplined antics betrayed an affinity for exactly the cultural politics he decried.[40]

The Panthers' critique, though compelling in some ways, indicates the way in which notions of strengthening black culture had devolved into a search for a rather shallow identity, one based on self-defensive claims of authenticity and on image; culture itself, in fact, was defined here in the narrowest possible sense as the projection of ethnic pride.[41] Newton himself failed to see the contradiction between his critical view of a politics based on a stagnant notion of identity and his own embrace of the idea that the black struggle necessitated hyperbolic images of black male potency. If the guerrilla was both the ideal man and the ideal weapon, as he argued, then the war would be fought largely on the terrain of the mass media. Thus, in translation from theory to practice, the Panthers, like the Black Muslim leader Malcolm X, became symbols of the assertion of blackness, of identity unleashed (for some whites as well as blacks), even while they deviated in some ways from the growing consensus on the importance of identity politics.

Tom Wolfe's *Radical Chic and Mau-mauing the Flak Catchers* captured in absurd detail the logical consequence of the encounter between whites' attraction to the cult of authenticity and blacks' assertions of it. The fund-raising party for the Black Panthers presented a vivid portrait of the complex of white guilt, desire for belonging, and vicarious experience of an unfettered black identity. Wolfe's satire provided unstinting insight into whites' embrace of black militance: "What a relief it was—socially—in New York—when the leadership seemed to shift from middle class to . . . funky! From A. Philip Randolph, Dr. Martin Luther King, and James Farmer . . . to Stokely, Rap, LeRoi, and Eldridge!"[42] The most riveting moment came when the white party-goers looked on with envy as a Black Panther raised his fist to a black audience member in a "fraternal gesture": "Through every white cortex rushes the flash about how the world here is divided between those who rate that acknowledgement—right on—and those who don't."[43]

The historian and journalist Cathy Tumber sees a crucial division within the black power movement itself. While some adherents "urged the seizure of power through the countervailing force of intimidation, violence, and wholesale assertion of racial pride," other, more conservative advocates conceived of black power quite differently. Tumber argues that this latter group was exemplified by the sociologist and church leader Nathan Wright Jr., who called for "a moral and historical recovery of the economic and social base of black communities."

Although he believed that the emphasis should be less on integration than on "desegregated self-development," in his words, Wright urged blacks not to lose sight of their place in and obligations to the larger community. He asked whether "the emphasis upon self-awareness among black Americans" might "defeat the dynamics of national solidarity," and warned that, while black power could bring black strength, it needed to have "strict limits" and be judged according to its ability to serve "the common good." Instead of Wright's "theocentric vision of community," Tumber writes, a version of black power that appealed "to black rage and unappeasable white guilt" gave rise to the "militant politics of racial resentment, of violent rhetoric and menacing postures" that set the terms of the "language of empowerment" that dominated identity politics after the 1960s.[44]

The racial dynamics of the civil rights movement in all its phases are too complex to unravel here. Yet what is clear is the degree to which the therapeutic culture came to dominate discussions of issues one might think exempt from categorization as questions of identity and self-expression: justice, equality, decency. The problems faced by the majority of black Americans in the 1960s went beyond the shortcomings of white liberal opinion to involve poverty, community, economic and social organization, the role of the state, and the harsh physical conditions of ghetto life. In the end, though, therapeutic notions overwhelmed the movement to address these problems, subordinating its most promising aspects to its least and sacrificing its alternative ethos to the one that was fast becoming dominant in American culture.

The increasing amount of time and energy devoted to promoting or attacking therapeutic notions of racial identity and psychological motivations sidetracked the movement, distracting it from the serious task of institutional innovation, economic reorganization, community building, and moral rehabilitation. The continuing dominance of therapeutic discourse also goes a long way toward explaining why the issue of white participation in the civil rights movement could evoke heated, protracted discussion over twenty years later. The transition to a therapeutics of race helped sap the best potential of the movement, hijacked many real prospects for change, and allowed the civil rights movement—the largest interracial mass movement in United States history and one of the country's best hopes for democratic regeneration—to falter.

CHAPTER THREE

The Encounter Group: A New
Interracial Mode for Integration

T he ritual of black expression and white submission received a boost from the realm of psychology, which had turned to the issue of race before but never with as much fervor as in the 1960s and afterward. It was during the heyday of 1960s radicalism that Frantz Fanon, who spoke of the revolutionary potential of psychiatry to liberate colonial subjects, became a household name. Fanon's idea that a necessary part of political liberation from colonial oppression was psychological freedom resonated deeply among many American radicals.[1] Oppression by the mid-1960s seemed to many to involve a state of mind as much as economic and political imbalance. To remedy inequality, it appeared logical that society would have to rid itself of archaic, benighted mental habits or, in the language of the day, "hang-ups."

Though the slogan "The personal is political" initially called attention to how personal life was affected by political arrangements, it also captured the sense that transforming American life could begin at the personal level. Much of a generation was inspired by the idea that transforming, even revolutionizing America could start at the personal level—through interpersonal behavior. However worthy the goal of improving society through individual self-betterment, the definition of self-betterment and particular ideas for bringing it about ultimately sidetracked the struggle for justice and equality. Finding one's identity became more important than the political project of attaining equality or building community. And the subsequent age would suffer the consequences of the attempt to translate revolutionary fervor into concrete changes in the realm of conduct by engineering attitudes under the auspices of democratic change.

A major expression of this fusion of therapy and radical personal politics was the human potential movement, which came of age in the 1960s and 1970s but continued to have an effect in the decades that followed. Social critics have described how this movement symbolized the trajectory of American culture as a whole. A cult of personal "growth," part of a broader ascendancy of therapeutic modes of thinking about nearly everything, spawned a new literature, new institutions, and a buoyant sense of unlimited possibility. But the link between the human potential movement and race relations has been all but ignored.

Conventional understanding has it that the human potential movement took root in the liberationist milieu of the 1960s and flowered in the 1970s. Tom Wolfe's famous essay "The Me Decade," for instance, explained the new therapies as the result of a heightened religiosity coming out of the counterculture's cult of "authentic," intense personal experience. But more obscure histories trace the origins of the sensitivity training movement further back, to the years directly following World War II. In fact, sensitivity training, the paradigmatic institution of the human potential explosion, initially arose precisely in the attempt to address interracial (as well as interreligious) tensions in the postwar era. This suggests a whole new reading of the shift from the early civil rights movement to the so-called black liberation or militant movement—as well as the counterculture. The stage was actually set for the shift to therapeutic politics years before the 1960s, and the experts were well poised to take advantage of it. Their machinations ensured that the therapeutic strain would win out.

THE BIRTH OF THE T-GROUP

Thanks to the 1960s reportage on the new California fads in inter-personal relations and exposés on the absurdities of that culture by Tom Wolfe and Christopher Lasch, the sensitivity training model—its stress on growth and awareness, its "touchy-feely" emphasis on let-ting out feelings before other people, even total strangers—came to be seen as a product of the attenuated counterculture in the late 1960s and 1970s. In fact, the social psychologist Alfred Marrow's 1969 biography of Kurt Lewin illustrates how Lewin's work as a pio-neering social psychologist in charge of MIT's Research Center for Group Dynamics in the mid-1940s played a pivotal role in the birth of the "T-group" (short for training group or sensitivity training group). Faced with the difficulty of translating "latent forces of good will in communities into overt endeavors to overcome various forms of bias," the Connecticut State Inter-Racial Commission asked Lewin for his assistance in combating racial and religious prejudice. The result was the establishment of the National Training Laboratories, a facility whose purpose was to study the ways in which people might "deal more effectively with complex human relationships and prob-lems." Its method came to be known as sensitivity or group dynamics training.[2]

Lewin had already launched an organization called the Commission on Community Interrelations for the American Jewish Congress, and the group had amassed much information about group behavior. Lewin agreed to use his organization's limited resources to conduct a "change" experiment to fulfill the request for a training pro-gram by the Connecticut State Inter-Racial Commission. The experi-ment would involve a workshop that would simultaneously train people for community action against prejudice and conduct research on what changed the attitudes of the trainees in the program. This is significant: from the start, the sensitivity training idea rested on the questionable premise that those already in the program, who might have been deemed to be among the converted, required the same changes in attitude as the hypothetical bigot for whom the program was designed. In any case, Lewin led "a large team of trainers, observers, and researchers" in designing a two-week workshop in 1946 at Teacher's College in New Britain, Connecticut.[3]

As Marrow describes it, the workshop aimed to train forty-one people, mostly teachers and social workers and a few labor leaders and businessmen, half of whom were either black or Jewish. These participants professed a range of goals, including developing interpersonal skills, exploring the sources of prejudice, learning how to alter attitudes, and reaching an understanding of their own "attitudes and values."[4]

The workshop involved mainly open discussion by participants, whom the staff, in the spirit of egalitarianism, treated as equals. In the evenings, most of the participants joined their families, but those who did not asked to join the evening meetings during which staff members digested their daily observations. There was initial concern about having participants listen in on reports that involved their own behavior, but Lewin liked the idea. One staff member said that the result triggered "a tremendous electric charge . . . as people reacted to data about their own behavior." Marrow writes, "Thus, the role of feedback in a T (training) group was discovered."[5]

Both trainees and staff responded enthusiastically to the nightly sessions. The "feedback sessions" were thus institutionalized, becoming the high point of the training. These sessions added to the amount of time participants already spent in the daytime analyzing their own behavior. In the end, the consensus was that the workshop was a success. Six months later, approximately three-quarters of the trainees reported that they used the methods they learned in the workshop, especially role playing, and that they could handle group relations more skillfully, citing "increased sensitivity to the feelings of others," "greater optimism about making progress," and better "performance in working with people, in planning action, in bridging the gaps between good intentions and actual behavior."[6] The Connecticut workshop spawned the formation in 1947 of the National Training Laboratories originally in Bethel, Maine, an organization devoted to the practice of sensitivity training.

Looking back twenty years later on the origins of sensitivity training, its pioneers stressed what they viewed as the tremendous importance of the new method for addressing interpersonal relations. Warren Bennis wrote that the National Training Laboratories had become by 1967 "an internationally recognized and powerful force affecting almost all of the social institutions in our society."[7] Leland Bradford, a leader of the Connecticut workshop and director of the National Training Laboratories beginning in 1947, later boasted of "the vast growth of sensitivity training as a technique and of the National Training Laboratories as a center of continuing research in the field." "Lewin's great concept of creating 'here and now' data, analyzing it, and using feedback," Bradford wrote, "remains the essential element in all the many variations of sensitivity training and encounter groups that have developed on every continent and in almost every land."[8] Carl Rogers also stressed the importance of the new workshop style, proclaiming in 1968 that sensitivity training "is perhaps the most significant social invention of this century. The demand for it is utterly beyond belief. It is one of the most rapidly growing social phenomena in the United States. It has permeated industry, is coming into education, is reaching families, professionals in the helping fields and many other individuals."[9] These observations might best be dismissed as boosterism on the part of sensitivity training's proponents, who assumed the method's omnipresence was a positive development. Strangely, though, they also capture a basic truth that has not been fully examined: the sensitivity training method did become all-pervasive, in ways its early proponents could hardly have foreseen.

A Higher Awareness:
The Human Potential Vanguard

In the late 1960s, observers cited the vast increase in the use of sensitivity training in the human potential movement. The journalist Jane Howard's book *Please Touch: A Guided Tour of the Human Potential Movement,* published in 1970, built on an article she had published in *Life* in 1968. It gave extensive evidence for her claim that the movement constituted a cultural development of major influence and significance. Reflecting thoughtfully on her numerous experiences with it, Howard captured the spirit of a movement that claimed, with unabashed exuberance, to be in the vanguard of social relations of all kinds—by allowing people to develop a higher level of awareness of their feelings. At the end of her book, a ten-page list of the "growth centers" and related institutions where human potential work was currently conducted established just how prevalent the new philosophy and techniques had become.[10]

"Human potential" came to refer to a range of eclectic approaches aimed at eliciting what adherents thought was the untapped capacity for some kind of transcendence. What they were transcending was not always clear, but it generally involved numbness or tension resulting from the repression of everyday existence. Rescue would come through a personal awakening to the full range of human emotions and sensations—and even "extrasensory" capacities. The movement's general premise was that with new, particularly noncognitive experiences an individual could achieve a level of self-awareness not ordinarily imaginable. This self-awareness, enshrined as an end in itself, represented a potential source of social progress. If the general population tapped into this source, social and personal problems could become figments of the benighted past.

Typical of the movement's hubris, but capturing to some degree its cultural import, the psychologist Carl Rogers, one of the most prominent advocates of personal "growth," claimed that it was "the most significant social invention of this century."[11] George Leonard, another major adherent, thought the movement was in the process of ushering in a whole new form of education that promised to do nothing short of bringing on a "new age." "Education's new domain is not bound in by the conceptual, the factual, the symbolic," he wrote in his 1968 book on the new movement, *Education and Ecstasy:* "It includes every aspect of human existence that is relevant to the new age. To move into it, we don't have to wait for the twenty-first century."[12] *Look* magazine, in turn, called Leonard's work "the most influential book on education in modern times."[13]

The human potential movement was an unwieldy collection of practices and approaches. Its diverse field of advocates included everyone from Frederick Perls, the German psychiatrist who founded Gestalt therapy, to Abraham Maslow, Paul Tillich, Erich Fromm, and many others.[14] Despite their eclecticism, the human potential advocates often shared the belief that growth could best occur in the sensitivity training group. By the time the movement took off, the National Training Laboratories had already practiced the T-group for two decades. In the experimental, no-holds-barred atmosphere of the 1960s, the T-group's emphasis on the expansion of horizons through intense encounters with other people—hence the rise of the term "encounter group," used frequently as a synonym for training group—caught fire. As Jane Howard put it, the movement's "most salable commodity is the 'intensive group experience,' known in some quarters as the 'encounter' and in others as the 'T-group' (T for training), or sensitivity-training workshop or training laboratory."[15] The formal task of such groups involved concentrated explorations into interpersonal relations and other factors in individual psychic well-being. Howard captured the essence of the small-group encounter as a gathering of roughly a dozen

> personable, responsible, certifiably normal and temporarily smelly people. Their destination is intimacy, trust and awareness of why

they behave as they do in groups; their vehicle is candor. Exhorted to "get in touch with their feelings" and to "live in the here-and-now," they sprawl on the floor of a smoky room littered with styrofoam coffee cups, half-empty Kleenex boxes and overflowing ashtrays. As they grow tired they rest their heads on rolled-up sweaters or corners of cot mattresses or each other's laps . . . . Some of them shout, seethe, sob, attack and eventually embrace each other. All of them survive long spells of silence.[16]

Eventually touching people from nearly every walk of life, including "businessmen, psychologists, ex-weightlifters, professors, dancers and theologians," another article announced, encounter activities were conducted under the auspices of "the major social institutions: church, factory, school and state." T-groups took place in a growing number of locations, from church basements, universities, and corporations, to those places more formally designated "growth centers." The small-group activities of the movement were at times supplemented by conventions of thousands of people. The movement grew tremendously in the late 1960s, with thirty-seven actual "growth centers" estimated in 1969 to over one hundred in 1970. This long list included such communities as Kairos in San Diego, GROW in New York City, Oasis in Chicago, Espiritu in Houston, Quest in Washington, D.C., Adanta in Decatur, Georgia, and Sky Farm Institute in Calais, Vermont.[17] Attempting to capture the essence of the movement's appeal, Howard cited its ability to address a wide range of perceived needs. The human potential movement "is many things": "It is a business, a means of recreation, a subculture, a counterculture, a form of theatre, a philosophy of education, a kind of psychotherapy, and an underground religion, with its own synods, sects, prophets, schisms and heretics." She added, "Depending on who is assessing it, it is also a passing fad, a godsend, a silly collection of parlor games or a menace."[18]

As Howard implied, the movement had not only its advertisers like George Leonard and Carl Rogers but its detractors as well. In one damning instance, the writer George Steiner gave a seminar at a human potential center and expressed his skepticism at what he had found, or failed to find: "What's the point of self-discovery if there's nothing, or very little, there to discover? All that's accomplished by having them go even deeper inside themselves is to show them what bores they are."[19] Wolfe's "The Me Decade" displayed what he concluded was the movement's absurd obsession with the self, particularly with minor personal problems. In *The Culture of Narcissism,* Christopher Lasch delivered a more sustained attack on the folly of what he called "pseudo-self-awareness," which he thought appealed to the narcissistic personality of the age, the main characteristic of which was an infantile inability to see where the individual self left off and the rest of the world began. To Lasch, the human potential movement represented both the belief in the primacy of the self's impulses and the ultimate sense of meaningless and despair attendant on the inevitable disappointment resulting from such a belief.[20]

While critics have explored the negative consequences of the human potential philosophy for American culture, few have made any link between the movement and how race relations played themselves out in the aftermath of the civil rights movement.[21] This is a peculiar omission. The way race relations came to be thought of and dealt with had everything to do with the rise of the therapeutics offered by the human potential movement.

The T-group or encounter group had its heyday in the 1960s and 1970s. A humorous exploration of two couples who flirt with group sex and spend time at Esalen getting in touch with their deepest feelings, the film *Bob and Carol and Ted and Alice* beautifully captured the enlistment of the encounter group in the counterculture's crusade to question received strictures on interpersonal conduct and explore all available avenues of personal fulfillment and intense emotional experience.[22] The original T-group faded from use after that period, primarily retained only in a less dramatic incarnation in group therapy dedicated to addressing inter-personal problems. Although it is no longer the popular, discrete insti-tution that it used to be, it does live on. If anything, its influence has grown. In fact, in many settings it has become the dominant mode of expression, a style of interpersonal interaction that helps set the parameters of social relations.

The encounter mode aims at nearly instant results: the breaking down of interpersonal barriers through uninhibited communication and the breaking down of individual barriers to self-development and self-fulfillment through total self-disclosure. To grasp its resonance for Americans since the 1960s is to weigh the effects of the convergence of major political crises and demands for reform, especially in the civil rights and antiwar movements, and the longer-term cultural changes that had brought all hierarchy, control, and authority into question. In this setting, the individual became the appropriate unit of social change. The notion of consciousness or awareness seemed intriguing and unlimited. Heightened sensitivity to outside stimulation became an end in itself, and laying bare one's inner being represented an assault on the mind-numbing sensory-deprived world the older gen-eration had passed down. The convergence of protest against political hierarchy and the decline of traditional cultural authority helped transform the self into a political project, lending self-exploration a sense of higher purpose.

The mushrooming of the field of psychotherapy helped set the stage for this new preoccupation with self-awareness. By the 1960s, a number of new therapies vied for Americans' attention and helped cast the individual as a new frontier. Therapists often had distinctive approaches, but nothing kept the clients from experimenting with one after another of the new therapies, causing overlap in the area of reception even when not in dissemination. Moreover, new institutions like the encounter group were less a "technique" than a "unit of treat-ment."[23] The encounter group represented an eclectic intermixture of therapeutic practices. A brief look at the trends in psychotherapy helps show this by laying out some of the strands that came together in the encounter group.

THE PSYCHOTHERAPY EXPLOSION

One of the most important developments in twentieth-century American life was the vast explosion of psychotherapy. The number of psychotherapists multiplied rapidly over the century, the number of Americans who sought some form of psychotherapy increased dramatically, and the number of therapeutic approaches abounded. Furthermore, psychotherapy gathered tremendous influence outside of clinical practice as a way of explaining personal and social problems. A drastic shift occurred as well when psychotherapeutic techniques became widely accepted as appropriate for an ever-broadening range of everyday issues or "life problems" rather than being reserved for seriously debilitating disorders. As psychotherapy became popularized and deemed generally relevant as a lens through which the world should be viewed, therapeutic approaches and assumptions came to blend promiscuously. Therapists of all stripes now practiced "hundreds of variants" of the major approaches, often combining seemingly opposed techniques, or varying the technique according to the client. Sometimes this conjoining and popularization of psychotherapy resulted in incoherent mixtures of techniques that were inherently at odds.[24] A brief look at the main trends in psychotherapy suggests how incoherent a form of therapy—like the encounter group—that randomly combined techniques could be.

As the historian Morton Hunt shows in his far-reaching survey, *The Story of Psychology,* psychotherapy by the 1960s bore the imprint of four overarching frameworks for explaining and addressing personal problems: dynamic, behavioral, cognitive, and humanistic psychology. Initiated in the 1920s and 1930s by the popularization of Freud's ideas and the neo-Freudians Erik Erikson, Karen Horney, Erich Fromm, and Henry Stack Sullivan, the movement for dynamic psychology took off after World War II and intensified the demand for psychiatrists and clinical psychologists. While the time-consuming and intensive endeavor of psychoanalysis itself, reaching its high point in the mid-1950s, was never practiced widely, its resonance was great within psychology and the broader culture, and its offspring, dynamic psychology, in the 1980s characterized a third to half of therapeutic practice, with its conception "of psychological problems as resulting from intrapsychic conflicts, unconscious motivations, and the interplay of external demands with components of the personality structure."[25]

Behavior therapy also came to the attention of the public in the late 1960s and became widely used in the 1970s and afterward. Howard Liddell, Joseph Wolpe, and Arnold Lazarus pioneered techniques designed to alter behavior with positive associations in Pavlovian style, or desensitization. Other therapeutic techniques of this school included aversive conditioning (association of undesirable behavior with unpleasant sensation), assertiveness training, modeling (influence on behavior through the presence of an individual practicing desirable behavior), or operant conditioning (rewards for desirable behavior).[26]

The third approach, cognitive therapy, emphasized that "flawed cognitive processes, rather than unconscious conflicts," caused personal neuroses and thus demanded "a method of getting the patient to rethink his or her faulty expectations and values."[27] Albert Ellis developed "rational-emotive therapy" in the mid 1950s, a method by which the therapist stripped bare the faulty reasoning that lay behind clients' emotional disorders. He believed a warm and accepting demeanor on the part of the therapist merely perpetuated clients' dependency, whereas direct confrontation achieved the desirable "unmasking" and change of world view. Through rational-emotive therapy, Ellis sought to lead clients to a "profound Basic Philosophic change" by altering "their dysfunctional Basic Philosophic Assumptions."[28] Another pioneer of cognitive therapy, who favored a much less confrontational style, was Aaron Beck, a psychiatrist and professor of psychiatry at the

University of Pennsylvania. Drawing partly on behavioral techniques like role playing and assertiveness training, Beck believed that the therapist needed to guide the client toward an understanding of his or her cognitive errors, which caused everything from inertia to self-doubt.[29] Their ideas made up a part of a larger "cognitive revolution" in psychological thinking that had occurred by the 1970s.

Finally, humanistic psychology, the school of thought that gave rise to the human potential movement, emerged in the 1950s and 1960s as a direct alternative to both psychoanalysis and behaviorism. It emphasized individual self-fulfillment and subjectivity, relativistic standards for behavior, and the presence in everyone of inner resources for change. Adherents of this philosophy said therapy should aim to "remove obstacles, such as poor self-image or the denial of feelings," to self-development.[30] Widely considered the guru of the human potential movement, Carl Rogers pioneered in "client-centered therapy," a clinical technique in which therapists often repeat or rephrase what their clients say in order to help convey a feeling that clients are "in charge of their fate." Popular in the 1950s and 1960s, it then waned dramatically and was widely lampooned later on. Frederick Perls's Gestalt therapy aimed to make patients aware of feelings they genuinely harbored and to acknowledge those that "were actually borrowed or adopted from others." He used highly confrontational exercises designed to "force the patient to acknowledge the truth about his or her feelings." Gestalt therapy was popular in the 1960s and 1970s, then largely faded from view as well. Transactional analysis, conveyed to the public via the best-selling books *Games People Play,* by Eric Berne, and *I'm Okay–You're Okay*, by Thomas A. Harris, sought to expose the part of the unconscious that was involved in a given social interaction—the child, parent, or adult (somewhat parallel to id, superego, and ego). Counselors helped clients analyze whether their transactions with others constituted genuine communication or social games that interfered with authentic interaction.[31] Primal scream was yet another therapy designed to heal a basic wound from childhood through uninhibited emotional expression—just one of a growing number of such therapies.

It was this milieu that gave rise to the encounter group, with its unusual mélange of ideas and practices. Like dynamic psychology, it stressed bringing into consciousness deep feelings, but at the same time sought to concentrate only on the "here and now" of Carl Rogers's humanistic therapy. Without going to deep roots in childhood, it attempted to resolve conflict through confrontational methods resembling Ellis's cognitive corrections and Perls's Gestalt therapy. And the encounter group constantly drew on behaviorist methods like role playing. It rested on the assumption that individuals needed to unearth and confront their deepest feelings, but also on the assumption they could do so in a very compressed amount of time. Thus people could undergo the kind of life-changing experiences over the course of a single weekend that would bring on a completely altered world view, in the way Beck thought possible. Encounters were based on the idea that honest and open communication of feelings—no matter how intense—would allow people to discover their authentic selves, break down barriers to communication with others, and enable them to choose which behaviors would fulfill them the most, all virtually overnight. This notion of an emergent consciousness undoubtedly owed some of its resonance to the long-term American revivalist tradition of the individual conversion experience, but was shorn of that tradition's crucial moral dimension.

The Race Diagnosis

One of the most important figures to popularize the notion that everyday experiences and tensions between blacks and whites could be explained in psychological terms and addressed with sensitivity training-like approaches was the black psychiatrist Price M. Cobbs. Cobbs coauthored the book *Black Rage* with the psychiatrist William

H. Grier, also black. Their book appeared in 1968 to such acclaim that it became not only a best-seller at the time but a widely read "classic in the field of African American studies" after that.[32] Born in Los Angeles in 1928, Cobbs received a B.A. from the University of California at Berkeley in 1954 and an M.D. from Meharry Medical College in 1958. On the basis of their clinical work with blacks in psychotherapy, Grier and Cobbs described what they saw as the effects of racism on the lives of individuals. The tremendous anger and frustration they observed in their patients, they wrote, was the price blacks paid to live in a society that systematically oppressed them. The team went on to coauthor another book, *The Jesus Bag,* which argued that religion had been employed as part of that oppression.

Interestingly, after *Black Rage,* Cobbs turned his attention away from clinical practice with individuals to approaches using small groups, including diversity training seminars. As president of Pacific Management Systems, a consulting firm he founded in 1967, Cobbs conducted workshops on race relations initially in schools, police departments, social service agencies, and community organizations and, increasingly, the business world. At first called "racial confrontation groups," Cobbs's workshops set the groundwork for his participation in the field of diversity training. The books by Grier and Cobbs and Cobbs's subsequent workshops provide an invaluable illustration of the consequences of viewing race through the lens of psychology and using a therapeutic approach to interracial interactions.

Black Rage mixes the notes taken by Grier and Cobbs on their psychiatric patients with excursions into history, sociology, psychology, and polemic that aim to explain the social factors the authors believe result in particular psychiatric disorders. Citing a variety of cases, from individuals with mild anxieties to those with full-blown diagnoses of schizophrenia, the book traces these disorders to white racism, something the authors considered all-pervasive: "For black and white alike, the air of this nation is perfused [*sic*] with the idea of white supremacy."[33] The authors traced current-day neuroses and complexes, large and small, directly to slavery, even though they were writing more than a hundred years after emancipation.[34] They believed that slavery created a set of interracial dynamics that led to a particular pathological mentality in slaves, and that those distorted psychological responses continued through the 1960s and would continue to exist after that, barring some revolutionary change.

The book delivered a powerful attack on white racism. It was part of a series of invectives against racial discrimination and the systematic exploitation of black labor under slavery—the long-term effects of which were still evident in the 1960s and, to a lesser degree, still are today. Like Cleaver's *Soul on Ice, The Autobiography of Malcolm X,* and Baldwin's *The Fire Next Time, Black Rage* was unrestrained in its condemnation of racism and unstinting in its articulation of the necessity of ending its effects. Like those books, *Black Rage* contained both implicit and explicit threats to whites that, if they did not bring an immediate end to white supremacy, they might be up against "the fire next time." Grier and Cobbs laid out the specific situations of several of their psychiatric clients, analyzed their problems as the result of the prevailing social relations corrupted by racism, and suggested that the symptoms blacks exhibited constituted a kind of psychic time bomb just waiting to go off.

As an example, Grier and Cobbs related the story of one young sergeant who had served in the military for ten years, three of those in combat, only to be subjected to an ugly racial incident. Returning to his small southern hometown, the young man accidentally found himself in a white neighborhood after drinking too much and falling asleep on a bus. When he asked a white man for help, that man in turn cried out for assistance and another appeared with a gun. The police arrested the black man for attempted robbery, and he spent three hellish years in jail, from which he never recovered. Ragged in appearance, he now had no residence and no steady job, only paranoid delusions that white men in the prison had somehow hypnotized him so that he heard strange voices.[35]

Grier and Cobbs saw the sergeant's decline as a direct effect of racism and presented the story as a cautionary tale. To them, the story bespoke the man's fall from a position of strength and promise: "Imagine the sustained pressure required to induce or trigger a schizophrenic response in a vigorous young man who had functioned successfully as a soldier. . . . This pressure must have offered him no chance of escape or even the hope of a chance." Yet, Grier and Cobbs found that "even years later, sick through and through," when the sergeant came in for treatment, "there was yet vigor and drive in his determination to get well." If he had not become a "severe chronic paranoid schizophrenic," they wrote, "consider for a moment what an enemy the white men *almost* had—a seasoned, resourceful, highly trained killer." Their threat took an even more direct form: "If blacks are often frightened, . . . consider what happens when they feel cornered, when there is no further lie one can believe, when one finally sees that he is permanently cast as the victim, and when finally the sleeping giant wakes and turns upon his tormentors."[36]

POLITICS THROUGH THERAPY

As a fiery invective against the nation's inheritance of white supremacy, the force of *Black Rage* can still be felt. However, the terms in which Grier and Cobbs chose to express their social criticism—and their image of a damaged collective psyche just about to explode into rage—are what concern me here. Beyond the questions this way of appraising the causes of serious medical conditions like schizophrenia might raise, these psychiatrists' depiction of the problem—that black men and women suffered from various emotional afflictions resulting from social conditions—put their own enterprise into a strange light. If their patients' afflictions were not so much abnormal as appropriate responses to the many manifestations of racism they encountered, it would seem they would be in need less of therapy than of changed social conditions. The logical conclusion would be that political activists, rather than therapists, were the answer. Only political change would guide the nation out of the psychological morass described by Grier and Cobbs, a morass that included a number of overlapping symptoms they considered nearly universal among blacks, ranging wildly from paranoia to depression. However, Grier and Cobbs concluded that it was a kind of radical therapy of race relations that was needed.

Activists like Grier and Cobbs sought to resolve this paradox through therapeutic intervention: they recast their professional work, in this case psychiatric practice, as social reform or even revolution. Grier and Cobbs implied that the psychological effects of racism, if left unattended, would continue to lead either to severely damaged psyches among blacks or to repressed hostility against whites. This festering hostility threatened to erupt at any moment. In fact, Grier and Cobbs thought that the race riots that were so prevalent in the mid-1960s were the inevitable result of white supremacy. *Black Rage* implied that, if other avenues for catharsis were not found, the nation could expect much more violence and disorder. The catharsis hinted at in *Black Rage* would be a racialized therapy, which Cobbs developed later, with different roles for whites and blacks.

Notably, Grier and Cobbs's conclusion was based on an argument against racial discrimination that rested not on religious, moral, or political rationales for social justice but on psychological ones. The historian Daryl Scott has recently explored the distinctiveness of this point of view in his impressive genealogy of the idea of the damaged black psyche or the use of "damage imagery" both by those who hoped to preserve the status quo and by those who sought to improve conditions for African Americans. Scott believes the cost of this approach is enormous. By single-mindedly focusing on the negative psychological effects of racism, racial liberals paved the way for conservatives to use those same concepts of black pathology to argue for blacks' inherent or temporary inferiority.[37]

While Scott's admirable study brings our attention to the dangers of "damage imagery" to the cause of racial equality, dismissing any and all evocations of the idea that racism has caused psychological damage does not reflect the ways in which racism has obviously inflicted at least some such "damage." Furthermore, the "imagery" of damage cannot fully characterize what was so lethal about enlisting psychology for the cause of civil rights. The replacement of the religious or moral arguments for equality with ones based on the psychological disorders of discriminatory institutions altered not only the means by which change could be seen to come about but also the ends themselves. The desired goal was no longer civic equality and participation, but individual psychic well-being. This psychological state was much more nebulous, open to interpretation, difficult to achieve, and controversial than the universal guarantees of political equality sought by the early civil rights movement. What is more, the movement for psychic betterment involved an interpersonal project that spawned many new problems of its own.

Perhaps most important, *Black Rage* exhibits the overarching preoccupation with repression for which its age became known. Cries for black liberation, women's liberation, sexual liberation, gay liberation, and the liberation of colonial people—just as a start— were not only simultaneous but often seen as one. Criticism of the larger repressiveness of society potentially undermined the assertion that white racism was the culprit for the strictures on black expressiveness.

But Grier and Cobbs were determined to see inhibitions in racial terms alone. They delivered a particularly strong attack, for instance, on a personality they deemed afflicted by "the postal-clerk syndrome." Not the same syndrome that came into currency later with the phrase "going postal," the "postal-clerk syndrome" was merely another way of describing the stereotypically passive black toady, yes-man, or Uncle Tom. "Granting the limitations of stereotypes," Grier and Cobbs still went on to "sketch a paradigmatic black man":

This man is always described as "nice" by white people. In whatever integrated setting he works, he is the standard against whom other blacks are measured. . . . He is passive, nonassertive, and nonaggressive. He has made a virtue of identification with the aggressor, and he has adopted an ingratiating and compliant manner. . . . He is a direct lineal descendant of the "house nigger" who was designed to identify totally with the white master.[38]

As an example of this kind of person, Grier and Cobbs cited the husband of one of their patients. The patient herself suffered from such "melancholia" that she had tried repeatedly to commit suicide. But it was her calm and well-mannered husband—a "leading Negro citizen"—who came under the scrutiny and, ultimately, disapproval of Grier and Cobbs, to the point where they seemed to suggest that the root of the wife's depression was her husband's reticence. The wife "was angry with her husband and berated him for never opening up and exposing his feelings," they wrote.

For his part, the husband remained "nice." He never raised his voice above a murmur. His wife could goad him, but he was the epitome of understanding. He was amenable to all suggestions. His manner and gestures were deliberate, studied, and noninflammatory. Everything was understated. During the course of treatment he was involved in several civil rights crises. His public life was an extension of his private one, and he used such words as "moderation" and "responsibility." His entire life was a study in passivity, in how to play at being a man without really being one.[39]

Grier and Cobbs went on to explain that this man could not be dismissed as just "an isolated passive individual," but had instead to be seen as someone who tried "to conceal his drive." Predictably, the next paragraph invoked slavery to explain that black men had to discover expressive forms that did not threaten whites, so they invented the

"posture of 'playing it cool.'" Grier and Cobbs saw this style as resulting from a fear of "the eruption of repressed feelings" and the "swift
punishment" that would result.[40] They interpreted the symptoms they
observed among their patients, such as "weeping without feeling," to
be the exorbitant "cost and suffering" inflicted from emotional repression. Many male patients cited incidents in which they witnessed a
"triumphant man"—whether it was a speech by Martin Luther King
Jr. or someone else's "moment of personal glory," perhaps an athlete's
triumph—and felt tears begin to well up in their eyes, but with no
attendant thoughts or feelings. Grier and Cobbs interpreted this as a
result of a man's not allowing himself the "forbidden feelings" of "sad-
ness" for "what he might have been." But white racism had commanded him "not to excel, not to achieve, not to become outstanding, not
to draw attention to himself"—"to remain anonymous."[41]

While one can surely detect a generalized portrait of victimization
in this line of thought, along with a concentration on the pathological
effects of racism, what has gone the most awry in such an interpretation—what rings false—is its single-minded focus on race as a key to
an entire personality structure and beyond that, the key to the personality structure of a whole group of people. Even more, tracing the
entire racial experience to slavery caused *Black Rage* to draw conclu-
sions about symptoms among blacks in the 1960s according to the
master-slave dynamic of a century before, and to a set of uncompli-
cated and unexamined assumptions about the dynamic at that. The
notion of a unique black self represented a continuation of differential
or racialist thinking.

From this set of assumptions, however, Grier and Cobbs went on
to prescribe what they thought was needed to address this "psy-
chopathology." Rather than fighting politically to end any last vestiges
of social inequality, the psychiatrists proposed new therapies. They
called for psychiatric revolution: "a profound convulsion of society"
that would address the "contempt and hatred of black people" that "is
so thoroughly a part of the American personality." Therapists were

ideally situated to be in the vanguard of this struggle because of their love for their patients, because, besides therapists, "how many people, black or white, can so open their arms to a suffering black man?"[42]

The new racial therapy, one gleans from *Black Rage,* should have several dimensions. First, directly in line with the sensitivity training group's self-referential obsession with "feedback," racial therapy should demand that therapists themselves turn inward. It is not enough just to increase the number of black therapists, for a black therapist whose manner mimics the "tentative, hands-off" approach of a "reluctant white therapist" is of no help to blacks. "The black clinician's own inevitable problems of identification," combined with the disengaged white "milieu" in which he was trained, "make it difficult for him to be comfortable with his blackness" enough to offer real help, unless he "begins to grapple with his own feelings about being black, ineffective, and victimized in a powerful white nation."[43]

Second, Grier and Cobbs sought to "enter a plea for *clinical* clinicians" who can differentiate the traits necessary for survival under white racism from real mental disorders—who can tell the difference between "a sick man and a sick nation."[44] To practice effectively, "clinicians who are interested in the psychological functioning of black people must get acquainted with" what the authors called "the *Black Norm.*" A level of paranoia, depression, masochism, and lack of respect for "white men's laws" is part of normal adaptation to being black in America. Grier and Cobbs put forth a formula to help therapists apply this knowledge: "to find the amount of sickness a black man has, one must first total all that appears to represent illness and then subtract the Black Norm. What remains is illness and a proper subject for therapeutic endeavor."[45]

Traits that would be considered disorders in others thus become norms for blacks—not only understandable but justifiable adaptive behaviors: "To regard the Black Norm as pathological and attempt to remove such traits by treatment would be akin to analyzing away a hunter's cunning or a banker's prudence."[46] Grier and Cobbs ended this discussion with a contradiction. "Too much psychotherapy involves striving only for a change in the inner world," rather than for "a change of the social order." Yet, a "good therapist" can help a patient "more effectively change his outer world." So, while the authors seemed to admit the limits of clinical therapy, they still held to a therapeutic approach to the larger social context they saw as the root of many of the emotional problems of blacks. The roles of the sympathetic therapist and emotional disclosure remain paramount:

> The essential ingredient is the capacity of the therapist to love his patient—to say to him that here is a second chance to organize his inner life, to say that you have a listener and companion who wants you to make it. If you must weep, I'll wipe your tears. If you must hit someone, hit me, I can take it. I will, in fact, do *anything* to help you be what you can be—my love for you is of such an order.[47]

While alluding to Martin Luther King Jr.'s belief in agape, or love of community, which King described as a love for a higher purpose that transcends individuals and could move blacks and whites from division and bitterness to the "beloved community," Grier and Cobbs cast this love completely in therapeutic terms. Rather than a love of something outside individuals that bonds them together, this love of the therapist embraces the individual against the outside world. Therapeutic love does not call on individuals to triumph in their inner moral wars against evil but encourages them to reveal their weaknesses in order that they be accepted unconditionally. The unleashing of the emotions, rather than mastery of them, constitutes progress. This is not the theory that drove civil rights, but the one that drove the countercultural and human potential movement's revolt against the supposed repression of the authentic self and its unbounded needs for fulfillment.

At the same time Cobbs was formulating his ideas for *Black Rage,* he was becoming increasingly involved in the human potential movement. When he was first approached to participate in this therapeutic movement, his response showed that he saw it as removed from the black movement. The irony is that he eventually was one of those responsible for connecting the two movements and helping to steer the black movement in a new direction.

"RACIAL CONFRONTATION AS TRANSCENDENTAL EXPERIENCE"

Cobbs's involvement in the human potential movement seems to have originated in an invitation by George Leonard to conduct interracial workshops at one of the most famous growth centers, the Esalen institute founded in the early 1960s in Big Sur, California, a stunning coastal town south of Monterey. Leonard, a white southerner who served as vice president of Esalen starting in 1966, had become an integrationist after serving in the army air force in World War II and had gone on to participate in school desegregation and civil rights marches. He later attributed his involvement in the human relations movement to his growing awareness of racial discrimination. In a 1983 history of Esalen, called *The Upstart Spring,* Walter Truett Anderson, a freelance writer on politics and culture, wrote about Leonard, "Having discovered that his society and its authority figures could be wrong on something as important as race, he remained open to the possibility that they could be wrong on other subjects, as well."[48] Leonard believed that he and other visionaries, such as Esalen's president and co-founder (with Richard Price), Michael Murphy, with their unbounded enthusiasm for the possibilities for human growth and education through innovative types of experience, were riding the crest of a "great social transformation."[49]

Worried about the race riots of the mid-1960s, Leonard included in his vision for this vast transformation a change in American race relations. According to Anderson, Leonard first discovered Cobbs when he read a newspaper article that detailed the problems that the black psychiatrist and his wife had faced in moving to an all-white neighborhood in San Francisco. Leonard called the story to the attention of his editor at *Look* magazine, where his own article about the human potential movement had appeared in 1964. In the process of getting *Look* to run an article on the situation, Leonard, Cobbs, and their families developed a friendship. Then Leonard asked Cobbs whether he would conduct interracial workshops.[50]

Anderson writes that Cobbs's initial reaction to the idea of conducting an interracial encounter group was ambivalence. Apparently, Cobbs even worried that Leonard's motive was to have "a suitable black friend to demonstrate his own liberalism." Later Cobbs accepted the idea that his friend was involved in Esalen. For his own part, Cobbs viewed it "as a playground of middle-class white dilettantes." Even after agreeing to conduct a workshop with Leonard, he nearly canceled in order to attend the Newark black power convention set for the same weekend.[51]

Price Cobbs and George Leonard conducted their first encounter group at Esalen in July 1967, while Cobbs was at work on *Black Rage*, which would be published the following year. In Leonard's *Education and Ecstasy,* also published in 1968, Leonard revealed that the impetus behind the workshop idea lay not just in interracial tensions but also in the utopian belief that Esalen methods could diffuse or at least alter them. "Since so much of Esalen is truly experimental," Leonard wrote, "nothing can be guaranteed to 'work.' Yet, most people who participate come away with the conviction that they have somehow been changed." Esalen "experiments" shared a "characteristic sense of hope" for solving even the "most intractable human problems."[52] At a time when the blood and fire of race riots were becoming regular features of American summers, one could certainly have argued that one of the most "intractable" problems of all was race relations.

While the black power conference took place in Newark, with more than 400 representatives of forty-five civil rights groups,[53] some 35 individuals gathered at Esalen for an interracial workshop entitled

"Racial Confrontation as Transcendental Experience." The brochure cast the racial problem as a matter of individual alienation and integration as a predominantly psychological project. The goal of the workshop was an interpersonal encounter that was free of inauthentic inhibitions—a form of collective transcendence. The publicity for the event read:

> Racial segregation exists among people with divided selves. A person who is alien to some part of himself is invariably separated from anyone who represents that alien part. The historic effort to integrate black man and white [sic] has involved us all in a vast working out of our divided human nature. Racial confrontation can be an example for all kinds of human encounter. When it goes deep enough—past superficial niceties and role-playing—it can be a vehicle for transcendental experience. [54]

Leonard later admitted that such language was hyperbolic and that, as the weekend began, he and Cobbs were nervous. However, Leonard recalled that they had been motivated by a sense that something had to be done "to show a way, even if a small one, through the racial impasse that had almost brought the civil-rights movement to a halt." Leonard spelled out this impasse as he saw it—in the terms of the encounter movement: "The Black Power militants screamed their hurt, anger, and hatred. By revealing themselves and voicing the truth, they begged for encounter. The white leaders responded with conventional language, revealing nothing of their own feelings." [55] As a result of their emotional pain, in this line of thought, blacks and whites alike sorely needed the therapy the encounter method could provide.

Both blacks and whites, according to the encounter group philosophy, required emotional release—though of different emotions. Leonard thought blacks needed to release their anger, and whites their racism and fears. In the absence of such release, stilted, phony behavior typified interracial settings:

> How could there be understanding without self-revelation? Didn't the whites feel outrage, fear, repressed prejudice? The measured, judicious response seemed to us a lie. Nor was there real encounter in the biracial committees set up in some cities. Blacks and whites sat around tables, mouthed slogans, established "positions" and made "decisions" of an intellectual and political nature. They generally left the meetings unchanged. Little education took place. What would happen when we ventured into the dangerous territory where nothing is hidden?[56]

What happened, as Anderson put it in *Upstart Spring*, was "a heavy weekend." The group consisted of thirty-five participants and the three facilitators—Leonard, Cobbs, and Cobbs's wife, Vad. Whites outnumbered blacks, and black men outnumbered black women, and some Asians participated. The mostly middle-class group had many professionals, including therapists and teachers. The session was a weekend "marathon," which meant that participants met Friday evening, broke for the night, resumed the session on Saturday morning, and continued on until Sunday noon, with only a break for meals and a visit to the natural hot springs, a big attraction of Esalen. This schedule meant participants did not sleep Saturday night, which was often the case in the encounter experience. The assumption was that deprivation of the usual comforts might also strip people of their unneeded inhibitions.

Leonard gave a vivid description of the encounter group in *Education and Ecstasy*, which Cobbs later said was told "brilliantly."[57] On Friday night, Cobbs and Leonard opened the weekend by having participants sit "in a circle in a rustic meeting room, warmed against the cool sea air by candlelight and an open fire," introducing the weekend's plan, and leading the group through introductions. Participants' introductions, in Leonard's eyes, involved pat accounts of their reasons for attending the seminar, accounts that would be, like everything else, subject to intense scrutiny by the end of the encounter.[58]

Next came an exercise called a microlab, a technique of William Schutz's designed to elicit the quickest possible expression of feelings. Separated into four separate circles, participants received instruction in the "encounter rules":

(1) Be completely honest and open. Forget about conventional politeness and reserve. Express anything you wish, no matter how shocking it may seem. (2) Relate on the level of feelings. Don't theorize or rationalize. (3) Stay in the here and now. Don't escape into past events or future plans. Only one prohibition: No physical violence, please.[59]

Then the conversation began. Initially, this conversation was nothing more than "the kind of chatter you hear at cocktail parties." Cobbs and Leonard stopped the activity after only a few minutes, inaugurating the running self-analysis for which the T-group was known. The facilitators had listened in on the four groups and heard some unconstructive tendencies which they thought had to be displayed and halted before any fruitful work could begin. The resort to humor, charm, excursions into personal history regarding race, or intellectual abstraction was nothing but a "cop-out," a way of evading prickly emotions in the present.[60] Chastened, the groups returned to their work with greater seriousness, but still fell back on facial expressions that cushioned the impact of their words in order to avoid inflicting pain.[61]

Leonard and Cobbs thus stopped the discussion and moved on to the next exercise. Here each group stood in a circle, and, one at a time, members stopped in front of each other person in the circle, looked the person in the eye, touched the person "in some honest way," and told the person what they "felt about him at that moment." Next, the groups sat and communicated for ten minutes silently. Most participants held hands. "Complete dialogues transpired without words," Leonard wrote later: "People learned." Finally, the groups stood and moved closer together. Most put their arms around the others' shoulders. Sitting again, they were to "express true, here-and-now feelings" in anything from words to sounds or touch. "Entirely departed was the cocktail-party chatter. A few barriers had been crossed and a few eyes were moist with the wonder or relief that often accompanies such crossings."[62]

However, on Saturday this closeness shattered. Real confrontations broke out, initially among blacks, who hurled the terms "racist," "Uncle Tom," and "fink" and exposed "the games that black people played," such as "the militant game, the middle-class-brother game, the hip-dude-out-to-make-the-white-chicks game."[63] This viciousness was taken as a sign that the activities had devolved into mere accusation, not "true encounter."

The long marathon session of the weekend began after lunch, with part of the group engaging in a "sensory awakening" activity outdoors in which, with their eyes closed, participants touched the others to communicate and get to know them directly, without racial stereotypes (since such stereotypes presumably originated in feelings about physical differences, and physical differences were mainly detected through sight). Noises from this activity could be heard indoors, including "loud sobbing and wailing." Inside a confrontation had broken out between Cliff, "a personable light-skinned Negro," and "a beautiful young white schoolteacher named Pam." Pam told Cliff she wanted to be his friend but Cliff rejected her " 'pitiful, condescending' overtures," whereupon she pleaded tearfully, "*Please. What can I do? I'm trying. Please help me.*" Cliff replied, "No, baby, I'm not going to help you. I'm not going to take you off the hook. I want you to feel just what I feel. I want you to feel what I've felt for twenty-one years. Go on. Cry." Silence followed, becoming "in itself a powerful medium of communication. We began to *know* each other," Leonard wrote.[64]

Black-white confrontation dominated the session going into Saturday night. The focus at that point was "the Negroes' hurt and anger and despair, their absolute distrust of all whites." Leonard received an exemption when Cobbs said that he did trust Leonard—"something always wished for in the hot and heavy of an encounter, but regretted afterwards," presumably because it got in the way of facing the universality of black rage and white racism. (If so regretted, however, it is interesting that Leonard included this detail in his account.) More pleasing to Leonard seemed to be one black woman's bitter response to his suggestion that whites, too, faced misfortunes: "I just can't buy that. Whatever's wrong with you, you can do something about. But I can't do *anything* about the color of my skin—or my children's. Compared to us, you've got it made."[65]

Spleen poured out, and the mood of the whites was one of deepening despair. One white woman said, "My best friend of fifteen years is a Negro, and I had no idea she felt these kind of things, and now I know she does and has just been keeping them from me to spare me. I don't want to go back home. I'm afraid to see my friend. I don't see how the race problem can *ever* be solved." Leonard's response was that he "was glad it was all coming out in the open," since "the race problem could certainly never be solved so long as we *didn't* know and feel and experience the truth."[66]

The climax of the Esalen encounter came when a young man in his twenties, "almost jet black" and with a "body as taut as a steel spring," announced to the group he had moved beyond the issue of race. He continued that he lacked all wrath against whites, refused to believe incidents of racism were widespread, and had rarely experienced racism himself. Incredulous, the group unified—even Cliff and Pam—against him, trying to "get through to Chuck." Leonard himself, at someone's suggestion, fulfilled his urge to yell at Chuck. Nothing had any effect on Chuck, who continued to profess nothing but good feelings. Later in the session, however, Chuck also claimed he had extraordinary "sexual prowess": "I could take any woman here."

"How would you take Pam?" I asked him.

"I'll tell you."

"Tell *her*."

He turned toward the teacher. "All right. First I'd rap you, then I'd take you."

"Rap?"

"Talk. You know, establish rapport. I'd rap you, then I'd take you."

This did not go over well with Pam, who said, "You'd never take me. I wouldn't let you *touch* me. *Ever*." A black woman chimed in likewise that Chuck had no chance of sleeping with *her*, adding, "And I'm going to tell you why. . . . Because you're just a dirty little black nigger." This triggered a violent response.

> Chuck almost leaped from his chair. Clenching his fists on the armrests, he loosed his hidden fury in a savage and frightening tirade. Finally, he caught himself, looked around the room with dazed eyes and covered his face with his hands. He sat that way as members of the group comforted him. Then he looked up and smiled.

Later on, Chuck said, "I want to thank all of you. I've learned more in the last two hours than in the last two years."[67]

After breakfast on Sunday, the session completely changed direction, as whites began pouring out the tragedies of their own lives. This started when a white woman said that she dated only black men and, when pushed, cried and admitted she had "given up" on white men. At this point, the group stopped accusing her of "white liberal trickery," and a black woman went over to comfort her with a hug.[68] "*And the Negroes wept for the whites,*" wrote Leonard. "Without question of race, they *felt*, they *knew*. One after another, the revelations poured forth. The group took on a life of its own. There were no leaders now. We were all swept along." As tragedies poured forth, the tears flowed.

Almost everyone in the room was crying. We were unashamed of our
tears . . . . For many of us, that morning was transcendental. . . . At
one-thirty, the dining-room crew came and told us we would have to
go. We rose and moved, without a word, to the center of the room in
a mass, moist-eyed embrace.[69]

Anderson wrote that Leonard, Cobbs, and Vad exulted at the way the
session had achieved the resolution that was not a given in encounter
groups, some of which "never broke through" but "only broke up."
"Late that night," Anderson wrote, "Cobbs called Leonard and said,
'George, we've got to take this to the world.'"[70]

Cobbs and Leonard went on to conduct interracial encounter
groups through the Esalen center in San Francisco—sponsored in part
by the Episcopal diocese of California. Two black psychology students,
Ron Brown and Michael Brown (no relation), assisted in the technique.
Anderson's assessment was that they were "extremely successful."
Those participating in the interracial encounter work became so close
that they gathered for a picnic a week after Martin Luther King was
assassinated, while much of the rest of the country was torn by racial
conflict.[71] A turning point, however, occurred shortly thereafter when
a crisis—not without its ironies—caused the program to implode.

Real Life: Not According to Protocol

Ron Brown, who helped run the interracial encounter groups, triggered the crisis when he pushed for more money than the standard
$125 both the white and the black leaders received for running a ses-
sion, according to Anderson's account. As Brown started his appeal
over the phone, an administrator of San Francisco Esalen, Bill Smith,
allegedly replied, "Fuck you," and hung up. When Brown rushed over
to Smith's office, Smith said he would call the police. " 'Shit, I was just
doing some confrontation,' Brown told his friends," Anderson wrote.

"Confrontation was the big thing around Esalen, he said. People were shouting at people all the time. . . . But nobody ever said, 'I'll call the police.' "[72]

Ron Brown and Price Cobbs interpreted the threat to call the police as a racial slur and demanded an apology from Smith, whose unwillingness to give one seemed to some to be possible grounds for removal from his job. Instead, Leonard and Cobbs proposed an encounter group session to deal with the difficulty. Michael Murphy, who was in New York City, traveled all the way back to Cobbs's office in San Francisco to participate in the group of five other whites and three blacks, all male. One woman had driven up from Big Sur but was allegedly told this encounter was about racism, not sexism, and was kept from attending.[73] Other tensions simmered below the surface because the San Francisco contingent thought the interracial group approach lacked support at the Esalen at Big Sur.[74]

In Anderson's telling, Bill Smith, the target of the allegations, tearfully protested against them in a conversation with Murphy before the encounter, denying that he harbored racist feelings and talking about his participation in the civil rights movement. Reluctant to participate in the encounter group in the first place, Smith was predictably lambasted. Less predictably, Smith held his ground. Anderson went on,

> People yelled and got angry. . . . Murphy lost his temper and tried to tell them about what Smith had done on behalf of civil rights. The blacks didn't want to listen to that. That was the old stuff that always came up in the encounter groups: whites protesting that they were free of racism. The blacks wanted some concession from Smith that he was *not* free of racism, that there had been racist overtones to his treatment of Brown. Smith wouldn't give in. It had been, he insisted, just a conflict between two people.[75]

Smith stayed in the midst of the angry group for approximately an hour and then, under the pretense of going to the restroom, left the session. Members of the group who remained achieved a vague consensus that Smith should have to go on a retreat at Big Sur; then they went out for drinks. Meanwhile, Smith phoned Richard Price, who interpreted the effort as one in a series of power plays in Esalen and later told Murphy not to cave in to pressure. Murphy, in turn, called Leonard and proposed a milder approach toward Smith—he would have breakfast with Smith daily and be sure "there were no further incidents."[76]

Feeling let down because the encounter group had reached a different decision, Leonard resigned as vice president of Esalen. Anderson wrote that this ended the interracial encounters.[77] Smith was fired a few months later by Murphy. Cobbs and the other interracial leaders left Esalen, but they continued the style of work inaugurated there in their interracial work with organizations.[78]

The incident, in retrospect, serves as an example of a social script that emerged in the 1960s radical milieu and went on to have a life of its own in the subsequent antiracist movement. Brown's assertiveness apparently gave way quickly to anger, perfectly fitting Cobbs's notion that legitimate rage always lies just below the surface of blacks' personality, ready to spring on the white oppressor. Smith, in turn, seemed to refuse to give in to the demonstration of rage, acknowledge his guilt, and confess to having been motivated by racism in denying Brown the raise and threatening to call the police.

Perhaps this departure from the script stymied those involved. The encounter group sought to reduce tensions by allowing all of the explosive emotions to be let out. By permitting those involved to express themselves freely and openly, the activity aimed to transcend everyday problems by moving participants to a new plane on which they could encounter one another in a completely authentic fashion. But the notion of the authentic expression of emotion was by no means as free of social and political pressures as proponents of encounter groups thought. The encounter group, in fact, helped define the authentic black and white emotional reality—when stripped of all artificial social convention and pretension—to be rage and guilt, respectively.

The interracial encounter at Esalen collapsed when Smith would not act according to the new script and admit to hidden racist proclivities. This insistence that whites were only authentic when they admitted to their racism translated into a truism of the subsequent antiracism movement: Any white person (and eventually, in some versions, any individual at all) who did not admit to being racist was in denial of a basic truth about his or her inner self. Likewise, blacks who failed to conform to the dictates of the new black rage were suspected of being alienated from their own feelings.

ETHNOTHERAPY

After Cobbs left Esalen, he continued to conduct interracial encounter groups. In the early 1970s, he and other group leaders conducted over one hundred groups involving some fourteen hundred individuals at the University of California at San Francisco Medical Center, funded by a research grant. In a 1972 article, Cobbs spelled out a "clinical model" he claimed could transform racial attitudes. He called the technique "ethnotherapy."[79] He explicitly traced his own efforts to his awareness of the T-group and laboratory method and "the great work of Kurt Lewin," which was a foundation for his own.[80] Cobbs bowed to Lewin's method but said that Lewin's interest in "social action" had faded after the inauguration of T-groups in the late 1940s, when the proliferating encounter groups focused more on individual growth and sensory exploration than on fighting prejudice. Cobbs also made a point of distinguishing his own efforts from group therapy. He saw the encounter group as innovative because it encouraged " 'normals' to participate in groups without fear of being labeled medically sick." It was this distinction between the T-group and group therapy, already practiced since the early twentieth century, that ironically allowed Cobbs and others to treat what they saw as the disease of racism in the population at large.[81]

Describing his practice of ethnotherapy, Cobbs argued for the infusion of race into therapeutic practice on the grounds that continuing racism still caused a festering wound for blacks. Blacks needed the encounter group in order to express and come to terms with their anger at whites, and whites needed it to confront their own racism. Cobbs argued firmly that racism was a disease, likening it to tuberculosis, alcoholism, and drug addiction in its disastrous effects, and therefore that it demanded the same kind of group therapy used to treat victims of those diseases. Citing the group approach used by Alcoholics Anonymous, he called racial confrontation necessary for the changing of attitudes.[82]

Cobbs's description of the typical ethnotherapy session or racial confrontation group bore the Esalen imprint. Ethnotherapy groups took place over two full days, usually over a weekend, in groups of about twelve to fourteen, with roughly half of the participants women and half of them blacks. The technique entailed the same emphasis on "the here and now," instant intimacy, intense emotional expression, and the stripping of one's defenses that were emphasized at Esalen. This emphasis would permit total disclosure of the "misguided feelings and attitudes" regarding race that could then come under analysis so that participants could "jar loose, dissect, and examine in fine detail" the "misinformation" underlying them.[83]

Cobbs's workshops began with a discussion of their own purpose and moved to personal introductions by the participants. Then commenced the "racial and personal exploration" phase, during which people discussed questions such as "what being black or white means to them personally" and "what thoughts and feelings" come up when they considered themselves "in light of social definitions of who is acceptable and nonacceptable [sic] in this country."[84] Next, a period called "black exploration" had only blacks talking about race while whites listened, followed by "black-white confrontation." Initial polarization eventually turned into a halting conversation, then slowly gave way to the total unveiling of intimate experiences, an intense sharing of private secrets and pain. This flood of repressed emotions, "intensified" and made "contagious" by the dynamics of a small group, constituted the final stage—the actual ethnotherapy.[85]

In this later description of his method, Cobbs made very clear the premises of the work, which rested on the idea that small-group confrontation would raise participants' awareness of the role of racism in their lives. While he warned of the potential dangers inherent in the unleashing of pent-up emotions, clearly it is exactly this unleashing that formed the crux of ethnotherapy. Therapy relied on participants' total honesty and openness, which Cobbs thought was the only method of bringing into the open attitudes embedded deep in the psyche. Finally, true honesty would bring out black rage and white guilt, without which expression there would be no progress. An even deeper set of assumptions underlay those premises: therapy was needed as the main way to deal with racial tensions; small-group confrontation of this highly personal sort, guided by trained leaders, was the optimal method to carry out this therapy; positive change in race relations was primarily a matter of technique; the ends were self-explanatory; and ordinary people required therapy as much as those who were designated mentally ill by society.

Over the course of this process, Cobbs said, leaders could come to expect several typical patterns in the ways whites responded to the rage of blacks. Early in the workshop, a black person inevitably attacked a white person, who responded with anguish. Automatically assuming that all whites harbor hidden racist proclivities, he dismissed this "peculiar sensitivity" of whites as a form of denial. Objections to the virulence of blacks' attacks and to accusations that whites hold hateful attitudes only proved whites' alienation from their own feelings.[86]

Cobbs went on to describe the response of the blacks in the group, who "counterattack, first with disbelief, then anger." Inside, blacks thought, "How can you take us to be such fools?" But outwardly they responded, "We know from long and bitter experience with whites that all are foes, that you in this room have the very same thoughts as the rest of the bastards. Why don't you own up to it. We already know. We know not by the words you speak, but by your actions toward us." Cobbs concluded that "the blacks are stunned as they realize that whites really believe the lies they tell themselves—and that blacks share belief in many of those lies."[87] Cobbs saw racism as a disease so pervasive in society that no American was immune from its ravages.

Whites continually tried to gain exemptions from inclusion in the class of bigots, for instance, by citing their civil rights work (as Smith had done in the Esalen fiasco) or by resorting to other forms of denial. Cobbs's virulent attack on this denial surfaces in a rare sample of transcripted dialogue of his therapeutic response in action:

Jane:	I don't relate towards you, towards color or anything else, I relate towards every single person here as an individual.
Cobbs:	You're lying, you're lying, you're lying!
Jane:	Why?
Cobbs:	If I would say, "You look like a little boy to me, I just don't see anything," you'd say I was crazy because you're a woman. . . . If I could neutralize you in some way this is exactly what white folks do to black folks. I don't see any color. How in the hell can you not see his color? . . . So stop lying![88]

THE ALL-BLACK ENCOUNTER GROUP: THE INTERPERSONAL IS POLITICAL

The same year Cobbs proclaimed his development of the new model of "ethnotherapy," other practitioners called the possibilities for applying sensitivity training methods to problems faced by blacks "exciting, challenging and frightening." Robert E. Steele, an M.P.H., and Kermit B. Nash, M.S.W., published a paper they had delivered at the 1971 annual meeting of the American Orthopsychiatric Association in Washington, D.C., in that organization's journal, entitled "Sensitivity Training and the Black Community." While Cobbs stressed the need for interracial confrontation, Steele and Nash criticized the sensitivity training movement for not addressing the tensions within the black community. Instead, current sensitivity training practice tended to employ black participants in order "to alleviate guilt for whites" and thus had little relevance beyond the middle class.[89] Steele and Nash thought small-group encounters were much more appropriate for intragroup discussion, whereas interracial problems resulted more from institutional racism and "interpersonal" dynamics and should thus be dealt with differently.[90] Yet their ideas about what blacks needed from encounter groups paralleled Cobbs's closely.

The authors argued that sensitivity training needed to confront the "emotional imprisonment of institutionalized black self-hatred," which they considered universal. Here they drew on the study of the psychologists Kenneth and Mamie Clark, in which black youngsters expressed a preference for white dolls over black ones. The Clarks thought the study showed the ways that racial discrimination had damaged the children's self-esteem, and lawyers in the *Brown v. Board of Education* case of 1954 used the study to argue against segregated schools. Steele and Nash proposed a "black behavioral model" for sensitivity training that rested on the assumption that racism had likewise emasculated black men. As a result of internalizing the demeaning stereotypes of blacks under white supremacy, blacks had adopted "a castrating type of adaptive passivity that encourages non-assertive, anti-social, self-destructive behavior on the part of the black male."[91] This passivity directly denied the inherent human emotional requirement of "self-assertion or aggression," which in turn led to low achievement, powerlessness, and problems within the black community, which could range from male-female recriminations to homicide. These authors prescribed sensitivity training to address this self-destructive behavior and the damaging attitudes in the black community and to inaugurate "personal growth" and the "improvement of self-esteem."[92]

Like Cobbs, Steele and Nash thought the crux of sensitivity training for blacks should involve the release of anger. Many sensitivity trainers aimed at establishing a "saccharine, idyllic, womblike state." But the situation of blacks in particular demanded the release of "negative, hostile, or angry feelings"—and only bona fide anger at that. Sensitivity trainers working with blacks needed not only to "be able to express and to deal with anger" but also differentiate real from artificial rage. Trainers had to get beyond the "cool" front and "well-rehearsed games" most blacks played, since "we [blacks] are accomplished con artists."[93]

Steele and Nash advocated breaking down this front through activities such as role playing and nonverbal exercises. One example was the common "Tug of War" exercise, in which equal segments of the group on opposite sides of the room pulled at an individual standing in the middle. In the example the authors cited, one side took the "Tom" and one the "militant" perspective in order to explore ideological conflict among blacks. Another example was the "fishbowl" exercise, in which an individual sat on a chair between two others, "representing his alter egos," one in the role of the middle-class black individual and the other in the role of the black nationalist.[94]

Steele and Nash disapproved of the emphasis on ideology over competence, stressing the need for trainers who were "not blinded by ideological rhetoric." Yet they also wrote approvingly that "the black power movement has had great psychotherapeutic value"[95] and that sensitivity training should "support the positive aspects" of black power or it might become "counter-revolutionary." Sensitivity training could build confidence and a sense of efficacy for a group by permitting the "psychological safety" that was necessary for the breaking free from old "behavior patterns." Through interaction in the group and feedback on behavior, individuals could locate what habits should be changed. Steele and Nash believed that the sense of trust and efficacy developed in the group could be translated into action outside the group aimed at community betterment.[96] They thought the continuing problems of the black community included economic and social conditions that needed to be addressed.

The approach of Steele and Nash brought many of the contradictions of the sensitivity training approach to race to the fore. They blamed several discrete entities for blacks' problems: a dysfunctional black personality entailing passivity and self-hatred; institutional white racism; disruptive and destructive black behavior; and social and economic conditions. They prescribed the black power movement's problack emphasis, the heightening of individual self-esteem, collective trust building, and self-confidence as a program for bringing about change.

This kind of diffuse, multicausal interpretation of blacks' remaining problems paved the way for a nebulous set of beliefs about what small-group activity could achieve and how. The result was a confused blend of an older tradition of small-group mobilization for social reform with a newer therapeutic notion of the small group as a prime locus for personal growth. As is well known, the use of small-group organizations to forge civic-mindedness and larger political and social reforms was common in the nineteenth and early twentieth centuries, in movements ranging from abolitionism to progressivism. In the first half of the twentieth century, many movements for social reform, as diverse as the settlement house movement and the civil rights movement, drew on the potential for small-group activities to develop a sense of individual efficacy crucial to further civic involvement and social change. What we see in the small-group activities of the late 1960s dedicated to the amelioration of racial problems is the infusion of this tradition with the new emphasis on therapy for the individual, which in turn reflected the shift in the T-group movement from group dynamics to personal growth.

The concern with personal growth never replaced the concern

with group dynamics; rather, they came to be seen as intrinsically con-nected. On the one hand, the building of self-esteem was recast as one goal—when not recast as *the* goal—of improved group dynamics. On the other, improved group dynamics would occur only through indi-vidual "growth" through various forms of therapy. At the same time, the group dynamics movement had helped equate changes in group dynamics with social changes. Although it has been well documented that the story of 1960s and 1970s reform was the new popularization of the idea that the personal was political, the restating of this equa-tion fails to get us beneath the surface of the reform milieu of the time. More revealing is a look at how and why reformers thought the personal became political. Not only did they rightly believe that even the intensely private reaches of personal experience could be affected by political—often equated with power—arrangements, which thus demanded political redress, but many of them also confused the proj-ect of self-development—recast as personal growth through the new therapies—with political action.

The idea that small groups could provide a laboratory in which to study social dynamics and ways to improve them in microcosm gave way to the idea that individual healing was itself a social and political project that could be achieved in the small group. While some, like Steele and Nash, still spoke of personal self-esteem and the efficacious group that allowed it to flourish as a means to an end—revitalized black neighborhoods and social and economic equality and power—others came to use the new equation of the political and the personal realms as a rationale for viewing individual change through small groups as the end of reform. The self-esteem movement, for example, seized on the notion of the psychological damage wrought by social hierarchy and brutality; mistaking cause and effect, it cast heightened self-esteem as the goal of reform, thus enshrining personal reform and imbuing it with higher connotations as though it automatically had an implicit social and political dimension. Concern with self-image, per-sonal motivation, and therapy ultimately displaced concern with increased personal efficacy aimed at civic participation and social change.

The premise that the small group is political was apparent in another little-known attempt to apply T-groups to race relations: the Encountertape. By means of this method, one could conduct encounter groups in the absence of a leader by using audio-tape recordings. It is revealing as a harbinger of the support group as well as the use of motivational tapes, both do-it-yourself therapies that came into widespread use in the late twentieth century. Betty Berzon, an encounter group enthusiast of the 1960s and early 1970s, worked extensively since at least the mid-1960s on the idea of the "leaderless" or "self-directed" group. In the early 1970s, she wrote about applying this method to race relations.

LEADERLESS ENCOUNTER GROUPS

Betty Berzon's ideas about the self-directed group drew on research she conducted with Lawrence N. Solomon, a psychologist who also pioneered in encounter groups, in the early 1960s at the Western Behavioral Sciences Institute. In their program, adult volunteers (clients in a vocational rehabilitation program) met regularly with only a therapist on call in another room. They believed that this approach could allow "many who would never encounter a professional mental health worker" to experience "personal growth," which could help them at work. Despite admitting that not much was actually accomplished, Berzon and Solomon maintained that such groups were "feasible."[97] After two initial studies, they experimented with booklets that would help inspire inexperienced groups by directing the program with particular exercises. Later they turned to tapes that would guide the group process.

Berzon and Solomon declared the intention of their early work to be the enhancement of the individual's social life and job advancement through better self-knowledge and interpersonal relations.[98] Though they had some technical suggestions for improving technique, they were content that both professionally led and self-directed groups witnessed a rise in positive "self-concept," emotional revelation, and self-assertion. They believed that aggressive "self-disclosure" could only enhance relations.[99]

Berzon and Solomon revealed the new therapies' tendency to take mundane insights and elevate them to a kind of scientific practice as they laid out the "two dimensions" of group behavior to be elicited: "talking and listening." Their description of the steps on the way to greater awareness of the relationship between behavior and feelings revealed their assumptions about what kind of talk would benefit both interpersonal relations and the individual. They listed a set of goals, along with the "intermediate behavior" necessary for the "criterion"— or ideal—behavior that had to occur if the goal was to be met. An excerpt from their description of the encounter group process illustrates this:

Goal: To experience more fully in awareness one's own feelings.

Intermediate behavior: Talking about public aspects of self.

Talking about private aspects of self.

Talking about private aspects of self with description of feelings.

Criterion behavior: Talking with direct expression of here-and-now feelings. . . .

It is clear that the more complete the disclosure of private feelings in the group setting, the more therapeutic Berzon and Solomon deemed the activity.[100]

They summarized the content of the encounter sessions, beginning with a consensual group ranking of "a list of ten characteristics employers look for in a 'good employee.'"[101] A tape playing in the room presented a number of exercises. For instance, the "Unfortunate

Circumstance" had participants go around the room to discuss their feelings about their worst life experience; "Self-Appraisal" had them discuss which of ten traits of good employees they should work on the most; "Feeling Pooling" had them write out anonymous notes about strong feelings harbored toward another member of the group, with the notes then read aloud and elaborated on by the group; "Confrontation" had members go around the room telling each person exactly what they felt about him or her. Clients revealed greater "transparency," which meant the experiment was a success in the eyes of Berzon and Solomon. They reported that people became "more open, sensitive to others, self-accepting, and self-motivating."[102]

Perhaps what was most noticeable about the activities in both the directed and the undirected encounter groups Betty Berzon was involved in was what seems to be their sheer uneventfulness. Transcripts from one of the interracial encounter groups based on Berzon's techniques present detailed conversation about how the participants felt initially ("I don't feel exactly afraid but I feel comfortable within the group"); what they felt initially about one another while touching the others one at a time ("Hank, you seem like a very warm individual"); what they felt about sharing those feelings ("There was a feeling within me related to how the people that I was talking to really felt"); how they felt about an exercise in which the group stood in a circle around a person, held hands, and would not let the person break out of the circle ("I didn't think about race at all"); and how they felt at the end of the workshop ("Why don't those of us here have lunch together?")[103]

The lack of direction evident in encounter groups as they actually played themselves out pinpoints what is disturbing about the lens of the therapeutic sensibility more generally, when used to as a mode of understanding the social world. Despite all of the hyperbole and bluster about the potential of the encounter group to let loose the wrongfully corralled facets of our inner beings, what happens in practice seems notably uneventful. The encounter group was the epitome of the long-term shift from what the historian Rochelle Gurstein calls the "reticent sensibility"[104] to the therapeutic one, with its premium on emotional transparency. The sociologist James L. Nolan Jr. has captured the nature of this sensibility well: it centers on the self and its impulses; it conceives of society as "something the self must be liberated from"; it celebrates release rather than self-denial; its "emotivist motif" appeals to the emotions above other faculties; and it casts the self as victim and human behavior primarily in terms of psychic health or pathology.[105] Even when presented as allied with a movement as committed to a moral vision of justice as the civil rights movement, this approach shows a clear tendency to cheapen and trivialize the depth and complexity of human emotion as well as the content of social bonds.

Richard Sennett has written that centering on the self in this fashion, besides degrading relations with those who are our intimates, erodes the very basis of our relations with those who are not. The measurement of all of social life in "psychological terms" rules out the vital impersonal standards of conduct and the social "masks" that allow us to differentiate our public from our private selves—the very distinction that makes it possible to live up to these standards. Here, "intimacy is a field of vision and an expectation," he notes, that actually diminishes the quality of social relations by investing them with undue pressures and false expectations. In so doing, the public world itself is denied legitimacy as a place and a forum for different kinds of pursuits and connections from those appropriate to the private sphere. "People seek out or put pressure on each other to strip away the barriers of custom, manners, and gesture which stand in the way of frankness and mutual openness," and assume that the absence of such barriers will lead only to "warm" relations.[106] The result is inevitable disappointment, which only worsens social isolation—the initial catalyst for emotional disclosure. The highly touted authenticity of behavior in actuality leaves individuals dry, since it fosters transitory emotional revelation rather than the richer expression that takes place only when private boundaries have been maintained. In the absence of any real inner life, the emotional expressions to be shared become purely self-referential, a matter of technique and not content, and ultimately devoid of meaning.

CHAPTER FOUR

Racial Identity Theory:
Groundwork for a Renewal
of Suspicion

The use of the encounter group model to address racial issues was part of a larger movement to adapt psychiatric insights to the realm of race relations. Initially this trend brought highly credible examinations on the part of Kenneth Clark and others of the real psychological dimensions of racial discrimination, but increasingly the terms and mode of the new therapies—including the twelve-step programs and the larger recovery ethos, the movement to free the "inner child," and the like—became mixed in with the racial struggle indiscriminately. The idea that therapy could and should help bring about political change, at the very least by helping one individual at a time confront his or her own psychological inheritance—the legacy of racism and oppression—spawned a number of initiatives that fused race and therapy. A rough consensus over what came to be known as a perspective dedicated to "empowerment" united the disparate approaches: therapy could help blacks and whites take charge of their own lives, ridding themselves respectively of the scars of oppression or their racism.

Mainstream psychotherapy increasingly adopted this perspective as it formed new institutions and approaches to push what advocates saw as the interests of blacks and addressed the racial dynamics of counseling. Meanwhile, a host of new therapies sprouted up, claiming with varying degrees of explicitness to be carrying out the mandates of the revolution of the 1950s and 1960s. The militant turn away from that movement in the mid-1960s increasingly validated those approaches deemed most radical. Under the benign guise of healing, such initiatives often escaped rigorous examination or public debate as the indeterminate notion of empowerment harked vaguely back to the civil rights movement, which few Americans had any cause or desire to challenge. In fact, the self-help renaissance and growing popularity of New Age therapies gave fresh credibility to peripheral approaches that were now recast as alternatives of equal standing to more established approaches. This atmosphere allowed movements that for good reason had hitherto existed on the fringes to work their way unbidden and unnoticed into the mainstream. This application of varieties of pop psychology to the issue of race has deep ramifications. The growing acceptability and respectability of approaches that should be recognized as outlandish both heightens and reflects our lack of clear-sightedness and common sense about race.

The Founding of Black Psychology

At the same time Price Cobbs was moving from the encounter group to his program of ethnotherapy, many others within the therapeutic professions were also carving out new orientations that dealt with race, drawing on or pioneering new theories of racial identity and difference. Although the whole issue of psychological and intelligence testing had exploded with the advent of the civil rights movement, and the idea of elemental racial differences justly received a fatal blow (or near-fatal blow, as *The Bell Curve* debate later showed), a belief in racial differentiation drew new sustenance from movements for a black psychology and multicultural counseling.

The black power movement's shift in emphasis from integration to self-sufficiency helped trigger the establishment of separate black organizations. Black caucuses, for instance, proliferated within professional organizations, and as a direct result, from 1968 to 1971, roughly twenty new black national organizations were founded.[1] This push for black coalitions had different meanings for different participants; some saw it as a temporary way to build a foundation from which to work in more integrated settings, some as an end in itself—a way of generating a viable economy and community among blacks—still others as a repudiation of white racism and white liberalism in the form of deliberate separatism. This mobilization had much to do with the growing number of black professionals in education, politics, the social services, and other arenas. New jobs and a more militant ideology dovetailed to create a unique course of professionalization for blacks. The formation of new institutions, disciplines, and approaches among blacks in the late 1960s and early 1970s fits the pattern other scholars have well marked for how new professions form, establish methods of credentialing members, carve out a specialized niche, and define or create a new body of knowledge.

The new field of "black psychology" emerged out of this context. In the late 1960s, a group of black psychologists broke from the main professional organization of U.S. psychologists, the American Psychological Association (APA). Charging at the APA's 1968 meeting in San Francisco that the association had not responded to the needs of blacks, a group of approximately two hundred black psychologists formed the Association of Black Psychologists, an independent professional organization whose membership is now around fourteen hundred.[2] The initial concerns of the organization included the low numbers of blacks at all levels of the field of psychology, the misuse of psychological testing, and the failure of the APA to use its resources to battle racism. The black association submitted a "petition of concerns" that asked the APA to take particular actions on behalf of blacks: endorse the Kerner Commission's conclusion that white racism triggered the urban riots; reorganize itself to include more black representation; direct its energies to combat racism; study the misuse of psychological testing; reevaluate its certification and training; address the problems of the "ghetto"; add to the numbers of graduate and undergraduate students in the field "by whatever means necessary"; and establish a committee with representatives from the Association of Black Psychologists. In an article on the founding of the new organization, the Washington University professor Robert Williams wrote that the APA's response was, despite several positive actions it agreed to take, "for the most part evasive and non-productive."[3]

To herald the arrival of the new field, a new journal was also founded, entitled the *Journal of Black Psychology,* whose first issue appeared in August of 1974. In an opening statement, its editor, William David Smith, defined black psychology as "the study of Black behavioral patterns": "It deals with the total behavior in all situations of Black people throughout the world." He added, "It is erroneous to assume that because Black Psychology has not been completely developed that it does not exist," and promised that "a more definitive explanation will emerge as we investigate and learn more in this area."[4]

Books and articles in the new field followed in a veritable flood. Differing and often disagreeing about theory and method, these works nevertheless shared a common understanding of the uniqueness of the black experience. While it was obvious that African Americans' historical treatment had been unique, it was not at all clear that their future had to remain so. To use terms familiar to the emerging adherents of black psychology, just because the diagnosis was that blacks' historical inheritance led to psychological differences, it was not a given that therapists should assume a continuation of those differences or prescribe treatment that assumed they were ineluctable. Yet, the simultaneous, broad reorientation in American culture to a preoccupation with individual identity helped ensure that the prognosis would rest on the same premise of basic racial differences.

A central treatise in the emerging movement was the book *Black Psychology,* edited by the psychologist Reginald L. Jones and published in 1972. With chapters on everything from the misuses of psychological testing to the roots of white racism, the collection of essays assembled the writings of a number of black social and behavioral scientists. Hardly all in agreement about basic matters, the essayists nevertheless shared a commitment to reinterpret psychological theory and practice relating to blacks and to pose new directions for thinking about race and psychology. In his preface, Jones pointed to several themes: an emphasis on the "positive aspects of black behavior which have permitted survival—though not without scars," rather than a focus on black "deficiency"; a rejection of the white experience as the norm for judging blacks; and a location of "explanations for black behavior" in social and economic conditions and not just psychology. Jones insisted that the new subdiscipline did not accept the notion of inevitable racial differences in psychology when he wrote, "It may appear that categorical black-white differences across social and personal domains are being made. Nothing could be further from the truth." Despite this caveat, he went on to say that environmental "forces . . . shape and influence black Americans."[5]

Jones's assertion of environmentally based differences, a view that had its origin in the turn-of-the-century cultural anthropology of Columbia University professor Franz Boas, was typical of the thinking that underpinned not only the explosion of black psychology but the social sciences more generally, not to say identity politics inside and outside of the academy. While rejecting the idea of innate psychological or mental differences, adherents of black psychology agreed that history and social conditions had created differences. It would be ludicrous to argue that these "forces" had no role in black life, or that the different environments that blacks and whites encountered failed to result in any differences in behavior or psychology at all. However, the eagerness with which social and behavioral scientists embraced the environmental explanations, stemming in large part from their well-intentioned recognition of the pernicious role racism had played in black life, amounted to a new kind of determinism.

In the 1990s, the Harvard sociologist Orlando Patterson criticized liberal social scientists for a deterministic or "over socialized" point of view that downplayed any possibility of black autonomy or responsibility, even while he took conservatives to task for their "under socialized" view that failed to see any social and economic factors in explaining black behavior or experience.[6] One important side effect of liberal environmental determinism was its promotion of an unexamined assumption of black difference. Another was an even less examined premise that the best way to understand the black experience and address black needs was through identity. In the context of the late 1960s, influenced both by the "rage" school of black invective and interpretation of the black struggle and by psychological and cultural trends that stressed the value of emotional catharsis and saw the inferiority complex as a crucial phase of life, this search for identity took on a distinctly personal nature. The idea that blacks should separately free themselves to discover and create their own identities—to become empowered—replaced the moral universalism of the civil rights crusade.

THE DEBATE OVER BLACK EMASCULATION

The psychiatrist Alvin Poussaint, one of the main spokespersons for a black psychology, helped reorient questions of racial justice to the realm of psychology. Taking issue with the leading black American psychologist Kenneth Clark, who headed the APA in the 1970s, Poussaint argued that the primary psychological problem blacks faced was not so much a self-hatred or inferiority complex, resulting from life under white supremacy, as an "'aggression-rage' constellation." The urban riots that occurred continually throughout the 1960s appeared to him to be less a form of "community suicide," as Clark put it, than a result of suppressed anger. To argue this point, Poussaint offered an analogy between the mood of all blacks and his own feelings upon being stopped, frisked, and publicly humiliated by a white policeman in Jackson, Mississippi, in the mid-1960s. Accompanied by his black secretary, he was tormented by his sense of impotence in the face of authority: it revealed publicly his inability to fulfill the mandates of his masculinity and protect his female companion. Because Poussaint was called boy, addressed by first name alone, and threatened with violence when he hesitated to comply with the policeman's commands, all of the blacks witnessing the incident were "psychologically 'put in our place,'" he observed, concluding, "What was I to do with my rage?"[7]

Poussaint's main argument, which surfaced repeatedly in his work and that of many others at the time, was that slavery and segregation had led to black men's "castration"—the stripping away of their very manhood. Blacks had developed "docile and unassertive" personalities in response to continual humiliation and the omnipresent threat of punishment for any sign of aggression. Even religion had "fostered passivity," by merely teaching blacks they "must love their oppressor." White racism had thus resulted in "a trained incapacity to be aggressive."[8]

This idea that one of the primary—if not *the* primary—results of racial oppression was black men's "castration" has, of course, been widely discussed and debated. The notion that a main thrust of black liberation needed to be an assertion of masculinity—as defined in terms that were increasingly coming under attack by the emerging women's movement, the counterculture, and the therapeutic culture—rang false to many black women, including prominent feminists.[9] Entangled in this debate over masculinity was the divisive issue of whether the traditional attacks on black men had contributed to an abnormal matriarchal social structure among blacks. Even those who condemned the emasculation of black men but failed to accept the idea that a black matriarchy existed were interpreted as arguing that the problem with black communities was the overweening power of

116

women, and its eclipse of black manhood. Michelle Wallace, in her 1979 work *Black Macho and the Myth of the Superwoman*, was one feminist writer who questioned the claim that the primary casualty of racism had been the black male's natural right to aggression. She traced that view to the sexism prevalent in the 1960s Left and its cult of masculinity.[10]

The controversy over the emasculation theory and the notion of a black matriarchy was heated and long-lasting, and it still rages in the work of some black feminists and some social scientists. Orlando Patterson's most recent book, *Rituals of Blood,* which returns to the emasculation theory, clearly touches on this sore spot. His analysis of what he sees as the profound problems afflicting black families—high rates of divorce, desertion, separation, loneliness, and social isolation— illustrates how the discussion of emasculation, and the implications of that discussion for the role of women, have also been intricately entwined with the debates over the so-called pathology of the black family and black culture. To call the black family pathological seems to many to demean the heroic efforts black women have often had to make—sometimes as a result of desertion or maltreatment by their male partner as much as of racism. But to deny that the disruptions in black family life and personal relationships are abnormal has appeared to others as a failure to grasp the problem with a situation in which black men have an insignificant role. Patterson believes that a crisis of "gender relations" is the most important remaining problem facing poor black communities today: destructive behavior, disagreements over values, layers of misunderstanding, recriminations, and a "love and trouble" tradition all make for an increasingly antagonistic situation between men and women. He thinks that a "hip-hop" street culture, with its oppositional attitudes toward all authority and its embrace of promiscuity, receives support from mainstream culture's fixation on the black man as a kind of American Dionysus—a figure whose superhuman physical prowess helps whites counter the repressed hyper-intellectualism of the corporate world.[11]

The debates have revolved around whether the black family was pathological or not, whether the emphasis should be on black men's emasculation or on black women's "double jeopardy" of being oppressed on two counts, being black and being female (or even triple jeopardy—black, female, and poor), and whether the role taken on in the family by black women in the absence of their mates was a desirable or undesirable development. These debates have been engaged elsewhere at length, though hardly resolved.

What must be recognized is how the usual terms of the male emasculation and female self-assertion debate keep the discussion centered on vague generalizations about the mood of all black women or all black men, and a sense of particular grievance and victimhood vis-à-vis one another, all of which pave the way for a therapeutic approach that surprisingly exacerbates tensions rather than resolving them. To argue over whether black men or women were hurt more by slavery, segregation, or by racism—given our knowledge that victimization was so extreme for both—itself seems tied to more recent agonies and disappointments, of the sort that Patterson describes. But the casting of these conflicts as entirely the long-term result of racial oppression misses a more recent dimension of both sides of the argument—that the current prescriptions might actually worsen the problem. Whatever their particular emphases, the identity theorists and the self-esteem crusaders hypothesized a perennially victimized self whose need for emotional expression was of supreme—even exclusive—importance. This version of self is ultimately detrimental for all arenas of collective life, including American race relations.

The emasculation theory has thus been criticized for downplaying the ways in which women suffered because of racism and focusing primarily on the victimhood of men. But a less understood problem with the theory is its view of aggression as the natural, authentic emotional mode of men and adoption of the pop-Freudian notion that the inhibition of impulse can lead to neurosis. Though its proponents never intended it to, the emasculation theory not only renewed the stereotype of the angry, sexually dangerous black male, but also gave support to the emphasis on individual emotional release or immediate gratification that meshed perfectly with the increasingly therapeutic strain of mainstream culture. This new orientation helped give racial differences a new lease on life. If it was no longer believable that there were physical, or at least mental, differences between blacks and whites, it increasingly seemed to make sense that there must be psychological and emotional ones.

THE PSYCHOLOGIZING OF EVERYTHING

Intellectual developments in the social and behavioral sciences and the social upheavals of the 1960s underpinned the fixation on individual emotional life and personal identity to the exclusion of numerous other aspects of life. In the post–World War II period, social psychology's concern with the social context of personality development and collective patterns of behavior, anthropology's culture and personality school of thought, and sociology's preoccupation with delinquency and alienation, all stressed the importance of personality. Theodor Adorno's *The Authoritarian Personality* and Erik Erikson's work on the concept of the identity crisis both had deep ramifications across the disciplines and outside the academy and inspired whole arenas of social thought, adding weight to discussions of the importance of personality structure and psychological motivation and equilibrium. The generational revolt, the turn to black power, and the attendant reaction of the parents and the "establishment"—along with everything else that happened at the time—came under scrutiny for how they manifested psychological impulses. *The Authoritarian Personality* left an indelible mark on the way racism would be viewed. Increasingly racism was considered a pathological condition inextricably tied to an entire psychological complex based in a repressive, hierarchical, and

119

rigid world view. And Erikson's depiction of the individual's quest for identity helped cast the youth revolt, in the eyes of many within it as well as outside observers, as a search for identity.

Social scientists who considered themselves part of a radical van-guard seized on the new emphasis on black power in the late 1960s. Influenced by Adorno, Erikson, and others, they interpreted the black power movement as involving questions of identity. In his study *Contempt and Pity,* the historian Daryl Michael Scott has argued that in the late 1960s what distinguished the thought of these leftist social sci-entists was their rejection of images of pathology and victimhood, their embrace of black pride, and their reading of the African American past and present as characterized by cultural resistance. He writes, "By the mid-1970s, in the wake of the radical onslaught, the social science image of the black psyche, along with black culture, was largely divorced from therapeutic concerns."[12] But the therapeutic sensibility ran deeper than the images of pathology. In fact, many rad-icals adopted language touting the need for positive self-images through group pride precisely as part of a therapeutic project, eschewing balance or realism about the readily observable destruction that racism had left in its wake.

The new myopia—however refreshing an alternative to the over-generalizations and the hyper-victimization tone of liberal pathology theories—made it difficult for these leftists to account for continuing problems. The identity tack made it nearly impossible to move beyond a simplistic polarization between white oppressors and the black oppressed (recast as heroic resisters). As a result, those in so-called radical ranks—let alone those of other political positions—found it onerous to discuss race at all when observers' language, demeanor, and intent did not seem to mesh with the therapeutic project of black pride. Although it comprised a limited assault on the received liberal view of the time, this therapeutic project fit perfectly into the larger personal growth and self-esteem movements and departed dramati-cally from the strain of civil rights and even black power that emphasized institution building in the black community. It was a politics of posture that relied on an integrated audience.

Even the theories about racial identity that adopted a definite scientific pose reveal the dramatic—and intentional—conflation of this political agenda and ideas about individual psychology. Of the many theories about racial identity to come out of the 1960s and 1970s, one of the most important was the concept of black racial identity as "negritude," as developed by William E. Cross Jr. Cross presented his highly influential theory while still a graduate student in developmental psychology at Princeton University, having received an A.B. in psychology from the University of Denver in 1963.[13]

LIFESTYLE AS RACE IDENTITY

Cross outlined his ideas in conference papers and articles that drew much attention, publishing work in Reginald Jones's *Black Psychology* and Joyce Ladner's prominent *Death of White Sociology,* whose role in proclaiming the importance of a black emphasis in sociology was similar to that of Jones's book in psychology. Cross's theory, which he elaborated on in a later book, was simple—to a fault. Clearly inspired by the concept of consciousness-raising prevalent at the time, he proposed that blacks go through four distinct stages "when they encounter blackness in themselves": "preencounter," "encounter," "immersion," and "internalization."[14]

In the preencounter stage, Cross and his coauthors wrote, society has conditioned blacks to see themselves as inferior and uncivilized, having adopted notions of white supremacy, so they adopt preferences for white norms of expression, beauty, and the like. Such an individual has difficulty trusting blacks and believes that whites are more intelligent. Furthermore, this psychological profile predisposes the individual to a self-destructive ideology of "incorporation, integration, or assimilation."[15]

In the encounter stage, an experience related to race makes an individual question his or her self-image. This experience leads to an "obsessive search for black identity." Now he or she develops a "black perspective" and turns to the project of self-validation, which comes in the next stage, immersion. Here, Cross and his coauthors argued with certainty, "everything of value must be relevant to blackness." They elaborated at length:

> This person involves himself in a world of blackness—e.g., he participates in political meetings, rapping sessions, black theater, seminars, art shows, television programs, etc. . . .
> This person feels and behaves as if the white world, culture, and persons are dehuman—e.g., whites become honkies, pigs, devils, etc., to him. . . .
> This person hungrily consumes black literature and devotes much contemplation to the forms of being black—e.g., he wears dashikis, cultivates an Afro, takes on an African name, etc.
> This person turns inward and withdraws from everything that is white.

As a result, the individual at the encounter stage stops deifying whites and begins celebrating and analyzing black culture, creating a "new life style."[16]

In the final stage of "internalization," the newly conscious individual exhibits "security" and self-satisfaction and "feels a great love and compassion for all oppressed people." Here Cross's theory bears unmistakable traces of the Protestant tradition going back to the Puritan conversion experience, in which the individual is prepared to better the world (the final Puritan phase of "sanctification," during which the new convert embarks on the erection of new churches). The individual's newfound identity leads to active community involvement on behalf of the "development of black power."[17]

It is a truism that even scientific theory is affected by time, ideology, and cultural context. But it must be admitted that the constraints on most such theories, which by their very nature as theories make at least some claim of transcendence of these markers, are not usually so transparent. The time-bound and ideological nature of Cross's theory bears the stamp of contemporary trends. Of all the theories proposed at the time to explain the formation of black self-identity, it is striking that ones like this, imbued with an adolescent tone of self-discovery, survived at all. That this theory was received by some as equally legitimate as the others proposed in *Black Psychology,* such as the psychologist Edward Barne's assertion of the important role of the black family and community in socializing children into a positive self-concept, testifies to the extent to which the paradigm of consciousness-raising had pervaded the American mind.

Coming in equal shares from the political movements of the era, which had yielded a valid basis for a large-scale awareness of past wrongs and future hopes—in the civil rights movement, the push for female equality, the growing opposition to the Vietnam War, and budding environmental, Native American, and gay rights agitation—and from the therapeutic movement, the cult of awareness was a strange hybrid. In the early 1970s, the belief that one's style—attire, possessions, housing, and other aspects of one's self-presentation—was an all-important and quasi-political phenomenon helped make personal identity seem intrinsically tied to one's political stand. In this context, Cross's ideas might have sounded eminently logical both to blacks who were open to the diminished conception of the black revolution as a lifestyle revolt and to sympathetic whites who believed, or wanted to believe, that outward expressions of black power sentiments like these constituted the only authentic voice of newly liberated blacks.

One might assume that theories like Cross's would burn quickly, like a candle flame, and then die out. On the contrary, this notion of a natural and universal course of black self-discovery has been enshrined in recent psychological treatments. Perhaps the best-known example is Beverly Daniel Tatum's *"Why Are All the Black Kids Sitting*

Together in the Cafeteria?" and Other Conversations about Race, which epit-
omizes the problems with racial identity theorizing along the lines of
Cross's model.

BLACK CHILDREN IN THE CAFETERIA

Tatum is a professor of psychology and dean at Mount Holyoke
College as well as a psychologist in private practice. Her book had
tremendous resonance when it came out in 1997 because of the climate of controversy about race that characterized the 1990s. After a
period of relative quiescence in the late 1970s and 1980s, the issue
of race was again catapulted to national attention by the Rodney
King beating in 1991 and the ensuing riots in Los Angeles, the growing critical mass of black conservative thought, the challenge to
affirmative action, the O. J. Simpson trial in 1995, and other controversies. Observers from across the political spectrum differed
dramatically in their evaluations of the racial climate, arguing over
the extent to which racial progress had really occurred. Some
expressed consternation, in particular, at what they saw as a continuation of patterns of racial segregation, observable everywhere,
from urban neighborhoods to school cafeterias. That much of this
segregation appeared to be at least in part chosen by blacks and
other groups themselves came as a tragic realization to many who
were committed to an integrated society.

In the introduction to *"Why Are All the Black Kids Sitting Together in
the Cafeteria?" and Other Conversations about Race,* Tatum describes the
long-term origins of the book. Initially a clinical psychologist interested in racial identity among black children, she agreed to teach a
course called "Group Exploration of Racism," which her university
colleagues had passed on because, in Tatum's telling, they were used to
teaching lecture courses, whereas she had experience leading "emotionally difficult group discussions" and relished "group interaction

and self-revelation." Using a manual of the post–civil rights "antiracist" sensitivity training movement from the late 1970s, Judith H. Katz's *White Awareness: Handbook for Anti-racism Training,*[18] Tatum began teaching the course. In fact, she speaks of having taught the course, retitled "The Psychology of Racism," to hundreds of students in a variety of formats, in order to help students discover how "racism operates in their own lives and what they could do about it." She says she has taught another course of this kind to hundreds of schoolteachers and administrators. In addition, she has led numerous workshops on racism for parents.[19] In the context of these classes and workshops, she has repeatedly heard the question about why black students frequently sit separately in school cafeterias, these many years after desegregation.

Tatum's book offers a sustained answer to that question. She makes a special case for the application of racial identity theory to our understanding of both white and black racial attitudes, claiming that such a perspective has been absent and is sorely needed. She decries the scarcity of racial identity discussions in psychology. She sets herself to redressing this "neglect" by deliberately popularizing identity theories, which she thinks are unfortunately "confined to scholarly journals and academic volumes." Even further, she argues that psychology as a whole has neglected race.[20]

There is only one problem with Tatum's assertion about the absence of psychology from the "public discourse" on race: it is not true. As Daryl Michael Scott and many others have shown, psychology, at least in the form of quasi-psychological simplifications from pop psychology, has actually been the *primary* lens through which race has been understood in America in the late twentieth century. The hegemony of pop psychology, in fact, goes a long way toward explaining why a figure like Tatum, whose theories barely glaze the surface of the complex story of race in this country, would be so sought-after that, heady with her newfound celebrity status, she would effuse publicly about her chagrin when yet another lecture invitation arrived.[21]

Another possible factor in the persistent difficulties in discussing race in this country continually eludes self-professed experts like Tatum: their own ministrations. From their position in the alleged vanguard, these writers cannot entertain the possibility that it is precisely their own theories and methods that have helped lead us to this impasse. What they are peddling as new and progressive is in fact at least a generation old. And what validity racial identity theory ever had, it had in a very different context. Despite the claims of the race experts that they are on the cutting edge—and their audience's seeming willingness to go along with this fiction—they are merely rehashing black power pieties. In their hyperbolic claims of diagnostic accuracy, the experts ignore the possibility of self-fulfilling prophecy. After having been exposed to the pervading American culture of diversity workshops and classes like Tatum's, many Americans have obediently learned to view race through the lens of identity.

Déjà Vu

For what Tatum is peddling is déjà vu quite simply: it is Cross's racial identity theory reincarnated, but with a few gratuitous insults to whites thrown in, delivered in the same breezy and jocular tone as the rest of the text. Tatum's answer to the question about self-segregation among black high school and college students is simple: they are experiencing a natural phase of their identity development. Building on the premise of an unchanged racist society, Tatum leads us through Cross's stages. In the preencounter stage, the black child adopts the norms of dominant, white society, including "the stereotypes, omissions, and distortions" of the "Eurocentric culture" that "reinforce notions of White superiority." Next comes the "encounter," or a set of experiences an individual has as part of an oppressed group—often beginning around junior high school or high school. In response to his or her awareness of racism, the individual frequently develops an "oppositional social identity," tries to assimilate to white society, searches for "alternative images," or turns to "seek support" in the "psychological safety of their own group" (thus the segregated cafeteria tables). Next comes the immersion in black culture, during which, Tatum eagerly informs us, "the developing Black person sees White people as simply irrelevant." This stage leads to a final phase characterized by a strong sense of one's racial identity, commitment to blacks, and supposedly a concomitant ability to "transcend race."[22]

Tatum gives a number of examples of what triggers this "encounter" stage, which she sees as naturally and justifiably characterized by anger. In one illustration, a teacher keeps encouraging a young black woman to attend a school dance. When the student declines, the teacher says, "Oh come on, I know you people love to dance." The student automatically interprets this phrasing as a deliberate racial slight. When she confides her humiliation to her white friend, the friend says, "Oh, Mr. Smith is such a nice guy, I'm sure he didn't mean it like that. Don't be so sensitive." Tatum thinks that the white friend's failure to reinforce the black student's feelings and interpretation of the event explains why the black student would seek the company of her fellow black students at the cafeteria table. Tatum says the friend misses the importance of the teacher's remark altogether.[23]

Tatum's analysis illustrates the faults in this line of reasoning. The real problem is not so much the separate assembly of black students, which really might be a fairly expected, even natural phenomenon resulting from shared neighborhoods, friends, and experiences. But adults like Tatum are helping children put a particular spin on their experiences. In explaining self-segregation as rooted in anger and withdrawal—which she considers valid responses to the many racial slights experienced daily in racist America—Tatum exaggerates the climate, makes all slights traceable to an intentional, relentless hatefulness, and blurs indiscriminately minor and even crude faux pas with heinous acts of racism. It seems rather important, for instance, that in the above example neither the teacher's remark nor the classmate's response is actually racist. Tatum dismisses the classmate's realistic counsel not to be overly sensitive—good advice for most adolescents. Tatum writes,

> Perhaps the White friend is right, and Mr. Smith didn't mean it, but imagine your own response when you are upset, perhaps with a spouse or partner. He or she asks what's wrong and you explain why you are offended. Your partner brushes off your complaint, attributes it to your being oversensitive. What happens to your emotional thermostat? It escalates. When feelings, rational or irrational, are invalidated, most people disengage. They not only choose to discontinue the conversation but are more likely to turn to someone who will understand their perspective.[24]

Tatum also ignores other possible readings of the initial event: "you people" could as easily refer to eighth-graders, this class, young women, or those students inclined toward dancing as to all African Americans; the broader context was one of inclusion, so if the teacher's enthusiastic invitation did refer to African Americans, it might not have been malicious in intent, but quite the opposite; the teacher's age, region, or nationality might not have provided for a complete familiarity with the taboos of today's racial etiquette, so a friendly or humorous correction might have been in order; the comment might have been a mistake for which the teacher is already humiliated but thought the student might not have noticed, or instead have been forgiving; or it might have been a misplaced attempt to make humor out of a stereotype that the teacher assumes is dead and buried at this point in history. Of course, there is the possibility—the one that Tatum assumes—that the teacher actually believes the stereotype, which seems like the most remote possibility, but a possibility nonetheless. However, rather than give the exchange the benefit of the doubt, counsel fortitude, or encourage students to practice the skills of civil engagement they will need throughout life in an integrated nation, Tatum encourages withdrawal and self-absorption. Even granting that a mere charge of over-sensitivity from a spouse or friend could actually trigger the ire and withdrawal Tatum thinks is a given, it is not so clear that it *should*. The idea that any slight, large or small—even if not actually intended as a slight—should be experienced as a deliberate withholding of emotional validation is one to be challenged, not supported. But Tatum legitimizes this hypersensitivity and overreaction by casting it as a legitimate stage in the forming of a racial identity.

White Identity as Therapy

Even further, Tatum sees "race consciousness" as a panacea not only for blacks but for whites as well. She holds up white students' inability to "identify with any particular ethnic heritage" as a mark of never having had to face racism. Whites need to "achieve a healthy sense of White identity," she believes.[25] Tatum draws on a model put forth by the psychologist Janet Helms, which delineates six stages in the formation of "White identity." In the "Contact" stage, according to Helms, whites first discover "the idea or the actuality of Black people," so they generalize about all blacks from this experience and measure their acquaintances against inherited stereotypes. Forced to acknowledge that blacks are treated as inferiors, whites then enter the "Disintegration" stage, during which there arises a "conscious, though conflicted, acknowledgement of one's whiteness." Whites suddenly experience a series of dilemmas as it becomes clear that their most cherished beliefs are at odds with the injustices of racism. During "Reintegration," whites move on to admit their whiteness, but define it in terms of their superiority to black people.[26]

Next, Helms writes, the "Pseudo-Independent" stage brings the stirrings of a more "positive white identity." Questioning the notion of black inferiority, whites examine themselves for signs of racist behavior. They misguidedly direct their efforts mainly, however, to helping blacks, on the basis of their narrow "white criteria for success." The "Immersion/Emersion" stage brings a search for information—through reading "biographies and autobiographies of whites who have made similar identity journeys" or participating in "white conscious-ness-raising groups." Whites can now turn to the more laudable goal of changing whites instead of blacks, as they experience "emotional" and "cognitive restructuring," as well as "emotional catharsis" of feel-ings previously "denied or distorted."[27]

After the "negative feelings are expressed," whites are free to expe-rience "a euphoria perhaps akin to a religious rebirth." This is a cata-lyst for forming a full-fledged white identity and beginning "to tackle racism and oppression in its various forms." The final stage, the cul-mination of self-development, is "Autonomy." At this point, whites experience "racial self-actualization or transcendence," which Helms describes as "an ongoing process" involving continual accumulation of information about race and other cultural groups. This stage "involves an awareness of personal responsibility for racism, consistent acknowledgement of one's whiteness, and abandonment of racism in any of its forms as a defining aspect of one's personality." The premise of this theory is that denial of the omnipresence of racism prevents whites from having "a positive white identity," which, in turn, makes them uneasy with the "racial consciousness" of others. The ultimate goal is for whites to develop a sense of the "Self as a racial being." The inability to do so in positive ways is one of the hidden injuries, writes Helms, of racism, which harms not only the victims but also the "per-petrators of racism" themselves.[28] Beverly Tatum informs us that only those whites who have developed their own racial identities as whites can have positive or "authentic connections with people of color."[29]

While many of Tatum's observations capture general truths about the racial tensions that still exist in our only newly integrated world, her attenuated and time-bound theories fail to account for improvements that have occurred. It is true that our current racial climate demands many subtle behavioral adjustments from both blacks and whites, especially from children and adolescents, and much social awkwardness remains. The racial identity theorists fault society for socializing people into racism, but their own ideas now play a distinct role in the process of socialization. Experts' theories and sensitivities enter the broader culture through classes, workshops, and publications, helping to set the terms by which young people understand and express their anxieties about race. The popularization of theories like Tatum's is disconcerting. Tatum makes claims about our collective "silence" regarding African American history, universal images and attitudes of white superiority, and lack of black role models, despite the tremendous advances in racial attitudes and the new visibility and the truly stunning achievement of blacks in nearly every arena imaginable. Recent polls, for instance, show a dramatic change on basic issues such as how much black history is taught and attitudes toward interracial marriage.[30]

The language and terms of the recovery movement—so apparent in this line of thinking—leave no room for an acknowledgment of progress, however incomplete. If we acknowledge that the majority of Americans are no longer in recovery but have recovered from most of the truly virulent racism underpinning slavery and segregation, these experts rightly sense that we might have little need—indeed, little patience—for consciousness-raising workshops and identity facilitators. They are probably right. Still, they undoubtedly harbor a nobler fear that we will abandon the fight for racial justice. Here they are also right in thinking that racial justice, like all of our other ideals of justice, requires constant vigilance. But these experts mistakenly confuse their efforts on behalf of identity— the diminished version of identity prevalent in the new therapies, a transitory emotional security—with the struggle for justice.

THE PSYCHOLOGICAL, RACIAL SELF

In assessing the application of the encounter group to interracial tensions, we note that one of its main consequences was to help legitimize the notion of race-related personality traits, different psychological and emotional needs and makeups. Out of the maelstrom of racial politics in the 1960s thus crystallized a newly racialized self. Certainly the concept of black and white racial identity was nothing new. The white defense of slavery and segregation had long rested on whites' sense of belonging to a race separate from that of blacks, and, in response to white oppression, blacks had developed a sense of identity as a race as well. What was new was the particular racial identity that integration created.

It is not sufficient to see the shift in the 1960s as a move away from an emphasis on citizenship rights to a "black consciousness"—called by some the rise of the "black voice." There were endless possibilities—as infinite as human variation itself—for what black Americans would think about the past and current strictures of their lives and how that would influence their sense of themselves as individuals. The idea that there exists a single, unified black consciousness, beyond a shared sense that wrongs had been inflicted upon blacks in the American past, was a product of the radical milieu as it unfolded in the cultural context of the age. That race was a preeminently psychological matter had become so widely believed by the 1960s that the notion of an individual's coming into racial awareness—or a society's rising consciousness of race—was reduced to narrow models for blacks and whites. For blacks, this consciousness involved freedom from psychological and emotional repression, mainly self-affirmation through the release of rage or another form of self-assertion. For whites, it meant freedom from the alleged psychological debilitation of their own racism.

The increasing weight of psychology as a tool for addressing race relations thus underpinned the shift in notions of interracial conduct by positing narrow interpretations of how the self responds to a social world pervaded by racism. Psychologists, psychiatrists, and pop psychologizers were a major flank in the army of social engineers who sought to prescribe or legitimize certain behaviors as responses to this reality. The prominence and appeal of their work spoke to the continuing anxieties Americans harbored about interracial conduct, but also ultimately served to exacerbate those tensions by contributing to a kind of cultural lag—a delay in Americans' realization that the civil rights movement had indeed changed, or represented a change that had already taken place in, many whites' attitude toward blacks—and by promulgating psychological resolutions that rested on a double standard of behavior. Furthermore, the racialized self—in shorthand, the angry black self and the guilty or imbalanced white self—that was implied in the specifically psychological form of consciousness that emerged furnished a severely limited range of validated emotional expression for both. The experts' narrow and backward-looking sense of the self's response to interracial life ironically constricted the choices available for interpersonal interactions by providing the underpinnings for a dominant model for such interactions, even while promising individual liberation.

The idea that race relations were fraught with problems that could be dealt with and understood only with the aid of insights from pop psychology helped carve out a sphere for experts and, in so doing, obscured broader cultural sources for anger and anomie. The psychological racial self, with its frustrations and anxieties, could, after all, begin to recuperate only through therapeutic approaches developed by these race experts.

CHAPTER FIVE

Revolt against Repression:
New Age Therapy from the Fringe
to the Mainstream

Alternative therapies originally associated with the human potential or personal growth movement quickly transmogrified into the New Age movement after the 1960s. The New Age therapies developed in a cultural context characterized by a number of factors: the 1950s outcry against growing homogeneity and conformity; a recognition of the egregious misuse and corruption of authority, prompted by the civil rights and antiwar movements; the counterculture's ensuing stylistic stance against all authority; the loosening of mores in the sexual revolution and rising acceptability of divorce and separation; trends in psychology, from new schools of thought, the explosion of counseling and psychotherapy, and the demand for short-term counseling to a growing hybridization of therapeutic techniques; the larger preoccupation with individual identity; the loss of political direction and will after the late 1960s and Watergate in the early 1970s; outrage against the growth of large governmental and corporate bureaucracies; the spiritual crisis prompted by growing materialism and secularization; and the triumph of a consumerist outlook on life. The antiauthoritarian character of their search for individual identity made many Americans receptive to new therapies promulgated both by formally credentialed psychiatrists, psychologists, and clinical social workers and by persons with little or no formal training. Even when defiance against authority translated into an attack on professional experts, Americans merely turned to newer, self-proclaimed authorities for guidance in living their lives.

Blacks were not immune to the attractions of such therapies. But these therapies have had a cumulative effect on race relations that reaches far beyond their effect on those individual African Americans who willingly sought their assistance. Multiplying uncontrollably and driven by a promiscuous blend of pop-psychological theories, many of these therapies increasingly cast themselves as techniques to deal with problems relating to race. Their frequent association of personal growth with political transformation prompts them to offer an ideological program along with their therapy.

The critical look here at the nature and implications of some New Age race therapies certainly does not rule out a proper or legitimate role for more venerable forms of therapy or social betterment through individual transformation; rather, it questions the particular way these therapies thought this could be done and to what end. A sampling of these therapies indicates there are good reasons for suspicion about the degree of ideological intrusion into individual therapy, even if one allows for the normal subjectivity humans inevitably bring to any social task. Even beyond the shortcomings of any particular therapeutic practice, we should ask what the cumulative effect of these new modes of interacting is on individuals already hard pressed to live amicably in society. The massive social therapeutic project masquerades as an attack on the stodgy old grandfather of the field—psychoanalysis—as well as an assault on the established traditions in psychology and nearly every other social authority, all in the name of personal growth and freedom. This project nevertheless perpetuates a therapeutic mind-set, even for those who have no special difficulty coping with everyday demands.

The accumulated effect of these new therapies is a sense that we

are all perpetually in a process of recovery and that we owe it to our-selves to seek the assistance of the helping professions (or nonprofes-sions). Ironically, the result is dependence on the very antiauthoritarian experts who claim to be able to liberate us. In order that we continue to believe we need their services, they stop short of bestowing actual autonomy. The meaning of "empowerment"—the mantra of the move-ment—is assumed rather than spelled out. For the therapeutic socie-ty, such a goal continually recedes beyond the horizon. These therapies share many of the new assumptions about race: racism continues unabated; all slights are equal; anyone who endures racial slights of any kind or degree is a victim or survivor who needs help; racism is an illness shared by all oppressors, who also need therapy; and small-group interactions and emotional catharsis are the primary ways in which the racial problems of the country should be faced. That there is never an end in sight—racism remains completely unchanged—handily gives the new therapies the rationale not just for persevering but for proselytizing through pamphlets, books, journals, classes, workshops, and retreats. Not so conveniently for the rest of us, they mire us ever more deeply in a new cultural quicksand.

The Reevaluation Counseling Idea

Just one example of these alternative therapies that threaten to work their way into the mainstream is reevaluation counseling, also called co-counseling (and sometimes peer counseling). It is worth looking carefully at this counseling method since it illustrates so well the pit-falls of the broader therapy culture by taking them to their logical extreme. Harvey Jackins, the pioneer of reevaluation counseling (called RC in the movement), has described its technique in numer-ous books and pamphlets. His 1975 *Guidebook to Re-evaluation Counseling,* published by the movement's publisher, Rational Island Publishers, calls reevaluation counseling a complicated theory and method but describes a quite simple idea. The theory is that each time an individual experiences some kind of "distress" or hurtful experience, he or she naturally turns to another person for emotional venting or "discharge." If venting does not occur, the stored-up emotional pain later surfaces in "compulsive patterns of behavior, feeling, and verbalizing," and new experiences can "restimulate" the original feelings. At any point in a person's life, discharge to another person, serving in the role of counselor, can permit a proper reevaluation (hence reevaluation counseling) of the original experience. Once this discharge occurs, an individual can become completely free of "accumulated distress patterns."[1]

Jackins's premise is that contemporary society inflicts all sorts of restrictions on individuals that cause them to become emotionally inhibited, thus disallowing the natural course of emotional discharge after painful experiences. If allowed to occur initially, discharge would lead to immediate "rational evaluation and understanding" of the experience. However, Jackins believes, our culture fails to confirm the need for emotional release so that individuals get the message: "Don't cry. Be a big boy. Get a grip on yourself. Don't be afraid. Watch your temper." The result is that inner "recordings" of the distress experience store the emotional "information," and these recordings then get replayed continually throughout individuals' lives. Jackins believes that those pent-up feelings are responsible for "all observable irrational behavior." Proper discharge typically involves anything from crying to yelling, and even sweating, stretching, or yawning. The result of discharge is "re-emerging into full humanness."[2]

This theory of emotional catharsis as the solution to all irrational behavior and the salve for all lingering memories of emotional pain rests on Jackins's idea that the natural emotional state of humans is "zestful" and that they are predisposed to "loving affection, communication and co-operation": he titled a book of his poems *Zest Is Best*. What distinguishes human beings, he thinks, is "rational human behavior"—the ability to offer an altogether spontaneous and *"new* response," to each daily experience. Stored-up emotional pain gets in the way of this gusto, preventing this rational response to each new situation from occurring. Because society has stunted emotional discharge for so many generations, each new child is subjected to the collective illness.[3]

Besides its optimistic view of human nature, reevaluation counseling is striking for its association of personal therapy with social change and its ostensibly egalitarian notion that anyone can serve as counselor for anyone else. On the first point, Jackins dismisses all social problems as merely "distress patterns" writ large. He sees no natural reason for conflict, since humans are naturally rational and thus able to pursue their interests through "mutual co-operation." Reevaluation counseling, Jackins thinks, can achieve this harmonious state by getting rid of all lingering emotional pain and can end "social irrationality" and transform all realms of life. Thus the solution to social problems like racial tensions, class exploitation, and warfare is a kind of wholesale therapy program.[4]

To work toward this goal, counselors belong to an organization called Re-evaluation Counseling Communities, whose guidelines state that the only requirement for membership is a commitment to the task of using reevaluation counseling to try to regain one's "occluded intelligence" and help others do the same. The guidelines insist that members of the community are all *"peers"* who can counsel one another, usually "one-on-one." Recruitment is part of the way that reevaluation counseling plans to address social problems: "This method will enlist enough communicators to reach the people of the world." The reevaluation counseling experts, in sum, believe that their therapeutic techniques have potential for widespread social change.[5]

Although he thinks reevaluation counseling holds the solution to our social ills, Jackins warns co-counselors that outside of the movement they should convey their ideas without explicit reference to reevaluation counseling. As co-counselors become increasingly rational, their desire to apply reevaluation counseling in the "wider sphere" to address the "nonsense and misfunctioning around them" grows. Jackins urges what he calls "the 'permeation' of society." In order to get outsiders to assist in "interrupting the patterns that infect our society and social organizations," co-counselors should avoid using the internal "jargon."[6] The principles and habits of reevaluation counseling can thus quietly infuse the rest of society without its knowing that it has given in to a political-therapy movement.

PROFESSED ANTIAUTHORITARIANISM:
COUNSELING BY PEERS

The counseling technique for reevaluation counseling itself is also distinctive. The fundamental method involves the sharing of therapy sessions between co-counselors. Even if one participant has considerably more experience in this form of therapy than the other, the relationship is deemed basically one of equals. Undoubtedly this aspect of the movement strikes many as refreshingly egalitarian and accessible, especially as an alternative to what is usually the greater expense, time commitment, and degree of reliance on professional expertise of traditional forms of counseling.[7]

Less common variations on reevaluation counseling include the more traditional one-way counseling between counselor and client, apparently the original form reevaluation counseling took in the 1950s and 1960s. This kind of session usually takes place over two hours for a fee, but can become as long as twenty hours a week with a team of counselors.[8] The counselor is expected to receive counseling from someone else. More traditional couples or relationship counseling with a single counselor or in group therapy sessions, in which members take turns being the client and the rest of the group acts as counselor, are also used. Group sessions employ several techniques, from participants' taking turns working against their usual emotional tendencies and then discharging, to "farewells" near the end in which participants assess the experience, and "validation circles" where participants take turns "expressing validations or approval" while involved in a group hug.[9]

Other group activities include conducting counseling sessions before an audience, separating the larger group into small groups by sex, race, age, class, and religion to discuss the advantages and disadvantages of belonging to that group then reporting back to the larger group, spending time alone and then coming back and reporting to the group, performing before the group, engaging in an environmental beautification or other collective project, engaging in "validating, non-competitive sports" where everyone gets an equal number of turns and no score is kept, and the like. Group games are also used to encourage discharge, such as "passing an orange from chin to chin," and many others.[10]

While Jackins's approach appears egalitarian and open—even to a fault—the reevaluation counseling guidelines reveal an attempt to establish the distinctiveness and authority of this counseling technique and community of practitioners. Jackins writes that he prefers not to discuss other therapies when questioned about them, and advises people outside his movement who wish to mix its methods with other therapeutic approaches to call their blend something else. And insiders in the movement are instructed not to bring other approaches into their reevaluation counseling work.[11] A carefully outlined process for handling disagreements through consensus recommends first a one-on-one counseling session between those who disagree then a group session, then a debate. If that does not work, discussion ensues about which view is most valid and compelling. In the absence of resolution, an International Reference Committee or, eventually, the international reference person can make judgments. A section of the *Guidelines* called "Process of Achieving Correct Positions" says that "all co-counselors are encouraged to illuminate, examine and arrive at correct intelligent positions on all issues facing humanity, including the most controversial ones." Conferences and publications can assist in this, although the guidelines point out that, even when the whole community holds them, such positions are not "binding."[12] An implicit assumption underlying the reevaluation counseling philosophy seems to be that those who have undergone the most therapy must be the most rational and thus presumably best poised to make decisions.[13]

Jackins's theory is dedicated to rooting out what he calls the gap between the repressive society without and the natural rational human within. Through "reemergence," individuals and society will throw off the pressure and dysfunction of traditional society. Reevaluation counseling is a method and an organization expressly dedicated to blurring the line between counselor and client, a blurring that goes against traditional psychiatric practice, with its forms of accreditation, professional debate of technique and theory, and authority of experts. At the same time, it implicitly posits a new authority of reevaluation counseling, with its own views and methods of decision-making.

COUNSELING RACIAL OPPRESSORS

In applying reevaluation counseling to social issues, Jackins pays particular attention to those coming from traditionally oppressed groups, since he thinks oppression leaves just the kinds of accumulated "distress patterns" that reevaluation counseling seeks to address. Though stating that the principles of reevaluation counseling are applicable to all human beings, the 1975 *Guidelines* end with "An Important Clarification," which was added after a special set of "Liberation Workshops" that had raised the question of counseling between members of historically oppressed and oppressor groups. Jackins concludes that a special counseling arrangement has to occur in this case. "Third World" counselors should not have to listen to white counselors express their feelings concerning race, since whites are liable to say something offensive: "You won't rape me, will you?"

or "You're so exotic" or "I'm so glad, glad, glad you're here! *We've needed you!*"[14]

These latter examples remind one of the misguided "liberalisms" that the interracial etiquette guides discussed in chapter 1 warned against. Echoing those guides, the reevaluation *Guidelines* make it absolutely clear that, even in a therapeutic context, whites need to keep past inequalities at the front of their minds and use a different set of rules. Speaking their feelings openly is not sufficient in this case, because their comments result from their own "restimulations" about race—they cannot get beyond their own racism to treat the other person as more than a stereotype. Whites sometimes even expect gratitude for the difficult task of speaking openly about race and ask how they can transcend racism without mutual counseling. But meanwhile, the wounds of the black counselor, who now feels "hopeless" and ready to quit reevaluation counseling, get reopened. The white co-counselor's desire to discuss race in interracial settings is dismissed as part of his or her "pattern."[15]

Jackins thinks whites should instead discuss race with white counselors. Seeming to go against his own warnings elsewhere that counselors should not guide or hold preconceived ideas about what a client should discuss or how a client should do it, Jackins has a very specific prescription for interracial, male-female, and other relationships he generalizes as all historically characterized by oppression. White counselors must aim at "the client's digging up, facing, and proudly proclaiming" the worst racist attitudes they can think of. Analyzing or renouncing these attitudes is not sufficient. Instead, counselors should demand the clients "shout proudly such sentiments as she or he would imagine a Ku Klux Klan cheerleader shouting at a lynching" in order to experience the pain of what it means to be "a conforming member of a racist society." Only through total emotional catharsis can the client stop being an "unaware racist."[16] In this schema, whites are unwilling and unknowing victims of their own racism and need therapy to overcome the resulting pain. Only through such expressions will clients bring their racism out in the open so that it can be considered. The result of therapy for whites is a recognition of their racism and of how they, too, even though on the side of the oppressor, have been harmed by it.

In the case of "Third World" counselors, the tables turn. Jackins asks rhetorically whether whites should serve as "respectful, permissive counselors" to blacks, listening to all of their attitudes toward "whites (including their stereotyping of that particular counselor)" and about racial discrimination. The answer is "Yes. Yes. Yes." The logic here is important. The reason for this special role is not that whites owe it to blacks, for this assumes an obligation born of guilt. Jackins considers guilt one of the undesirable patterns of behavior originating in childhood—just a "distress pattern" people need to overcome. Instead, he resorts to pragmatism as the only valid guideline for behavior. Why should black clients let out all emotion to white counselors? "Because it works." As whites silently take in blacks' outpouring of thoughts and feelings on race, blacks and whites alike can become free of "*all distresses in this area.*" Ideally blacks will experience their "discharge" right then and there, but whites will experience theirs later. Both will end up experiencing "re-emergence" of their original, unconflicted inner selves. After this bravado, Jackins goes on to justify this double standard as he asks, "Is this 'fair'?": "There should be nothing 'fair' in our treatment of patterns." His point is that it is a service in itself to try to counter the enormous unfairness of the past. But unfairness seems to be a justifiable means to an end, according to this logic. If white counselors do not have the "correct attitude" toward blacks, Jackins says, they should not counsel them until they do. This "correct" attitude and differential approach, he says, was what led to the mutual cooperation at the liberation workshops.[17]

THE PERILS OF TOTALIZING CURES

Jackins maintains that reevaluation counseling can cure individuals of the emotional distresses in their past; his sweeping claim that this racial therapy will do away with any remaining effects of racism and racial oppression is fully consistent with this. Another example reveals the extent to which he believes that reevaluation counseling offers total cures: his contention that counseling can end physical pain.

In a startling section of the *Fundamentals of Co-counseling Manual*, Jackins discusses "Counseling First-Aid on Injuries." In his view, the most important thing about physical pain is the emotional trauma it produces. Thus, he thinks that not just past emotional distresses but physical pain itself can be relieved through emotional discharge. If an injury is of recent origin, reevaluation counseling promises even quicker results, since the emotional trauma has not yet been "stored away." In this interval, while still in pain, one can let out one's feelings and "release" the pain right away.[18]

As stated here, the method has at least some superficial connotations of sadomasochism, which seems somewhat ironic, given that reevaluation counseling claims to offer a solution to all "human problems," including all "compulsive" and "irrational" behavior.[19] Emotional discharge of physical pain in the aftermath of injury comes quite simply through "experiencing the hurt . . . as thoroughly as possible over and over again while reviewing the actual occurrence of the injury."[20]

The wording is vague here as to what reexperiencing the pain really means. Most likely, in keeping with the rest of reevaluation counseling, it means reviewing it so that one feels it again, one hopes only emotionally or mentally. In one section, however, Jackins recommends actually heightening the physical pain. For instance, immersing sunburned skin in warm water or holding a burn near a heat source will intensify the pain. After the pain is experienced completely it will "be gone—for good."[21]

Failing to specify the nature and limits of the techniques that can help heighten pain in the service of ultimate painlessness leaves too much room for interpretation; Jackins does not spell out which types of injuries and pain intensification techniques are appropriate and which are not. Specific measures aside, this approach promises total pain reduction through emotional wallowing in the original pain. Perhaps it is meant simply as a harmless old wives' tale or a home remedy for superficial scrapes or burns, but without explicit qualification this method seems to be based on a lack of familiarity with the most extreme varieties of pain that humans can encounter and the uncontestable advances of modern medicine in addressing them. The results "appear almost magical. Pain is relieved permanently."[22]

FALSE INTIMACY

An independent scholar and freelance journalist, Matthew Lyons, says his own experiences with reevaluation counseling made him critical of the movement's approach. Coauthor with Chip Berlet of *Too Close for Comfort: Right-Wing Populism, Scapegoating, and Fascist Potentials in U.S. Political Traditions,*[23] Lyons worries that it is easy for participants to lose "critical distance" on the community because reevaluation counseling can appear to be "the answer to all social problems. . . . A 'rational island' in a sea of distress."[24]

Lyons has many reservations about reevaluation counseling, from its psychologizing of politics and social inequality to its tendency to assume or create false intimacy. His description of this artificiality is what concerns us here. It offers valuable insight not just into reevaluation counseling but into a particular quality of human relationships more and more frequently observable in a society in thrall to superficial, emotional unveiling as a style of interaction—the now familiar transparency of the human potential movement and its antecedents. Lyons gives a moving account of his own acquaintance with this emotional mode, which now strikes him as "confusingly intimate and impersonal at the same time":

> I remember the constant confusion I experienced within RC about personal boundaries: the unspoken pressure to share intimate

thoughts and feelings with virtual strangers; the unspoken expectation that I would help probe for intimate thoughts and feelings from those strangers in turn. I remember my reluctance and hesitation in counseling sessions, and the inner voice telling me: "*That's your distress.*" I remember people I had just met coming up to me at RC workshops and saying, with the best of intentions, "*Can I give you a hug?*" And me standing there, not wanting them to, telling myself: "*Go ahead—it's just your distress,*" and letting them hug me. I remember conversations with RCer friends where I tried to share thoughts and feelings in a direct, unselfconscious way, as friends do, until I saw that Counselor look come into the other person's eyes—that detached, patronizing, I'm-helping-you-discharge look—and I felt myself withdraw into silence in anger, frustration, and shame. And still that voice inside me was saying—"*That's your distress.*"

Lyons quotes the interview of a reevaluation counseling member in a book by R. D. Rosen called *Psychobabble*, to help explain his reservations about the effect of the reevaluation counseling mode: "Co-counseling levels the distinctions between kinds of intimacy." Another interviewee was shocked by the effusive affection that was all out of proportion or lacked any basis at all in actual relationships. This false intimacy, writes Lyons, "could make even real personal connections ring hollow, because all interactions started to sound the same."[25]

Once we abandon distinctions between different types of relationships, we alter the nature of intimacy itself and the qualities that make it distinctive. Furthermore, this quality of transparency—where all of one's private life is open to group scrutiny—is a well-known trait of authoritarianism, whether on the large scale of whole states or the smaller scale of utopian reform groups.[26] So its emergence anywhere is clearly cause for concern. But reevaluation counseling certainly does not have a monopoly on this blurring of distinctions between the varying degrees of intimacy appropriate to different kinds of relationships between individuals. It can be argued—as it has by several key theorists who have depicted our increasing inability to differentiate between public and private spheres—that this has become, if not the dominant mode, then certainly the one destined to become dominant if the trend is not intentionally reversed.[27] But it is vital that the public, in its deliberation over the crucial issue of what properly belongs in the public sphere and what in the private, be aware of deliberate attempts to spread this transparency.

WORLD WITHOUT GUILT

Even beyond its cheapening of intimacy and invasion of privacy, our culture of therapy often has no real place at all for emotions, though it elevates them beyond all recognition as a window to the individual. This is particularly evident in the philosophy of reevaluation counseling, which seems to lack any way of explaining or considering evil at all.

In a world devoid of emotion and drives—one in which all individuals hold the right views, are not victimized by their earlier distresses, do not have their rationality eclipsed by their distorted behavior patterns—there simply is no reason to be evil. There is nothing wrong with this utopian view as an expression of hope for another way—the vision of heaven in the Christian tradition—but when applied to human affairs it could be disastrous. A world without emotional depth, simply put, is a world without guilt. And a world without guilt in turn is a world without moral conscience.

Jackins explicitly states that reevaluation counseling adherents renounce "thousands of years of cultural mistakes and hundreds and hundreds of religions and theories which assume, for understandable reasons, that the human being is a mixture of good and evil." Instead, he writes, "THE HUMAN BEING, AS A HUMAN BEING, IS INTEGRAL, IS WHOLESOME, IS GOOD . . . distinct from the distress patterns which parasite on it and infest it." Thus, "EVERY SINGLE

HUMAN BEING AT EVERY MOMENT OF THE PAST, IF THE ENTIRE SITUATION IS TAKEN INTO ACCOUNT, HAS ALWAYS DONE THE VERY BEST HE OR SHE COULD DO AND SO DESERVES NEITHER BLAME OR REPROACH FROM ANYONE, INCLUDING SELF."[28]

The problems with this line of thinking are legion, as revealed in Jackins's explicit references to racism, which he lumps together with all other forms of "oppression." To Jackins, the root of racism is not a particular racist individual or group, or a morally wrong racist act, but the generalized injustice of the molds into which society forces all of us. He seems to think being subjected to racism is almost a matter of choice: were it not for our "distress patterns," we would not "submit to being oppressed." Indeed, in this view racial oppression is no different from what all individuals experience: "We're oppressed as workers, we're oppressed as women, we're oppressed as children, we're oppressed by racism, we're oppressed by many other oppressions." If we were not "first hurt as children," we would not have taken on negative behavior patterns that cause us to "play an oppressor role."[29]

Absent any emphasis on moral wrong or culpability, racism thus all boils down to playing roles. Whether one chooses the role of racist or victim is determined by the nature of the predisposing "hurts" one has endured. No matter what one's role, one is automatically blameless.

"Colonizing the Next Planet"

Perhaps this entire framework should be dismissed as the rantings of an offbeat but charismatic pop philosopher. One could certainly point to reevaluation counseling's apparently small formal membership in order to assuage any deep worry about its effect on American life. However, the movement hopes to expand and, even if it does not, is closely related to more general trends in American culture that threaten to be reinvigorated by movements like this one. In spite of the incisive skepticism social critics have expressed about false intimacy, the decline of private life, and the decline of our moral understanding, this notion of guilt-free, emotional transparency continues to spread. And it acts to the detriment of race relations, to the point where it threatens to compromise the remarkable gains of the late twentieth century by worsening tensions and misunderstanding.

While reevaluation counseling has many of the traits of utopian reform movements of earlier times—such as the totalistic, perfectionist hubris and surety—it is very much a product of our own time. It shares a central tendency seen in today's recovery movement. That is, while reevaluation counseling posits the purge of the individual of all abnormal functioning resulting from original traumas as a goal, the actual attainment of this natural state—the "reemergence" Jackins preaches—seems located on an ever-receding horizon. We are all in recovery—but never recovered. Like the rest of the recovery movement, with its twelve-step programs to cure everything from alcoholism to "misery addiction," reevaluation counseling assumes all individuals are basically in a perpetual state of recovery. Everyone is a prime suspect for falling into self-destructive patterns of behavior and thus everyone needs to be in counseling continually, even the counselors—*especially* the counselors—for "no one should counsel without being counselled."[30] The point of reevaluation counseling is not over when a destructive pattern is eradicated: instead, therapy must continue even outside of actual counseling sessions.

In fact, Jackins considers his therapy "an ongoing process, a tool for living." It is not just a theory for co-counselors to apply in therapy sessions. Perhaps the major paradox of this notion of reevaluation counseling as a world view is that, despite an ostensible emphasis on individual autonomy and responsibility, a stated intention of freeing the individual from debilitating emotional burdens, and exhortations to "take charge,"[31] this world view seems to encourage a kind of dependence on reevaluation counseling. It falls in line with the broader recovery movement's increasing stress since the late 1980s on the idea that everyone is perpetually in recovery from something—if not from an addiction, the varieties of which have expanded exponentially, or from an emotional or "personality" disorder, the number of which has also grown beyond belief, then from affiliation with someone who has one of these in a relationship of codependency.[32]

It is revealing that, in a discussion of the need for individuals to set concrete goals for their counseling program, Jackins uses the imagery of imperialism: "One needs a clear picture of what one wants to do before one climbs the ladder to the space ship to colonize the next planet."[33] His writings are laced with advice to adherents to be on their best public behavior so as to represent reevaluation counseling favorably to prospective converts.[34] His handbooks state that a major goal of counseling classes is to expand the movement.[35]

But the goal of spreading reevaluation counseling extends well beyond expanding the organization itself. He sees the peer counselor relationship as a model for all relationships and says the movement's goal is to have its members in all social institutions and walks of life. Resistance to the incursions of reevaluation counseling is just a symptom of the behavior patterns that need to be overcome through its methods. Jackins writes with satisfaction of the ways reevaluation counseling members currently apply reevaluation counseling to many different occupations, such as teaching.[36] This would surely be a matter of concern to at least some parents, if they knew that their children's classrooms have become sites for counseling sessions.

Though its visions of expansion are most likely quite exaggerated, reevaluation counseling is succeeding in insinuating itself into at least one mainstream social realm—diversity training. Despite the far-fetched character of this counseling method's ideas, an organization with a national and even international reach, the National Coalition Building Institute, appears to draw extensively on them. This institute is a nonprofit organization that conducts "leadership training programs" and forms "anti-racism coalitions." It uses its combination of diversity training and conflict resolution to offer "prejudice reduction" workshops in a wide variety of settings—workplaces, universities, churches, law enforcement agencies, and community organizations. By 1996, it had established fifty city chapters, thirty "campus affiliates," and fifteen "organizational affiliates" in the United States, Canada, England, and Switzerland. A W. K. Kellogg Foundation grant allowed it to conduct pilot programs recently in Allentown, Pennsylvania, Birmingham, Alabama, Raleigh/Durham, North Carolina, and Washington, D.C. It has been involved in situations throughout the world, including post-apartheid South Africa.[37] It reflects its growing reputation that the National Coalition Building Institute was in 2000 one of the organizations listed on the Internet on the White House home page under "National Resources" related to President Bill Clinton's "One America" initiative on race. At the end of the list, the White House included a disclaimer saying that it did not endorse the listed organizations. However, the list was entitled "Promising Practices," giving the impression that these organizations were helpful ones.[38]

In addition, the work of the National Coalition Building Institute has been covered in the *Washington Post,* and the organization's founder and executive director, Cherie R. Brown, has had her philosophy featured in major publications. The most prominent of these venues, however, fail to mention that Cherie Brown is a fan of reevaluation counseling. To her credit, she does not obscure this connection. In materials geared to other diversity trainers like her, she includes Harvey Jackins in her acknowledgments and cites his work in her bibliographies. For instance, in *Healing into Action: A Leadership Guide for Creating Diverse Communities,* which Brown coauthored with George J. Mazza, she writes, "I want to acknowledge Harvey Jackins, founder of Re-Evaluation Counseling, who has spent a lifetime building a theory and practice of healing and liberation, which became an integral part of the work of the LDI [Leadership for Diversity Initiative, a project of the National Coalition Building Institute] teams. Many of the principles in this manual are derived from Re-Evaluation Counseling."[39]

A Politics of Parody

A short piece Brown wrote as part of a symposium in *Tikkun* magazine in 1996 betrays the influence of reevaluation counseling, making her treatment of the symposium's theme, the "politics of meaning," seem like a parody piece. She begins with the ominous assertion that "*at least* as much attention" needs to go to "*preparing* people for this transformation [her emphases]" as to "developing the vision of a politics of meaning."[40] She goes on to adopt recovery movement language— especially the concepts of reevaluation counseling, though with no reference in this particular article—to this effort. Brown's piece exemplifies the trademark self-referential quality and obsession with technique that reevaluation counseling shares with sensitivity training and the human potential movement.

To pave the way for a politics of meaning, we must begin by breaking our own reliance on comfort. Brown says she is referring to more than just material conveniences, but then goes on to speak only of Western women's complaints about the crude hotel accommodations at the United Nations Women's Conference in China. She concludes that a visit to Africa or Asia might help Americans transcend their "small, Western vision"—a surprising note, given her decidedly therapeutic vision, which is also decidedly Western, and has everything to do with seeking emotional comfort. Before we can progress to politics, she thinks, we need "to un-numb, grieve, and let our hearts break," since "our lives have been *ruined* by not being able to live lives of meaning," and we need "hundreds of hours to grieve the loss."[41]

Just as we cannot imagine meaningful politics without first letting out our grief, we cannot proceed without ridding ourselves of our fears—or at least this is how Brown interprets the words of a South

African leader whom she met at a tension-filled conference in post-apartheid South Africa. The leader confided, "Cherie, we don't need skills in prejudice reduction, conflict resolution, or coalition building. What we need is to learn how to reclaim courage." Brown interprets this remark not as rather blatant criticism but as a mandate for *more* training in these skills. She recounts how, at home, she now includes in every training institute for National Coalition Building Institute leaders a workshop on "reclaiming courage and breaking through the barriers from the past that keep us from being courageous."[42]

There is more. Brown's last argument is that we must do away with the oppression of leaders. She recounts a meeting with two leaders of Northern Ireland's Women's Peace Movement who had suffered attacks from within their own organization. This time she decided to add to all of her training programs a workshop for leaders on ways "to cherish other leaders," "to build support for themselves as leaders," and to stop "leadership attacks." She then mentions the editor of *Tikkun* itself, Michael Lerner, as an example of "a leader who takes enormous risks" with his bold ideas and thus "routinely gets attacked." She suggests that it is important for everyone "to back each other's leadership fully," and declares that she has resolved not to "allow any-one in my presence to attack Michael."[43] At the end of Brown's argument, Lerner adds a generous, but somewhat bemused, note: "Attacks, No! But Criticism, Yes! The difference? Time, place, and manner. In this journal, robust criticism is always welcome. But in a social movement, Brown's point is a welcome corrective to the anti-leadership tendencies that too often flourish."[44]

Lerner undoubtedly has no knowledge of the parallels between Brown's reasoning and reevaluation counseling: in both, views not deemed appropriate or useful seem at risk of being dismissed as incorrect—signs of one's personal "distress patterns." In the case of criticism of leaders, "we too often are simply rehearsing our own powerlessness." Brown writes: "We must adopt a correct attitude toward leaders—that leaders are to be cherished, even though they're not perfect."[45]

Daily Affirmations and Déjà Vu All Over Again

At first glance, it might be tempting to thank Brown for material that would fit nicely on the old Stuart Smalley "Daily Affirmations" *Saturday Night Live* skit by the comedian and political commentator Al Franken. But seeing the methods and theories of reevaluation counseling transposed to what seems like the benign "peer training" of presumably well-intentioned organizations dedicated to the laudable goal of "coalition building" is sobering.

In a 1991 article, Brown and a fellow National Coalition Building Institute associate, George J. Mazza, outlined six theoretical principles of the organization's "prejudice reduction model" and six corresponding methods for translating theory into practice in the workshop setting. Both theory and methods closely resemble the tenets of reevaluation counseling. One theory spells out the supposed origins of stereotypes. Juxtaposition of reevaluation counseling and National Coalition Building Institute principles shows the clear correspondence. Brown and Mazza write that individuals' prejudices are formed when they take in miscellaneous bits of "misinformation, often in the form of simplistic generalizations" about another group. "Every distorted piece of information concerning another group is stored as a literal recording, much like a phonograph record," despite experiences that might "contradict the negative recordings," they write. Here Jackins's book *The Human Side of Human Beings* (1965) is cited in a parenthetical note. This passage, of course, directly evokes Jackins's theory that unexpressed feelings of emotional anguish are like "recordings."[46] As Jackins puts it,

> One might say that, "reminded too much of" the old distress experience, we are forced to behave as if we were some kind of walking "juke-box." In effect, the new experience "pushes the button." The recording of the old, miserable experience then rolls out as if

from a rack onto a "turntable in our head." The recording now plays us![47]

The corresponding method that should be used in prejudice reduction workshops, Brown and Mazza write, is to let out the "first thoughts" that come to mind regarding a particular group (blacks, women, etc.) in a manner of free association. Working in groups of two, one partner says the name of a group to which neither partner belongs, and the other, "without hesitation, says his or her first uncensored thoughts."[48]

The stereotypes, epithets, or misconceptions that come out through free association indicate that all individuals harbor "negative recordings" and thus "no one person or group is to blame."[49] Even members of oppressed groups have much baggage to unload related to internalized stereotypes. These individuals sometimes turn on members of their own group for conforming to stereotypes or themselves act in a way designed to counteract these stereotypes. Emotional disclosure allows them instead to get in touch with their own feelings, such as that of "authentic group pride."[50] Why this pride is more genuine than other kinds is not clear, nor do Brown and Mazza explain why it is undesirable to refuse to conform to group stereotypes.

Other theories and methods put forth by Brown and Mazza closely resemble those of reevaluation counseling as well. Like Jackins, Brown and Mazza assume that racists have experienced an earlier injury, which caused their racism. They now need to heal their own "recordings of fear or injury." Their bigoted remarks are simply "a call for help." These comments must not be silenced; rather, these "recordings are healed by airing them."[51] Just as Jackins writes that all human misery will vanish if people are permitted to "discharge" in the presence of another person who listens with "aware attention and concern,"[52] Brown and Mazza believe that, "instead of quickly acting to silence a person who makes a bigoted comment," one should encourage the "healing" by listening attentively.[53]

155

Here, Brown and Mazza could practically be writing a handbook for reevaluation counselors. They state that once an individual has experienced emotional release, he or she can help heal others. Just as flight attendants urge parents to put on their own oxygen masks first before helping their children in the event of a drop in cabin pressure, Brown and Mazza warn, "in order to be able to assist another person, we must first give attention to healing our own painful experiences."[54] Similarly, Jackins advises counselors, "There is no limit to what you can accomplish . . . provided you see that you yourself have adequate counseling."[55] Even more explicitly, Brown and Mazza spell out that all trainers need a support group that is a "safe place" to develop their "prejudice reduction skills" and to explore the "emotional blocks that hinder them in leading workshops."[56]

Only by such "healing" can the real roots of racism be addressed. This healing supposedly occurs in the National Coalition Building Institute's prejudice reduction workshops by means of "effective communication," in which each participant can "speak and listen." Individuals can also meet in groups divided by class, sex, religion, and the like. The apotheosis is "the sharing of personal stories," since this gets the group's attention and can change attitudes. But Brown and Mazza go on to stress that the person divulging personal experiences also benefits, because the "public sharing . . . enables the storyteller to release the emotions that have often been buried since the initial incident": "The emotional release is usually experienced as healing."[57]

One of the institute's workshops was written up on the front page of the *Washington Post* in 1994. Taking place at Wilson High School in Tenleytown, part of Washington, D.C., the "diversity workshop" put these theories to work. A student leader began by saying that "diversity is not just about race" and asked the students "to reveal something hidden about themselves": "I'm anorexic, said one. I'm adopted, said another. There's a lot of alcoholism in my family. I'm a recovering cocaine addict. I'm a virgin. My mother is manic depressive. I was an abused child. I'm gay."

After this disclosure, the workshop proceeded to "first thoughts"—the "records inside our heads." The free association began: " 'Black,' one girl said. 'Africa,' the other replied. 'Martin Luther King. Ghetto.' They try another word. 'Asian,' one student said. 'Smart,' the other replied. 'Slanty eyes. Short.' " Next it was time to get all the sources of shame or stereotypes (assumed to be one and the same) about one's own group out on the table, and finally to root out the sources of pride. At the end came the "speakout," with the personal stories of "pain and discrimination." Although there were "painful moments, nervous giggling and tough talk," the *Post* reporter wrote, "by the end, one student, tears streaming down her face, told a secret about her mother that she had kept for years."[58] The assumption was (and the *Post* reporter seemed to share it) that such "discharge" spells success.

An old standby of most forms of psychotherapy, emotional catharsis is not necessarily a problem in itself. And perhaps it even has some role in healing group conflict. But we must surely be at least slightly wary of reformers who say that in this day, at the height of the television and radio talk show mode of total revelation, what we are mainly suffering from is reticence and repression. Even if it were true that we are, there is at least a lingering sense of irresolution pervading descriptions like these. Certainly, the technique of free association should, at a bare minimum, be used with great care. Telling the world one's most intimate feelings and experiences might make workers, classmates, and others more, not less, vulnerable to additional pain. And just letting out any and all feelings, including those based on hearsay, in the disembodied form of "recordings" seems to mean that no one has to take responsibility for them or for examining their meaning or their veracity. Emotional statements are taken on their own testimony and left there, unexamined, unchallenged. The idea that free association—"first thoughts"—is a valid procedure for turning up the real stereotypes or sentiments one group holds about another rests on a questionable application of the technique of free association and on a severely impoverished notion of the human mind that lacks *any* acknowledgment of the role or complex workings of the unconscious. The assumption that merely uttering spontaneously whatever comes to mind and airing any mean-spirited or misguided comments will naturally heal the original pain and thus cure all conflict, rather than, say, create new misunderstandings that can take on a life of their own, should be confined to New Age movements on the periphery of American life.

NONJUDGMENTALISM AND THE ASSAULT ON GUILT

Even if it were not so similar to reevaluation counseling, however, the National Coalition Building Institute's approach would bear the imprint of a problem that has become increasingly mainstream and is part of the larger infusion of the therapeutic mode into American culture. In his recent study of the nature of American middle-class culture, the sociologist Alan Wolfe concluded that one of its most prominent features was nonjudgmentalism.[59] Just as reevaluation counseling seems to have no concept of evil beyond a cycle of emotional pain allegedly established long ago in some nefarious collective past, the National Coalition Building Institute begins its "leadership guide" with an assault on guilt. Worried about the ineffectiveness of making people feel guilty for confronting racism, its vision is fixated on training techniques and emotional dynamics at the expense of moral distinctions. "Condemning people, shaming them, and making them feel guilty are all unproductive strategies: they increase defensiveness rather than creating an opening for change," writes Brown. This view fails to distinguish between superficial feelings of guilt and the profound fact of actually being guilty of a wrongdoing—and thus rules out the possibility of moral responsibility. In this amoral universe, in which guilt is merely assessed as to its worthiness as a strategy, moral conscience is nonexistent.

> Guilt is especially useless, because it thrives on our turning inward, focusing on our own bad feelings about ourselves, rather than directing our energies outward, toward the work of becoming an ally. People change more readily when they are lifted up and appreciated, not when they are made to feel guilty.[60]

Operating under the premise of a movement dedicated to the now attenuated and murky goal of social change, adherents assume that change in itself is always good. The exact nature of the desired change, however, receives little attention. The imprecise slogan of empowerment stands in for any real vision of what all these technologies of change are supposed to deliver.[61]

The therapeutic movement, with this ethos of empowerment, has trumped the civil rights movement, with its vision of the just society and the good life. The culture of therapy's view that the problem for everyone—bigots, oppressors, and leaders alike—is a lack of nurture, validation, and support has inspired numerous best-selling books and talk shows. The spirit of the movement is that we are all owed unconditional acceptance at all times, and that any weaknesses we have are not our own responsibility. Of course, there is some validity in the claim that individuals must at some level feel good about themselves in order to be generous contributors to their family, community, and nation. The problem is that this self-esteem philosophy discourages vital distinctions—or adds to the confusion that already exists concerning matters having to do more with morality than with pop psychology. The worthy dedication to the importance of each and every individual too easily translates into an inability, or reluctance, to see the difference between the truly egregious wrongs and the more minor, fleeting slights of everyday life.

This blurring of distinctions directly results from the abandonment of the integrity of conscience—from the ludicrous, but widespread, belief that guilt is of no practical value in making people change their views or behavior. This view of guilt as "useless" goes directly against those principles that underlie our very sense of justice. When a defendant has been proved to have committed a heinous crime, we still find the defendant guilty, even if he or she feels remorse. These basic concepts imply that, in legal thinking at least, there is still an important difference between being guilty of a crime and being innocent. Nonetheless, we do hope for remorse, knowing that it is only when we understand our real guilt that we take responsibility for our actions.

But in the world of diversity workshops, at least those that assume, as most now do, that we all (or at least all whites) harbor hidden racism, the language has shifted. The notion of incorrect attitudes—stereotypes—both expands and diminishes the extent of the problem. No one is truly guilty here—no one is actually at fault—because it is society that breeds wrong attitudes. Yet everyone must be subjected to self-examination, because everyone harbors these attitudes. Thus any distinction between a racially motivated act—like refusing to hire or promote someone or chasing someone out of one's neighborhood on account of race, or worse—and a passive misconception one might have about a group one has never known intimately gets lost. This focus on attitudes of nebulous origin, and the misleading assumption that they are universal and as lethal as racist acts, comes from a loss of judgment and proportion. This loss of proportion and inability to distinguish among wrong acts rests on the idea that stereotypes are responsible for racism, not individuals. After all, if one has truly committed a heinous racist act, one should not only feel guilty if one has a conscience; one should admit that one is guilty. It is this profoundly psychological aspect of morality that deters most potential wrongdoing and makes it possible for human beings to live together in society at all. We abandon it at our peril.

CHAPTER SIX

A World of Endless Slights: Diversity Training and Its Illogical Consequences

Diversity training, broadly construed to mean the whole range of ideas and initiatives regarding the diverse backgrounds employees bring to the workplace, has quietly become the most important movement related to race in the 1990s. At a time when affirmative action has met with significant criticism, the broader movement of diversity training has increasingly replaced affirmative action as the preferred focus of corporate management and diversity consultants alike. The consultant Mary P. Rowe at the Massachusetts Institute of Technology's Sloan School of Management argues in an article in *Change* magazine that, although she in fact supports it, "affirmative action still deals with the outermost layer of the onion. While it helps with recruitment issues, compliance-oriented affirmative action alone is not sufficient to achieve healthy diversity."[1] She goes on to elaborate on issues such as workplace harassment, poor employee retention, and barriers to promotion, which she thinks affirmative action alone cannot address. "If affirmative action is really going to work," she says, diversity initiatives need to attack "subtle discrimination":

> Subtle discrimination is made up of covert, ephemeral, or apparently trivial events that are fre-

quently unrecognized by the perpetrator and often not evident to the person injured by them. By definition they are not legally actionable; they happen wherever people are perceived to be "different." These "micro-inequities" interfere with equal opportunity by excluding the person who is different and by interfering with that person's self-confidence and productivity.[2]

Of course, not all corporate managers or diversity consultants share Rowe's embrace of affirmative action or agree with her that "subtle discrimination" or "micro-inequities" should be a basis for widespread corporate policy. Whether they agree or not, however, they have been forced to confront the general issue in the form of discrimination complaints or actual lawsuits. A 1994 article in the *Washingtonian* by one of its senior writers, Andrew Ferguson, states that over the course of the 1970s and 1980s such lawsuits in federal courts alone increased over 2,000 percent. Ferguson argues that this upsurge explains the widespread adoption of diversity training: "The smart employer, especially one with government contracts, is prepared to show he has gone that extra mile—not merely to make his workforce look like America, but also to change the *culture* of the company, or at least make people think he's changing it."[3] Another widely cited financial incentive for diversity training involves worker retention. Elsie Cross, president of a management consulting firm in Philadelphia called Elsie Y. Cross Associates, has conducted diversity seminars for major companies such as Eastman Kodak and Bell Communications. She argues that companies that do not conduct diversity training will sustain huge financial losses by losing highly skilled employees: "You're talking about spending $250,000 to $1,000,000 to replace *one* person."[4]

THE EXPLOSION OF DIVERSITY TRAINING

The sociologist Frederick R. Lynch illustrates how, in response to such pressures brought on by lawsuits and an array of other factors, the diversity training movement's parameters have expanded to such a degree that the movement has erected a veritable "diversity machine." In his superb survey of the movement's historical development, Lynch shows that self-proclaimed experts have created a diversity industry with a professional literature, university courses and programs, research institutes, and lucrative consulting firms. Their efforts have created a kind of "policy engine," with supporters in universities, government, and business. So effective have they been in pressing their interests, Lynch believes, that, despite his own and others' criticism and despite contested effectiveness, diversity training is "here to stay."[5]

Indeed, the statistics do suggest that the use of diversity training has become increasingly widespread in the last ten years. A 1992 study found that approximately 65 percent of major American companies conducted diversity training,[6] and in a 1995 survey of the top Fortune 50 corporations cited by Lynch, 70 percent of the companies reported that they had already initiated a formal diversity management program and another 16 percent expressed their intention to do so.[7] Ferguson estimated that there were approximately five thousand diversity trainers by 1994.[8] Not only are there proliferating positions for diversity trainers, but corporations are willing to pay well for their services. Trainers commonly earn from $1,500 to $2,000 a day, with sessions varying from a day or two to a month or longer for a full workplace "overhaul," which can cost from $200,000 to $500,000.[9] In an outstanding, but disturbing, critique called "The Diversity Industry" published in the *New Republic*, the writer Heather MacDonald revealed that the top diversity consultants commanded $8,000 to $10,000 per day in 1993 and that Elsie Y. Cross Associates "requires a five-year commitment from companies—at a total cost of more than $2.5 million."[10] In addition to consultation and workshop costs, there are training manuals, books, videos, board games, and a variety of other accoutrements that go at a high price. This explosion is particularly striking when one recalls that the profession was little known until the late 1980s.

Productivity Envy

The diversity training movement got underway in the 1970s and 1980s as civil rights prompted long overdue integration in many workplaces. In the late 1980s and early 1990s, however, diversity training enjoyed spectacular growth. In the context of worries about the capacity of U.S. businesses to compete with Japanese corporate successes, a highly influential study prodded American companies to pay serious attention to the issue of diversity in the workplace. Published by the Hudson Institute, a private, nonprofit research organization in Indianapolis, *Workforce 2000: Work and Workers for the 21st Century* contended that American businesses needed to come to grips with, among other things, an increasingly diverse workforce. In a section entitled "Demographics as Destiny," the report made dramatic projections for the 1990s: the labor force would increase "at a slower rate than any time since the 1930s"; three-fifths of new entrants to the workforce would be female; nearly a third of new entrants would be nonwhite; only 15 percent of new entrants would be white males. The combination of slowing rates of labor force participation and increasing globalization of markets, the report suggested, could seriously cut into American productivity unless diversity was taken seriously. Workers of diverse backgrounds would need to be fully integrated into the economy if the United States was to retain competitiveness.[11] By the turn of the twenty-first century, Americans had witnessed the Asian economic woes of the early 1990s and then their own unprecedented economic boom of the Clinton years, so these worries about competitiveness might now seem drastically exaggerated. At the time, though, they were palpable enough to add to the threats of litigation another major rationale for the spread of diversity training. And the recent dearth of skilled employees—a surprising twist after the downsizing at all levels throughout the 1990s—puts added pressure on recruitment and retention.

The actual content of diversity training, as it came into its own in the late-1980s to the late-1990s, reveals enormous variation. This lack of uniformity resulted partly because the industry formed and expanded so quickly, with little planning or coordination. According to Lynch, the diversity industry in the late 1990s had three major professional associations that oversaw and coordinated the field: the American Society for Training and Development, the Conference Board, and the Society for Human Resource Development. While the Society for Human Resource Development has now begun a credentialing program, critics charge that over the past decade virtually anyone who wanted to become a diversity trainer could.[12] But the inconsistency in the content of diversity training programs can also be attributed to the eclectic influences on the movement, given the changeable American cultural milieu since the 1960s and confusion over the issue of race itself.

Once diversity trainers and managers agreed on the need for diversity training, the more difficult questions became what the wrong attitudes about race were, what the new attitudes should be, and how exactly new attitudes were to be conveyed. Several diversity gurus took center stage as these questions came to the fore and different schools of thought emerged. The best-known diversity consultants included R. Roosevelt Thomas, whose American Institute for Managing Diversity operates out of Atlanta and is associated with Morehouse College, and Lewis Brown Griggs, who leads Griggs Productions in San Francisco. Along with a number of other consultants who worked through proliferating organizations, Thomas and Griggs helped shape the content of diversity training. Griggs, whose 1988 articles and videotapes with Lennie Copeland were among the most well known, pioneered an approach he called "valuing diversity." On at least one of these diversity training videos, Price Cobbs was a collaborator. Roosevelt, who published an important article on diversity training in 1990, changed the direction of the movement in calling for an approach that emphasizes "managing diversity."[13]

Lynch distinguishes between different strands of the diversity training movement. The "civil rights moralism" of the consultant Lillian Roybal Rose leads to efforts to raise "cross-cultural awareness" through techniques that raise the emotional level in order to increase awareness of what she sees as the main culprit of workplace problems—racial oppression. Lynch views Griggs as an evangelist who aims at getting managers to undergo a "conversion" experience to heighten sensitivity and challenge what he regards as workplace norms based on a white, male perspective. Lynch prefers the "business-demography pragmatism" of Thomas, who stresses acceptance of all forms of workplace pluralism, with the goal of greater overall productivity. In his scathing attack on the diversity business, Lynch is generous to make this distinction. He worries that some of the most moralistic approaches, drawing as they also do on everything from identity politics to encounter group emotional confrontation, heighten "ethnic and gender group consciousness, even among white males."[14] According to this logic, however, even the more sober and businesslike approach of Thomas could have this same effect. More than getting hired, the problem for women and members of minority groups is that now they often reach a plateau in the workplace hierarchy. Laudably calling on managers to create a work environment that allows every individual to perform to his or her potential, Thomas encourages a "cultural audit" and diversity training as partial remedies. The point of such an audit of "the body of unspoken and unexamined assumptions, values, and mythologies" is "not to assimilate diversity into the dominant culture but rather to build a culture that can digest unassimilated diversity."[15] This view just as easily paves the way for the engineering of attitudes—and thus for the ministrations of those self-appointed diversity experts who might lack Thomas's more balanced perspective. Moreover, in actual implementation there is no check on the overlapping and intermingling of approaches.

ATTITUDE CHANGE
THROUGH WORKSHOPPING

One of the influences on diversity training was the human potential movement, as discussed in chapter 3, which had already influenced the

American business environment with its notion that workshops for managers or employees could address personal matters such as self-image or interpersonal dynamics which might be compromising productivity. Encounter group–type activities often aimed particularly to get participants to express openly and honestly even their most personal feelings. Indeed, they sometimes resorted to extreme measures to do so, such as the notorious technique of wielding foam bats to let out hostility toward other participants. As diversity training was increasingly deemed a necessity, the workshop methods of the human potential movement, together with its focus on baring emotion, seemed a natural fit for what many trainers thought needed to be accomplished—a change in attitude.

As corporations rushed to address the issue of diversity in the workplace and diversity trainers rushed to fill the need, trainers drew from the available stockpile of information and resources on the issue of race as it is played out in social contexts. It is clear that they often drew on only the most readily available materials, that is, those already condensed or digested into forms that lent themselves to short workshops. Sustained or systematic study of the large body of literature and multiple perspectives on race, ethnicity, or social antagonism was eschewed, on the whole, in favor of the adoption of films or handbooks that promised quick fixes in the form of attitude adjustment.

An exploration of some of the available diversity training materials suggests that they have several common tendencies: they see negative stereotypes as the cause of tensions regarding racial or cultural differences, thus simplifying the issue drastically; they see the project of overcoming stereotypes as requiring intervention along therapeutic or behaviorist lines; they seek to replace negative stereotypes with a new understanding of group attributes; and they seek to replace old behaviors with new ones based on a more enlightened way of thinking about differences—in other words, the way prescribed by them. It is thus worth looking closely at some of these films and handbooks to see the manner in which themes come across and to see what problems these prescriptions might cause.

A common resource used by trainers, also used in schools and other settings, is one of three videos highlighting Jane Elliott, an Iowa schoolteacher who began conducting experiments in 1968 in which she divided her classes into blue-eyed and brown-eyed groups in order to teach about racism. *Blue Eyed* shows clips from her earlier films, including her original *Eye of the Storm,* a video showing this classroom experiment in action.[16] Elliott's idea was to label members of one group, say the brown-eyed one, privileged, beautiful, and superior and the others oppressed, unattractive, and inferior. She then observed the effects of this labeling on her students, noting that those in the group designated inferior became increasingly dejected, as evident in their glum demeanor and diminished self-image, which materialized in the self-portraits she asked them to draw. *Blue Eyed,* which is available for $295, shows Jane Elliott conducting this same experiment with a group of forty adult employees in Kansas City, Missouri, including blacks, Latinos, and whites.[17]

The film begins with a clip of a 1963 speech by Martin Luther King Jr., alluding to civil rights as a justification for Elliott's experiments. Elliott opens her employee workshop by stating that the purpose of the exercise is to let white, blue-eyed people understand the experience of blacks, women, gays, and others by assigning negative stereotypes to them and discriminating against them on the basis of eye color, a fact they cannot change. She removes the blue-eyed group while she prepares the brown-eyed participants to treat those with blue eyes in a demeaning fashion when they return. After asking the participants if they are willing to cooperate, she asks one woman why it took her so long to raise her hand. The woman tentatively responds, " 'Cause it sounds like rude behavior and I . . . would normally go out of my way not to be rude, so I will have to try to do this." Frustrated and confrontational, Elliott likens the woman's reluctance to volunteer to passivity in the face of discrimination, demanding whether she would "normally go out of your way" to help the oppressed.

Once the blue-eyed individuals have returned to the room, Elliott goes on the offensive, with the clear goal of humiliating them. Posted on the walls are various slurs, such as "Catch a blue-eyed by the toe," and the form of address for a blue-eyed man is "boy." Getting the audience involved in attacking the blue-eyed group, Elliott includes in her repertoire extreme rudeness, condescension, hurried speech, rule changing, self-contradiction, and blatant bullying. Both a blue-eyed woman and a man in the audience break under the pressure and begin to cry. To another woman who, unlike her dejected peers, still has some spunk, Elliott commands, "Get over cute," causing her to cry as well. When the participants begin talking about the stress that the experiment provokes—presumably exactly what they were supposed to feel—the session fails to move from confrontation to education. When the blue-eyed members speak of their stress, other audience members demean their experience by dismissing the whole exercise as a game, despite protestations from the blue-eyed members that it does not feel like a game. Elliott misses the opportunity to explore this exchange. The goal of an Elliott seminar seems to be silence on the part of all the white members as an admission of guilt, and an angry state of unresolved grievance on the part of blacks.

The video includes footage of Elliott in her home in the town of Riceville, Iowa, where she first conducted her experiments with schoolchildren and still lives. She recites her own story, which she casts as a tale of victimization as well. Townspeople protested against her activities not by confronting her directly, she says, but by attacking her own children and refusing to patronize her parents' coffee shop, forcing it to go out of business.

Nothing justifies the assaults on her children she alleges took place. However, when one views her experiments in action, particularly in the classrooms themselves, one can see how legitimate concerns might have arisen about Elliott's techniques. The experiments obviously disturbed Elliott's pupils deeply, at the time, anyway, causing tensions and fights among the children and periods of gloom and

self-deprecation for some of them. It is troubling to see Elliott, confident and brash, lead the class through the stages of the exercise: the
initial incomprehension as the very young children, for whom self-
respect and respect for others presumably had been the normal expectation, encounter Elliott's idea; the slow waning of the children's
sunny smiles as the experiment gets underway; the withdrawal of
some students altogether; the bitter bickering that breaks out when
the children are let go for recess. By any standard, such experimenting on schoolchildren raises questions because it would seem to run
contrary to the instinct of a caring teacher. For adult participants of a
diversity training seminar, the project's methods might be more
understandable, but they still raise doubts.

Those who purchase the film *Blue Eyed* are treated to a brief training manual by Nora Lester, a diversity trainer in the Boston area and
clearly a fan of Elliott. Rather than downplay Elliott's heavy-handed
approach, the manual parades it, all as part of the learning process.
Lester praises Elliott's indefatigable "ridicule and humiliation" of participants.[18] The manual underscores Elliott's belief that the best way to
get whites to understand the experience of being black is through a
simulation of an intense episode of active social aggression, so that
they are dislodged from their usual situation of "comfortable privi-
lege." The assumption is that racism remains entirely unabated and
that emotional pain is the only avenue to enlightenment.[19]

The Attack on Universalism

While Elliott feels "moral outrage" about the racial discrimination she
thinks remains unchanged in the thirty years since she began her
experiments, she seems to harbor no moral compunctions about sub-
jecting her audience to emotional manipulation as a means to an end.
The manual's study questions, heavily loaded to steer discussion

toward ends in keeping with Elliott's intent, are revealing. Anticipating the possible response to the film, the manual reads, whites may insist, "The color of one's eyes or skin is irrelevant to me. I treat everyone the same." Facilitators might respond to this concern, Lester writes, by raising the following questions for discussion: "Do you think that all people want to be treated the same? . . . Why do many white people think that the only way to be fair is to treat everyone the same?" The discussion should emphasize that many whites "were wrongly taught that to notice difference is offensive."[20] The entire premise for the film is that it is permissible to use a reprehensible code of behavior in service to a higher end. Elliott and Lester prove equally unaware of or unconcerned with the altogether new tensions that might arise from the social situations they recommend.

The *Blue Eyed* experiments also clearly seek to serve as a kind of ritualized group therapy. The manual anticipates another potential problem film viewers might have: blacks might unleash many thoughts and feelings they are ordinarily forced to repress, such as anger; alternatively, they may become silent. In the latter case, white people need "to stretch, if necessary, to hear people of color, no matter what tone or phrasing they use," while blacks should not have "to frame their ideas or feelings for the benefit of white people" or be expected to "bleed on the floor for white people."[21] In sum, a therapeutic environment should reign. The facilitator must "create an environment in which emotional reactions, including crying, are okay," and he or she "needs to be prepared to handle whatever kinds or level of emotion that gets expressed."[22] Yet the lesson is clear. Emotional expression from blacks—rage, silence, tears—must be embraced, but any turmoil whites might feel is part of learning about racial discrimination, not a new humiliation that might belong quite distinctly to the exercise itself.

Diversity trainers or consultants do not merely simplify racial issues by drawing on only the most easily condensed versions of ideas about race but often create new theories based on their limited experiences in training environments. Jo Vanderkloot, a social worker with British roots who works with an African American partner named Myrtle Parnell, believes that "one of the hidden rules in American culture is that you don't comment on differences, because it's assumed differences mean a deficiency." Rather than see this as an expression of egalitarianism or tact, Vanderkloot and Parnell think Americans are in denial about their discomfort. Parnell writes that "a major mistake is having a multicultural work force and pretending you don't."[23]

Despite their proclamations of attentiveness to differences among people, Vanderkloot and Parnell posit new generalizations on the basis of work they conducted at a mental health center in South Bronx, New York, which had equal numbers of blacks, Hispanics, and whites on the staff. A 1991 article in *Working Woman* quotes Parnell as arguing, "You can really divide the world into two communication styles":

> One is a style that connects to people through doing things together and revolves around task, structure and time. . . . In Hispanic and African-American cultures, the relationship is what's important. There is a need to have some idea of who that other person is in order to work together—what is your common ground? The whole issue of time—get it done now, be here by four o'clock—is so Anglo-American. In other cultures you have an obligation to honor the relationship first.[24]

Vanderkloot believes that such drastic differences in world view can lead to major misunderstandings in the workplace, since even the answer to what seems like a simple mathematical problem could come out differently according to the background of the worker solving it. Besides exaggerating differences by drawing on hypothetical cultural differences of this sort, such a perspective denies any validity to inherited, shared mores. To argue that all behavior is valid—lateness, disrespect—because it represents cultural difference sets workers up for disappointment, when they come up against those mores, as well as for possible failure.

ARE YOU A D, I, C, OR S PERSONALITY?

Other diversity trainers also draw on these kinds of pop-sociological overgeneralizations to typecast the workforce. The consultant Iris Randall gives managers the "Personal Profile System," a questionnaire created by Performax Systems International, so they can discover into which of four categories their own behavior falls: D, dominant; I, influencing; C, cautious; or S, steady behavior. According to Randall, whites, especially men, tend toward dominant behavior, which is decisive and geared toward results. African Americans, Hispanics, and women generally behave in an influencing fashion: "These types are very verbal. They are good at influencing and persuading. They are cheerleaders: 'I can, you can, we can make a difference.' They like people and they like applause." Those who exhibit type C behavior, supposedly often of Asian background, are "taught not to shoot from the hip, not to be confrontational, always to think before they speak, to make sure they are right." Finally, the S behavior characterizes many Native Americans, according to Randall: "For the most part, they show the high S behavior of a person who will hang in there. They are good team players and have no trouble recognizing the person in charge, whereas D-behavior types all act as if they are the boss."[25]

In the Vanderkloot-Parnell typology, there are two mentalities: one that respects "task, structure, and time" and one that values "relationships." In the "Personal Profile System," the influencing, cautious, steady behavior groups are all counterposed to the "dominant" one, which is supposed to represent the more familiar, businesslike style reigning when the workplace was dominated by white males.

While the influx of women and nonwhites into the workforce

undoubtedly calls for adjustments of various kinds to ensure fair and equal treatment, it is not at all clear that a renewed typecasting of people furthers this goal. These pseudo-theories, or at least the general propensity to figure out new categorizations based on vague notions of either cultural background or personality type, surface perennially in the materials used in diversity training. One can imagine that, rather than easing workplace tensions, such generalizations might create a whole new era of misunderstanding, all because of the false premises about group differences they purvey.

Several diversity training films illustrate this particularly well. Despite the different schools of thought in the movement, diversity training materials tend to follow a certain pattern. Usually they begin with the rationale for their own existence, which concerns the bottom line: since the globalization of the economy will mean that in the twenty-first century customers and workers will increasingly be non-white and female, anyone wishing to fit into the new economic scene, either as manager or as employee, must learn to get along with a variety of people, and managers must create a comfortable atmosphere or risk stifling the productivity of the isolated or offended individuals and thus lose profits. In these videos, much care is taken to show that diversity concerns not just white men's treatment of black and female employees. In fact, from viewing the films alone, a foreigner might conclude that in the United States blacks and women are most often in managerial positions.

It is worth looking closely at a typical one of these videos, *Managing Diversity,* for the various messages it conveys and for the assumptions about what kind of etiquette is needed and why. Released in 1990, this training film opens with this statement:

> Diversity in the workplace is a complex and demanding subject. . . .
> For the purposes of illustration and discussion, this training video
> focuses primarily on differences. This is in no way intended to imply
> or perpetuate stereotypes, or to value members of one group over

another, but rather to explore ways in which we can all meet the challenge of Managing Diversity together.[26]

Interspersed with authoritative statements by human resources experts, a series of dramatizations show the kinds of misunderstandings that arise ostensibly because of cultural differences.

In one cameo, a black male manager has to ask a Greek or Italian immigrant male assembly line supervisor of production, who is beneath him in the corporate hierarchy, how much his workers can produce. The line supervisor asks what management wants and, when he finds out, agrees to manufacture that amount. The black manager smiles and expresses contentment that they now have all of their "ducks in a row." On his way out of the building, however, he over-hears the immigrant line supervisor expressing anxiety about the possibility of producing that quantity.

The film's narrator intervenes here to give us some tips. We learn that individuals differ particularly on the following issues: how an individual relates to the group; how he or she views "power and authority"; and how he or she copes with "uncertainty." Supposedly because of his relaxed view of authority, the black manager assumed that the line supervisor could be frank with him, while the immigrant line supervisor thought he had better go along with management's original expectation at all costs. The narrator explains that following a few basic rules of behavior could prevent misunderstandings like these, which were supposedly caused by different cultural back-grounds: (1) communicate, (2) be clear and concise and avoid slang, (3) be aware that the cause of workplace tension might be cultural dif-ferences, (4) be alert for non-verbal messages, (5) accept different cultures as equally valid, and (6) make sure to explain your company's "culture" to employees.

Next, the black manager returns to the immigrant line supervisor and lets him know that a lower production quota would be fine. The supervisor relaxes visibly and makes a joke about how they now have all of their "ducks in a line." Both manager and supervisor clearly part on much improved terms.

Several things are revealing about this scenario. First, while the film's narrator stresses the manager's mistake in using slang or clichés, in the end it is precisely the cliché about ducks in a row (and actually the immigrant's mistake, "ducks in a line," resulting precisely because of his cultural difference) that provides for merriment between the two people involved. Second, cultural differences—different attitudes toward authority—are employed to explain why an employee might feel pressured and closed-mouthed around management. This sidesteps any inherent unfairness in the hierarchical corporate structure itself. Here we see how this approach can be seen as part of a larger trend since the 1920s to engineer social relations in the workplace by employing psychological theory and methods, which redefined genuine conflicts in interest as mere indications of the need for smoother, therapeutic "personal relations" efforts on the part of management.[27] Finally, we learn that blacks as a group supposedly have a relaxed attitude toward power and authority, whereas Greek or Italian immigrants are respectful to a fault. In materials designed to counteract stereotypes, then, rules for behavior are encouraged that are based on gross generalizations about groups.

TAILORING TREATMENT TO IDENTITY

Some recognition of the flaws of a modus operandi that categorizes individuals' traits according to their so-called culture, simplistically rendered, does appear in other training materials. *Valuing Diversity: New Tools for a New Reality,* a book edited and substantially written by one of the best-known proponents of diversity training, Lewis Brown Griggs, together with Lente-Louise Louw, advises managers to refine this cultural model a little: "We must gather as much cultural information as we can, and then we must hold it to one side as we look to see in what ways it may be relevant to the individual with whom we are dealing."[28] One chapter lays out four rules for managing people from different groups:

1. Acknowledge the differences.
2. Educate yourself about differences by reading, listening, and putting yourself in situations where the other group is dominant.
3. Figure out how the person you are working with is like what you have discovered about the group of which he or she is a member and how she or he is not.
4. Work to value those differences.

The chapter guides us through a script in which you, the reader, hypothetically a "Filipino-American woman," have an African American named Ed working under you. After you have listened carefully to his story of his experiences,

> your next step is to find out as much as you can about the culture. You go to the library and to bookstores, particularly those in African-American neighborhoods or the African-American Episcopal church in your community or go to an exhibit of black artists currently displayed in a museum near you. The third step is to observe how Ed is like the culture you have read about or met. How do the things you learned apply to him? This is best done by observing, not by asking Ed a million questions about himself.

Clearly, Griggs did not absorb the lessons of Sheila Rush and Chris Clark's *How to Get Along with Black People,* which warned against taking on the demeanor of a cultural detective. The result of all of your hard work, according to *Valuing Diversity,* is that "your employees" will not only "feel more valued" but "will work harder to see that goals for the whole organization are achieved."[29] Barring that, your workers are certain to feel more *observed.*

Even those diversity training materials that deliberately try to get away from group stereotypes cannot seem to do so. *Diverse Teams at Work,* a film based on a book by Lee Gardenswartz and Anita Rowe, tries desperately to encourage workers to see others as individuals, but cannot seem to imagine how to reconcile that tendency with group identity.[30] The film begins with the business rationale that became increasingly common in the movement. Diversity can be "an added value" in workplaces—that is, "good for business." A focus on diversity can help improve public relations and enhance market share while ensuring higher productivity through more effective cooperation between employees working in teams. In order to illustrate this last point, the film goes on to offer a dramatization of a diverse team at work—an imaginary diversity task force—along with interspersed guidelines for behavior. The dramatization is intended to show how an awareness of the differences in individuals' backgrounds is necessary for good performance in the workplace.

Diverse Teams at Work instructs viewers that it is necessary for each individual both to form a "diversity filter" through which he or she sees others and to know one's own "filter." This hypothetical filter comprises all the factors that make up one's identity: age, race, ethnicity, sex, and the like. As the fictional meeting unfolds, the narrator intervenes periodically to zero in on the current speaker with a cameo describing his or her "filter." These cameos are intended to explain why certain conflicts occur during the meeting, that is, why a particular speaker says what he or she says. One exchange between a black woman named Akilah and an older white man named Clete becomes particularly inflamed as the group considers the idea of celebrating holidays pertinent to different groups in order to improve tolerance of differences in the workplace.

Akilah proposes taking off Juneteenth, the African American celebration of freedom from slavery. When Clete says he does not know what the holiday is, Akilah defines it in a condescending tone and snickers, "We have *far* too many holidays for dead white men." When a co-worker asks, "What about Martin Luther King day?" the exchange continues,

Clete: "Right, you have that don't you?"

Akilah: "You know what? I am not here to represent the entire African American race."

Clete: "What did I say?"

Akilah: "Well you said, about Martin Luther King day, 'Well you have that one, don't you?' I mean, I take offense at the implication that I am only here to defend African American rights. . . ."

Clete: "Now don't get all emotional over it. I didn't mean anything."

Akilah: "And that's another thing. Because I'm a woman you say don't get all emotional. Well, I'm not emotional. I'm angry, which is probably how you'd see it if I was a man."

At this point, the narrator intervenes to try to shed light on the conflict. Cameos spell out that the black woman is forty-two, hails from Memphis, and was active in the black pride and women's liberation movements, while the white man is sixty-three, from the Midwest, hardworking, and a believer in tradition and family. The solution, according to the film, is that everyone needs to appreciate these differences.

Later Clete proposes the idea that, besides all of the standard holidays, the company should allow for three additional floating holidays that employees can take whenever they wish. Akilah fires back, "*You have missed the point!* I want the day to be recognized by the company." A little later, a Latina woman named Rosa recommends the same thing, though she adds that the company can do something further to teach employees about each other's holidays. Her suggestions, unlike Clete's, are deemed constructive and serve as the gist for further conversation.

The point here is not that such dramatizations and narration could under no circumstances serve as a springboard for intelligent discussion of issues of diversity, although the idea that employees have unlimited free time for these activities might be a good argument for a shorter workweek. These materials, by any account, suffer from serious basic flaws. In this case, different cultural norms or personal identities in communication style and content are designated a "filter" through which individuals see the world and others see them. You must keep your "diversity filter clean," the film commands, and goes on to suggest ten characteristics of successful workplaces: a shared sense of mission; a clear objective; an understanding of the role of different cultural norms in communication; shared values of dignity and respect; acceptance of different viewpoints and ways of doing things; ability to meet assignments; loyalty to the team; desire to be involved; openness to new experiences; and "shared laughter and humor." While it encourages these other goals, however, the film concentrates on the "filter" through which an individual sees the world. As in the case of the Elliott experiments, the assumption here is that simplistic negative stereotypes cause interpersonal tensions in diverse settings and that the main task is not so much overcoming them entirely as replacing them with other images of the identity of co-workers.

The problem with this procedure is threefold. First, the replacement of a negative or dismissive "filter" with only a slightly enlarged impression of individual identity represents no real advance, since it lends itself to superficial views of other people. Second, the filter concept assumes that the content of what individuals have to say results from unchangeable facets of their personal identity, such as age and race. This is a certain recipe for further reductionist thinking and problems in communication. Finally, the ultimate goal—not only tolerating differences but also continually focusing on them—is a project that needs to be given much deeper consideration than these materials usually do. In the process of this kind of cultural reeducation, it seems clear that many other things get taught.

The Problem with Brainstorming

Besides the content of the training materials used, reports from journalists and actual participants in diversity training seminars give a sense of how and what the movement teaches. Many workshops begin with, or include at some point, a component that seeks to bring about total disclosure of personal feelings—or at least a mock ritual of disclosure—for purposes that are represented as both personally therapeutic and productive for businesses. A 1990 article in *Black Enterprise* describes a seminar led by the diversity consultant Terrence R. Simmons, president of a management consulting firm in New Hope, Pennsylvania, called Simmons Associates, that begins with a typical urge to participants to be completely candid. Participants in the seminar, held at a Norcross, Georgia, center for diversity training, included thirteen senior-level managers from Unisys. Their first activity was to list "negative and positive stereotypes that are normally associated with various groups—including blacks, Hispanics, women and white males." The result is worth considering:

> After working for 10 minutes, the group, which has been divided into three teams, reads their list aloud. Although several positive stereotypes were listed for white males—they were labeled "leaders" and "decision-makers"—the group appears disturbed that a number of negative stereotypes were listed for the other groups. For example, women were viewed as "pushy," "bitchy," and "too emotional." Hispanics were seen as "lazy," "emotional" and "unskilled." African-Americans were described as "uneducated," "slow workers" and "militant." . . . "That was extremely difficult to do," says one manager, shaking his head. "A lot of our stereotypes," says another executive, defensively, "come from the media." A third participant asks, "What was the point?"

These responses hardly inspire confidence, and, in fact, diversity trainers have yet to prove the effectiveness of their methods. However, trainers like Simmons conclude that this kind of catharsis benefits everyone. "The purpose of this exercise is to allow managers to safely recognize and admit, to themselves and their peers, that they really do harbor some biases against minorities and women."[31]

There is a major logical flaw with Simmons's claim that this atmosphere of free association is the solution to the problem of workforce diversity. It is not clear at all that the "negative stereotypes" are actually held to be true by any of the actual participants in the seminar. Before the exercise, Simmons asks the managers, "Just jot down the things that you've heard, or the things that you've seen," not what they believe to be true of the chosen groups. The hypothetical nature of the stereotypes—and thus the whole mistaken scenario of managers bringing out into the open their deepest biases—does not prevent Simmons from claiming triumphantly that this airing of prejudices amounts to "a quantum leap ahead because it becomes obvious that those biases are adversely affecting their ability to manage a diverse work force productively."[32]

This method of using brainstorming sessions about any stereotypes or biases that diversity seminar participants might ever have heard to establish the premise for exploring further the issue of diversity appears frequently in diversity training. It is a troubling tendency for a number of reasons. For one thing, it trivializes the very real problems groups can have coexisting in a pluralistic society by reducing them to a problem of name-calling or of negative images that are alleged but never quite proven to reign in people's minds.

Like the racial encounter and therapy groups explored earlier, this diversity training approach also posits a world in which all of these hurtful stereotypes and images still exist and in which members of one group actively hold these views of other groups, whether they do or not. In essence, they threaten to give new life to old slurs and untold force and power to mere stereotypes. This is not to say that racial slurs are a thing of the past—would that this were the case—

but that it is possible that this wrongheaded approach to potential social conflict might actually instill new suspicion and inflict new pain and anxiety. This suspicion can then trigger defensive reactions, like icy recoil from interaction or new generalizations about groups, thus perpetuating an endless cycle of recrimination and balkanization. Instead of stopping the cycle of group animosity, these attempts to impose a new etiquette through a mock ritual of therapeutic group disclosure actually exacerbate tensions—perhaps even creating them where none existed.

A WORLD OF CONSTANT SLIGHTS

Another video widely used in diversity training, *A Tale of "O,"* displays the worst possibilities inherent in this creation of an imaginary, hyperbolic world of constant slights and degradation. From its terms and premises to its prescriptions, the film is imbued with a surreal quality. Its setting is a kind of world twice removed—a world in which unbridled racism, sexism, and other interpersonal hatreds are a given, but also a world where any objective measures of the kind of degradation and exploitation that are so weighty that they deserve all of society's mechanisms of retribution do not exist. This is an arena of perceived slights, suspected bias, and egos as fragile as blown glass.

The premise of *A Tale of "O,"* as the *User's Manual* accompanying the video says, is the following: "In short, nearly everyone has been an O at one time or another. All of us have experienced the feeling of being 'different,' whether because we are part of an ethnic/racial/age-group minority, because we wear the wrong clothes to a party, or simply because of foreign travel."[33] This idea that the overriding factor leading to problems for individuals in the workplace is "social rarity or relative numbers"—that is, whether they are part of only a small minority—bears the imprint of the guiding spirit of *A Tale of "O,"* the management sociologist Rosabeth Moss Kanter. Kanter's 1977 book,

Men and Women of the Corporation, studied the significance of the numbers of blacks and women in a company she called Industrial Supply
Corporation and concluded that, regardless of sex or race, individuals
in the minority in a particular workplace encountered major interpersonal problems.[34] This idea is taken to the extreme in *A Tale of "O,"* as
all ways in which one could consider oneself to be in the minority get
thrown together.

This lumping together of all members of potential minorities—
including even those who "wear the 'wrong' clothes to a party"—
allows the film to present a conglomeration of all behavior that
could possibly be interpreted as exclusive or hostile toward the person in the minority, without weighing the relative importance of different kinds of wrongs. To indicate the universal application of the
film's lessons about incorrect behavior, the generic character "X"
denotes members of any majority and "O" denotes a minority member. In this way, the film resembles Jane Elliott's blue-eyed/brown-
eyed experiments, which focus on racial discrimination but make
claims—mainly through innuendo—to apply to other kinds of discrimination. Nevertheless, *A Tale of "O"* proceeds through a number
of examples of group etiquette that read like a list of well-known
complaints raised in the context of discrimination against blacks and
women. Only someone unfamiliar with American culture in the late
twentieth century would fail to recognize these thinly veiled references. It is worth looking at a few examples.

THE SOCIAL SCENARIOS OF INTEGRATION

With an excruciatingly slow, patronizing voice—as if the audience
were a class of grade school children rather than a group of managers
or employees—the narrator recites a set of questions mixed haphaz-
ardly with abstract scenarios, each of them alluding clearly to well-

known issues of social etiquette. There is the "encountering a black person on a dark street" scenario:

> When you see an O . . . coming toward you . . . on a dark street just outside the office late at night . . . what thoughts go through your mind . . . about what the O is doing there? But maybe the O was just working late.

Next is the "black self-segregation" scenario:

> People also make different assumptions about O's than about X's—even when they are doing the same thing. It looks perfectly natural for a group of X's to be having a conversation around the water cooler, or over lunch. But when a group of O's does it, the X's get some different ideas.

Then there is the case where individuals use a term that is offensive to blacks or women, when sorry is just not good enough:

> They elaborately apologize before going on. Of course, that simply draws more attention to the O as someone different.
> The X's may think they are just being polite, but it puts the O on the spot anyway. [35]

Expectations of ingratiating behavior by blacks allowed into the white-dominated group form another example, predictably calling up the "Uncle Tom" image. As a sign of their appreciation for being accepted, these individuals must now establish their affinity with the dominant group's perspective, even to the point of denigrating or ostracizing those of their own group. [36] Along these lines, the "Uncle Tom" can achieve a precarious belonging among whites through "developing a 'good sense of humor'":

What that means is laughing at jokes the X's tell about O's. But, of course, the O doesn't dare tell any jokes about X's. That would make them X-it fast. [37]

To illustrate the narrator's simplistic set of scenarios—as if the viewer required more explication—a similarly condescending visual image of talking X's and O's appears on the screen. The professional calm of the narrator's voice is smug and self-assured. Together with the generic X's and O's, this tone allows the film to strike a pose of scientific objectivity, as though all of the vignettes and rhetorical questions derived from years of accumulated wisdom based on disinterested social observation. Instead, ironically, there is no check on the hodgepodge of real and invented—the makers of the film would say composite—situations.

Materials used in diversity training increasingly conflate all cases in which one might experience a social slight if one finds oneself in the minority. In turn, their scientific pretensions help purvey a sense that all such slights, real or perceived, result from the same urge toward discrimination that results in failure to hire, promote, and reward members of some groups. Furthermore, these materials imply that such slights, together with discrimination on the job, are but latter-day manifestations of the virulent racism that underpinned American slavery, Jim Crow, lynching, and other brutal institutions and behavior. This history of racist wrongs looms in the shadows of any discussion of discrimination in the present, as well it should. We need an undying reminder of what the human will to power and capacity for evil can achieve. But diversity training materials exploit this looming presence of racism's legacy to make their rendering of current slights seem more pressing than common sense would have it, to make their ministrations seem urgent and indispensable. They speak with an air of grave importance, as though they had the wisdom of the ages behind their diagnoses and prescriptions for human interactions.

One of the largest contradictions in the movement is that, despite experts' tendency to blur all the kinds and degrees of behavior that treat members of different groups differently, they do not find solutions in a code of behavior based on a single standard. Instead, after raising a whole litany of social tensions and quandaries, and blurring the lines between actionable wrongs and unintended slights, they turn for solutions to measures that heighten "awareness" of what they see as the omnipresent racist, sexist, or otherwise discriminatory urges underlying behavior in groups. At the end of *A Tale of "O,"* for instance, viewers hear that, as workers in the minority learn to "cope" and workers in the majority learn about the effects of their behavior, everyone can "stop playing set parts," return to work, and see one another "as just people."[38] Naturally, the need to raise this awareness of or sensitivity to differences creates a self-perpetuating rationale for diversity training programs.

A diversity training film that takes this goal of increasing sensitivity about differences to the extreme is *Let's Talk Diversity,* put out by the Human Resource Development Press in 1993. It begins with an ominous warning:

> This videotape was specifically designed to spark lively and emotionally-charged discussion. You will find that many of your participants will have strong feelings about the topics portrayed. Therefore, DO NOT play this videotape for participants if you:
>
> - are unfamiliar with proper facilitation skills
> - feel uncomfortable handling emotion
> - cannot remain objective about the topics being discussed
> - plan to abandon the participants
> (Do not play this videotape and then leave the room.)[39]

In a tone even more condescending than that seen in *A Tale of "O,"* this film's narrator informs viewers that the exercise will illustrate "how our own cultural programming" can get in the way of working with people who differ from one another. A series of particularly brief, simplistic vignettes follows, including ones in which a well-known reaction to stereotyping like "They all look alike to me" or "I'm not Mr. Affirmative Action" gets voiced. After each vignette, the narrator comes on and asks, "What do you say in response?" A longer example illustrates how superficial this treatment is:

[Black Woman:]	There's this guy I work with. I just can't get along with him. We can't see eye to eye on anything. He's just got that typical white male attitude. . . .
[White Man:]	There's this woman at work. We just never agree on things. It causes problems. She's just got that typical black female attitude.
[Narrator:]	Whoa, did I just hear some racist, sexist, derogatory remark? Do you think his remark is less acceptable than hers? Why, and why not?

While this kind of unresolved presentation of the issue of racial stereotyping might be defended as a legitimate starting point for an open discussion of the issue, the underlying assumption requires careful consideration. The premise here is that sensitivity in itself is an unquestioned good. One can legitimately hope that these fictional characters would be sensitive enough to know that dismissing individuals on account of a "typical white male attitude" or "typical black female attitude" is an unfair and ungrounded generalization about a whole group of people. But the value of merely bringing up at random any and all such phrases in hypothetical scenarios under a pseudoscientific guise is much less clear. It is not self-evident how a kind of extreme sensitivity to differences in itself would remedy situations of this sort. In fact, it could be argued that it is heightened sensitivity to differences that leads to such comments. The two speakers in the vignette, indeed, suffer from hyperawareness that the person they dislike has traits that put him or her in a completely different social group. Paradoxically, perhaps it is a kind of insensitivity to these kinds of differences in outward physical traits or long-term cultural heritage—or rather, not insensitivity so much as a temporary placing of these to the side—that is necessary if one is to be sensitive and respectful to others as individuals and treat them as full equals and fellow citizens.

Diversity training largely creates an atmosphere of hypersensitivity to differences in group attributes and evokes a generalized, looming, omnipresent threat of discriminatory treatment. As such, it has created a kind of tinderbox in which a wayward spark could create an explosion.

The Nihilism of "Making It"

Besides diversity training materials, many other sources aimed at managers proclaim to help blacks make it in today's workplace. In *The Black Manager: Making It in the Corporate World,* published in 1982 and reprinted in 1991, Floyd Dickens Jr. and Jacqueline B. Dickens advise blacks to "manage racist behavior by strategy." While some of the guidelines are similar to those given by diversity training materials, such as "Learn how to approach people tactfully, sensitively, and in a way that avoids unnecessary conflict," other directives differ substantially. The basic subtext of this book is that lack of communication is not the problem, but outright racism is. The black manager should follow a number of guidelines when facing interracial situations:

- Use effectively controlled anger as a tool for achieving results. . . .
- When whites are illogically resistant, lay out relevant data and let them think they came up with the idea. . . .
- When using whites as resources, show your appreciation by giving them a stroke or sharing useful information. . . .
- Watch and listen to whites in order to learn white organization norms and duplicate their behavioral approach. . . .
- When dealing with whites, be careful about what key organiza-

tional issues you discuss and how you phrase your needs relative to hot issues. . . .

- . . . Be sure you have all relevant information before stating your position. When you lack the pertinent facts or sit on the fence, racists can easily control you.
- Do not depend on organizational rewards. Whites tend not to expect or give public strokes and rewards. . . .
- . . . Ask key questions indirectly, to avoid giving racists a reason to react negatively to questions perceived as threatening or irrelevant. . . .[40]

The Black Manager's guidelines and the diversity training materials are particularly striking when juxtaposed. One can only imagine the confusion that would result in a workplace in which one worker learned the cardinal rule of "managing diversity"—"Be clear and concise and avoid slang"—and another read in *The Black Manager* that he or she should "ask key questions indirectly." What the two schools of thought have in common, however, is their acknowledgment that race relations require a new etiquette and that this etiquette needs to be spelled out in all its particulars. Furthermore, they share the idea that there should be a separate etiquette for interactions among different groups of people. Such an etiquette, based on a heightened awareness of differences construed as cultural facts, clearly relies on simplistic, stereotypical renderings of the groups involved, as well as a condescending assessment of and cynical resignation concerning individuals' capacities to learn, through experience, to get along with others. This resignation often translates into an unabashedly utilitarian or instrumental stance. *The Black Manager* goes on to advise blacks,

- Eat lunch with whites to get information from their formal and informal communications networks and make personal contact [but]
- Eat lunch with blacks to share information, keep in touch with the grapevine, relax, and replenish your psychic energy.[41]

Like those of the diversity training films, these guidelines are predicated on the idea that the primary reason why an elaborate etiquette exists is that each group requires the other in order to fulfill its economic goals. Since workers and customers will be increasingly diverse, lack of tolerance will compromise profits. Mere tolerance is the only goal that remains—not an inspiring foundation for any social world.

Even though many Americans spend more and more hours at work, the workplace is only a part of our social world. To allow or expect diversity training programs to solve our remaining conflicts or tensions over race is misguided and unrealistic. In fact, the management consultants Hellen Hemphill and Ray Haines declared in 1997 that diversity training was an unmitigated failure: "The evidence is overwhelming that diversity training programs have failed to significantly reduce discrimination and harassment in the workplace." They point to the record settlement of $176.1 million paid by Texaco in a racial discrimination suit although it had a diversity training program. Besides failing to reduce discrimination, they wrote, diversity training often "caused further divisiveness and negative labeling." Organizations sought tranquillity, but after spending billions of dollars on diversity training, they had worse tensions and ended up paying millions on legal fees, not just in cases of harassment in the workplace, but in cases involving "comments made by [diversity] trainers and employees in diversity training programs."[42]

While Hemphill and Haines present an impressive critique of the movement, they conclude that the problem is that diversity training sought to change attitudes, not behavior. Of paramount concern to them is continuing harassment and discrimination at the workplace. They point to the laws against these abridgments of workers' rights and argue for a policy of "zero tolerance" by managers accompanied by another massive training program, this one aimed at interpersonal skills training, rather than cultural change—or so they say. But next we find them outlining a program of "Managing MindTalk™," or the "conversations that take place inside ourselves, to ourselves, about ourselves and others." This initiative aims to "(1) Question our perceptions; (2) Challenge our clusters of perceptions; (3) Interrupt our habit patterns; and (4) Control our filters." These filters, or lenses through which we view the world, are closed when we stereotype others. To open our filters, we need to "feel safe, trusted, loved, listened to, free, respected, or appreciated." "When the situation is nonjudgmental or open," we "are free to be aware in the moment." And you guessed it, we must be taught by a new "Workplace Relationship Skills Toolkit™," that most arcane of skills, "listening to understand."[43]

Hemphill and Haines decry the billions of dollars they think were wasted on diversity training, but they are eager to redirect managers' attention to another program for engineering employees' attitudes. Though the experts and the catchwords may change, the structure remains largely the same. And it is this structure that requires examination. Before offering a new program of their own that will transcend the divisiveness of the diversity training programs by downplaying differences and highlighting social behavioral skills for all workers, Hemphill and Haines write soberly that diversity training caused new "social conflict" by trying to "deal publicly with sensitive personal and social human rights issues better dealt with elsewhere." They cite workshops that degenerated into angry confrontation and emotional outbursts. They write that trainers were misguided "to think that with three to five hours of diversity training, complex sociological and cultural principles could be easily understood, much less applied to all interpersonal relationships." But they themselves go on to spell out the principles and skills—the quick cure—they believe to be the keys to these relationships. "MindTalk™ controls our life!" they exclaim.[44]

That new programs for managing the emotional lives of workers—even the conversations we have in our own minds—accompany even the harshest criticism of past programs should no longer come as a surprise. Trends in management style come and go quickly, since they are part and parcel of the marketplace, an industry in themselves.

But we need to think seriously about whether we can leave matters of such importance to the corporate fads and gurus. Hemphill and Haines make no bones about it: the point of smoother interpersonal relations is greater productivity and global competitiveness. A point they do not make is that in recent years, while corporations paid billions of dollars for diversity training programs, only to see them crumble amid more conflict, the gap between the rich and the poor in this country has become the widest it has ever been. Corporate CEOs currently earn over 250 times what the workers in their own companies make. It might seem fairly convenient to some shrewd corporate managers that endless rounds of navel gazing about facets of identity, "filters," and interpersonal dynamics deflect attention away from this fact. Besides contemplating this waste of manpower and resources, however, even these managers—in their capacities as mothers, fathers, citizens—must be worried about the unintended consequences of seemingly benign employee workshops that claim to solve our social problems but in fact worsen matters by giving old attitudes a new lease on life. If they are not yet concerned, they should be.

CHAPTER SEVEN

In Perpetual Recovery:
The Problem with Multicultural
Education for Self-Esteem

The effects of the focus on racial iden-
tity, hypersensitivity to real and imagined slights, and
the need for emotional gratification and validation, to
the exclusion of other collective and individual goals,
were everywhere apparent in late twentieth-century
America, but perhaps nowhere as much as in the field of
education. These tenets of the therapeutic culture ironically found some of their most loyal and vocal champi-
ons among self-styled radical educators who drew on
theories of education as liberation from forces of oppression. In the aftermath of the massive felling of legal
obstacles to universal civic rights and privileges, what
exactly constituted these forces of oppression was inevitably left vague. Inspired by the truly egalitarian
ideals of the civil rights movement, a generation of educators unreflectively took the radical theorists to be the
embodiment of that movement, mistaking the fluff of
jargon and posture for the substance of revolution.
Lacking full appreciation of how revolutionary the civil
rights movement had been, these self-proclaimed heirs
of the revolution thought their mission was to enlighten
the masses to their own oppression and to give them the
tools—identity and pride—that would supposedly em-
power them, an end that was also left markedly vague

but that all agreed had something to do with heightened self-esteem. The radical posturing of the liberationist educators dovetailed nicely with the self-centeredness taught by the new therapies. The result was the institutionalization in education of two fundamental tenets: identity relies first and foremost on self-esteem; and education should revolve first and foremost around identity.

SELF-DESIGNATED RADICALS

The transformation of education into therapy came in the service of a project ostensibly aimed at expanding democracy to include non-mainstream populations through tolerance and multiculturalism, the new watchwords of the movement. Capitalizing on the spirit and moral force of the civil rights movement, the empowerment crusade made its incursions nearly unnoticed. By the 1990s, however, cracks began to appear in the new edifice, as controversies over curriculum, speech codes, course content, and numerous other topics erupted. Often issued from the right, but sometimes from the center and independent left, challenges to the liberationist educators often came in the form of attacks on intellectual and political conformity, dubbed "political correctness." A set of unwritten guidelines and taboos tended to tamp down dissent from the reigning left-liberal orthodoxy, fears about the decline of educational standards, and worries about the overemphasis on racial and other differences at the expense of commonalities seen as vital for the democratic project.

Defenders of multicultural education succeeded in defining their opponents as undemocratic critics of diversity rather than as thoughtful dissenters from the particular blend of politics and education that had come to dominate. Critics of education as empowerment in turn caricatured all defenders of multiculturalism as adhering to identity politics or radical theory, when actually many merely advocated a more inclusive definition of the canon and curriculum. The attack on "political correctness" could not do justice to the complexity of the competing positions on race that had evolved by the 1990s. The bitterness of the controversy stemmed in large part from the self-righteousness with which some radical theorists made their case. These self-designated experts in education as radical politics promoted their racial dogma with a vengeance and succeeded in penetrating the mainstream through their influence on schools of education.

THE FLAK OVER "NAPPY HAIR"

One news story that made a minor flap in the set of controversies over multicultural education in the 1990s illustrates the tensions that had accumulated over the seemingly innocuous matter of multiculturalism in education. In 1998, at a school in the Bushwick neighborhood in Brooklyn, New York, a battle erupted over a white third-grade teacher's use of a children's book called *Nappy Hair*. Ruth Sherman had been hired at the school a couple of years earlier as a volunteer reading assistant in an effort by the school's new principal to boost flagging test scores. A graduate student at St. John's University, Sherman gained success and popularity that earned her a full-time teaching position. A *Newsweek* article stated that, partly as a result of her efforts, the number of third-graders meeting state standards for reading doubled. To encourage students' interest in reading, Sherman read books on multicultural themes to them, including one titled *Nappy Hair*.[1]

Nappy Hair, written by Carolivia Herron and illustrated by Joe Cepeda, was published in 1997 to much acclaim. It is written in a call-and-response style traditional among many black preachers and audiences. It sets forth a story told at a backyard picnic and was based on "the fun" the author's "own family poked at her nappy hair when she was a girl," according to the book's dust jacket. The story celebrates "nappy" hair, a term traditionally considered an insult because it assumes that the soft, tight curls of many African Americans constitute undesirable, "bad" hair, as opposed to the manageable, silky, straight hair usually associated with whites. Herron, instead, portrays "nappy" hair as a desirable, beautiful feature that was created deliberately by God. Characters in the story try to straighten the heroine's curls, but to no avail, and her hair ends up being cause for great celebration and admiration.[2]

The students enjoyed the book so much that Sherman made photocopies for them to take home. When one child's mother saw the photocopies later, she spearheaded a protest because of what she thought were the book's degrading written portrayals of blacks and illustrations full of physical caricatures. The incident came to a head one day at a school meeting. Called from her classroom to the auditorium, Sherman encountered a roomful of angry parents, some of whom allegedly "yelled out racial epithets like 'cracker' and shouted threats," such as "You'd better watch out." *Newsweek* reported, "Anxious, Sherman smiled, a nervous habit. Her grin fueled the crowd's anger. When she rolled her eyes at the gathering, a woman in the front row lunged toward the stage. The principal and the school security guard intervened and Sherman was rushed out of the hall." Having told the children in her class she would return in ten minutes, Sherman was instead escorted from the school and neighborhood. She never returned. Despite school administrators' later pleas that she return, Sherman accepted a position at another school. The original school was embarrassed by the incident, especially when it came to light that the author of *Nappy Hair* was herself black and the story's message was about black pride. Many of the angry parents admitted they had not read the book before the protest or even afterward. *Newsweek* reported that the parents' objection to the teaching of the book was based in part on the belief that "a white teacher had no business raising such a culturally sensitive subject." Still others disapproved of its being raised by any teacher.[3]

In the contemporary climate of hypersensitivity about race, the incident not surprisingly drew a substantial amount of news coverage and commentary. It got the attention of public forums and talk shows. It also helped boost Herron's book sales. For our purposes, what is particularly revealing is the nature of the media and public response to the case. This response shows that, contrary to the dogma of the race experts, clashes over matters of race now defy the usual premises of white insensitivity and racism and the division of blacks and whites into clear camps. It is worth considering the situation in all its complexity, for only by doing so can we possibly get at the root of what has gone so desperately wrong that children were forced to pay for our unresolved problems over race with the loss of their teacher. Who knows what new seeds were planted here—and in incidents like this one—for future racial anxieties?

Before the day of the meeting that led to Sherman's removal from her position, by her own account, one of the parents angered about the photocopies of *Nappy Hair* apparently stormed into Sherman's room on parents' night, telling her that she expected to find a Ku Klux Klan hat sitting on her desk.[4] Later Sherman spoke of the contradiction between this attack, including racial epithets and threats she said she received at the parents' meeting, and the accusation that she was the one who was racially insensitive.[5] Although the school itself immediately realized its error in caving in to the mean-spiritedness of the parents' group and invited Sherman back to her position, Sherman pointed out that it would be nearly impossible to return to any semblance of normality in the classroom, given the objections to her teaching, let alone to feel safe going to and from work, given the intensity of the parents' behavior. "I don't want to be a prisoner," she said.[6] The failure of nerve in the educational system ensured that returning would not be an option. To his credit, an invitation to return to the school came from Schools Chancellor Rudy Crew, who stated that Sherman was "an outstanding" and "courageous" teacher and called the behavior of the parents "a serious violation of civil rights": "They stepped completely outside the scope of what good, responsible parenting means."[7] Newspaper editorials and articles, however, claimed that these words were not backed up by a further strong public show of support, reflecting an absence of the "bold leadership" required by the situation.[8] While Sherman was temporarily reassigned pending investigation, the parents were not apparently disciplined in any way.

In addition, New York City schools officials seemed to give mixed signals. A spokesman for the board of education, J. D. La Rock, said in the words of Lynette Holloway of the *New York Times* that "the book's title and illustrations could be perceived as insensitive if taken out of context."[9] The district 32 superintendent, Felix Vazquez, decided that the book was not offensive, but that Sherman should have obtained permission from the school principal for using it. This might be a way of saying that the principal would have had the sensitivity to veto the use of the book, a point more explicitly made by the president of the school board for the district, Dennis L. Herring. "If she had allowed the principal to view it, she would have been told that's not the best way to do it," Herring said. La Rock equivocated similarly: "We're not saying it should be banned. That's not what the parents want. The superintendent wants to make sure that staff review material with the principal. They almost always do that because it prevent [*sic*] incidents like this from coming up."[10]

The removal of Sherman from the school (even though quickly reversed), the lack of a strong show of support for her, and the failure to reprimand the unruly parents all illustrate a failure of leadership. The attack on Sherman was simply cruel. Racial epithets, public ridicule, threats: these have no place in either education or democratic civil society, which of course is supposed to provide for the open airing of divergent views without such tactics of intimidation.

Yet, the incident bears further contemplation. In the aftermath of the incident, editorials, op-eds, articles, and letters to the editor appeared in newspapers and magazines across the country. While many different points were made, the general consensus was that Sherman was treated unfairly and rudely. Most commentators blamed the parents. Except for a letter to the editor of *Newsweek,* which said that the attack on Sherman "dramatically underscores that not all bigots are white,"[11] nearly all those who later commented on the incident focused not on the parents' racism but on their lack of engagement in their children's education and their backwardness on racial matters. Lynette Clemetson, author of the *Newsweek* article, took this tack, pointing to the parents' belated discovery of the photocopies of *Nappy Hair* some two months after the class read it, their failure to attend an earlier meeting at the school on test scores, and their lack of awareness of the book's acclaim. "Recommended by institutions like the Teachers College of Columbia University," she wrote, "it is on reading lists in schools and libraries around the country" and "has been widely acclaimed by educators and critics (including *Newsweek*)."[12]

An editorial in the *Omaha World-Herald* shared this assumption that the endorsement of the book by Columbia Teachers College and the black columnists Byron McCauley and Clarence Page proved that the Sherman incident was "about parents and their involvement—or lack of involvement—in their children's education." "Many educators and critics," the editorial went on, "including many African Americans, have hailed Herron's approach," and "reading experts" have "endorsed it for classroom use." Herron wrote the book "to build self-esteem," and Clarence Page said that it "makes African American children feel good about being black." To the *Omaha World-Herald,* this stamp of approval had the final say: the parents acted the way they did because they had been neglecting their children's education: "Only four parents came to a meeting in October about test scores. . . . People who meet regularly with their children's teachers and help their children with homework are less likely to misunderstand something so completely."[13]

INTERNALIZED OPPRESSION AS LOW SELF-ESTEEM

An even more common explanation for the parents' unleashed fury focused less on their lack of awareness of the newest educational materials and more on their unenlightened attitudes about race itself. As one author of a letter to the editor of *Newsweek* stated, "I have to wonder about the parents at P.S. 75. It's tragic that they seem not to have even read the book, but it's absolutely horrifying that they're ashamed of their hair and their heritage."[14] It seemed clear to a number of observers like this one that what had triggered the parents' poor behavior was the very thing that *Nappy Hair* sought to address: low self-esteem.

Many commentators explained that the parents were acting out of a deeply rooted, but now outmoded, shame at their own hair. Isoke T. Nia, director of research and development at the Teachers College Reading and Writing Project, recommended *Nappy Hair* to the teachers she trained in summer institutes. "I would like to talk to the parents and ask them, 'what is it about your hair that you are offended by?'"[15] Jill Nelson, author of *Straight, No Chaser: How I Became a Grown-Up Black Woman* (1997) and *Volunteer Slavery: My Authentic Negro Experience* (1993), chimed in with even greater condescension directed at Sherman as well as the parents. She spread the blame liberally to include blacks as well as whites, but implicitly exempted the parents on account of their experiences with racism. Despite Sherman's "good intentions," Nelson wrote, her use of *Nappy Hair* "tapped into a well guarded secret in a community that is often under attack."[16]

Despite Nelson's insistence, it is difficult to accept that some African Americans' historically internalized notions that black "Afro-type" hair is less beautiful still constitutes a "well-guarded secret," considering all the exposure it has received: the well-known agonies of "conking" or straightening of hair described in Malcolm X's famous *Autobiography*; the "Black is beautiful" cry of the late 1960s, which spurred an embrace of natural hairstyles; the outpouring of autobiographical writing and social criticism attacking the old cultural message that the black physique is less desirable; the massive movement to remedy low self-esteem based on race; the incorporation in the media of television shows, movies, and advertisements of black images; the adoption of many black styles by whites; and the multiplying images of beauty held up in popular culture and sports as African Americans have become prominent and visible in arena after arena.

Yet Nelson persists. Although she might be right that "we live in a culture in which most women are fixated on hair," it seems no longer true that "long, straight hair" is the unchallenged standard of beauty. For one thing, women of this hair type are just as prone to spend vast amounts on perms to give their hair body, curl, frizz, and the like. The revolt against the natural styles of the 1960s and 1970s in the perm craze of the 1980s and the more recent boom in popularity of hair coloring and professional styling for women of all ages, and now men, even teenagers: these trends were not confined to blacks. Her conclusion that "most women of African descent are eliminated from the running" in aesthetic consideration is strange, given recent American culture's adulation of images of black female beauty (which has significant precursors even under segregation). This is not to deny that the damaging potential of the mass commodification of beauty is a serious matter, but only to refute an outdated racialized analysis that stops at the notion of stereotypes rather than questioning mainstream media imagery in a more fundamental way. Nelson's statement that "straight hair has historically been called 'good,' nappy hair 'bad,'" holds only if the years from at least the 1960s to the present are not considered a part of history. Much has changed in this time. Not only that, but even in the era of white supremacy, African Americans (and whites to some degree as well) varied in the degree to which they accepted or rejected the dominant, degrading images of them tendered by whites.

But Nelson sees no such nuances. She asserts that too many blacks believe "proximity to whiteness inherently enhances our self-worth" and argues that Sherman "had no inkling" that at times it is blacks themselves who foster self-defeating images of themselves. Nelson even wonders whether Sherman realized that African Americans think of "nappy" as an insult.[17] If Sherman had no idea that negative self-images come in part from within, why would she choose a book for her black youngsters that celebrates a trait of many African Americans with the declared purpose of raising their self-esteem? How could anyone read *Nappy Hair* and not *learn* that nappy hair was originally an insult, if he or she did not already know? The idea that all blacks still have internalized negative images is so deeply embedded in today's educational philosophy—the very philosophy that explains the craze over books like *Nappy Hair* by the educational establishment—that it is surprising Nelson believes she is letting us in on a "race secret." A San Francisco community leader, the owner of Marcus Books, Raye Richardson, similarly dismissed all questions about the book as deriving from obsolete racial attitudes: "Many people still maintain the idea that to be white is to be right. . . . They are living in the past. This culture has not affirmed black beauty or that a woman can have African features and be beautiful." Richardson found it baffling that "some black parents" refused to accept "nappy" hair, which Herron portrayed as invincible and resilient, as a "proper metaphor for them."[18]

There is no doubt that the parents acted hastily and meanly. They attacked a young and inexperienced teacher, an outsider to the community who was trying to make a difference in the lives of their children. However, dismissing the parents' behavior as complete backwardness, lack of self-esteem, and failure to take an interest in their children's education jars with some of the facts. Storming a school meeting because of photocopies found in a pupil's homework, after all, hardly denotes inattention. Rather, the rallying of passionate parents in response to a particular reading suggests, perhaps, over-excitement rather than apathy. Particularly striking was the continued resistance to the book on the part of the very parent who originally complained about the book (and was alleged to have distributed the photocopies of the book to other parents), only to admit later she had not read it in its entirety. Stunned by a photocopied page of the book where she saw illustrations in which it appeared that a bush was growing out of the girl's head, and descriptions of hair that sounded "like crunching snow," Cathy Wright said she asked Sherman, "Well, what was your purpose for using this book? . . . I want to understand what you were trying to convey." When Sherman supposedly said, "Well, I was trying to make her feel good about her hair," Wright wondered, "Who said my child had problems with her hair?"[19]

In the midst of the insanity over this incident, this question stands out for its sobriety. Intentionally or not, Wright's question implicitly calls into doubt the entire self-esteem enterprise of Herron, Sherman, and most of their defenders. It is perhaps the question that needs to be put to the whole company of self-proclaimed racial experts who persist, even in the face of studies and protests to the contrary, that low self-esteem is the main problem facing blacks today and enhanced self-esteem is one of the main solutions—thus a top priority for early education.

While nothing excuses the parents' actions, it is possible that their misgivings about the use of the book might have some validity, however much one might disapprove of their decision to take out their views on one particular teacher and book—and the pupils, in the process. To hear that a book called *Nappy Hair* was assigned at an all-black school, after all, could be the equivalent (only much more sensitive, given the history of racial oppression in this country) of hearing that a book called *Pasty Face* or something along those lines was assigned by a black teacher at an all-white class. To reject the reappearance of old, hitherto derogatory terms as a way of reclaiming them in the service of ethnic pride is not simply a matter of rejecting progress.

Yet it is important not to take Wright's comment out of context. Her behavior and other comments revealed that she perhaps also accepted the terms of self-esteem but merely differed over the question of who and what should properly build it. The book "didn't make me feel good about myself," Wright said ambiguously, "and I don't think it really made my daughter feel good about herself."[20]

THE INEGALITARIAN POTENTIAL
OF SELF-ESTEEM

Instead of renunciation of the newest trends in self-esteem education, was the parents' reaction instead exactly the kind of divisiveness we can expect to result from these trends? Are we down to fights basically over who and what best promotes self-esteem? Only two out of scores of commentators on the incident hinted that perhaps the whole myopic focus on feeling good about oneself—the essence of the therapeutic ethos—was the real culprit in this situation. John Leo in *U.S. News and World Report* faulted "the therapeutic culture permeating our schools" for the parents' bad behavior. "In that culture, it is incorrect to criticize feelings as wrong or bad. By the code of therapeutic culture, if a person feels affronted, then a genuine affront has taken place, even if the affrontee, like the Brooklyn parents, misunderstood the situation or got the facts wrong."[21] Certainly, this fits the situation; the school meeting sounds hauntingly similar to the emotional bloodletting of television talk shows like the *Jerry Springer Show*.

Another commentator, Jeff Jacoby, in the *New Orleans Times-Picayune* blamed Sherman herself for complying with recent trends of "racial boosterism and ethnic consciousness" rather than teaching her students the rudiments of reading and writing. Acknowledging the poor behavior of the parents and Sherman's good intentions, he asks whether teachers should encourage students to "dwell on their hair": "What kind of teacher tries to promote self-esteem with feelgood cheerleading for meaningless racial characteristics? What kind of teacher imagines that what is needed at P.S. 75—where 70 percent of the children read below grade level—is a patronizing affirmation that black is beautiful?" Jacoby's finger-pointing at Sherman—rather than, say, at the educational field, whose latest teachings she has merely mastered—is a bit extreme. We can assume that Sherman used many other books as well, on a variety of other subjects besides physical traits. Still,

Jacoby's analysis zeroes in on a fundamental premise that went unchallenged and unanalyzed in the dispute: education is fundamentally about self-esteem and identity. Jacoby believes that this, in fact, is the ultimate lesson the children at P.S. 75 will learn: "the technique of wearing their racial and ethnic identities like suits of armor—a defense against all criticism, a shield against high expectations."[22]

Both the parents and those who accused them of anachronistic racial and educational attitudes were similarly schooled, as was Sherman, in racial hypersensitivity. When Sherman found herself the subject of racial insensitivity in the midst of her efforts to be racially sensitive, she was caught unaware. When the black parents felt affronted, they did not hold back their own racial animosity.

The one who got out of the whole ordeal unscathed—perhaps laughing all the way to the bank, as the joke goes—was Carolivia Herron, the book's author. At the time of the uproar, *Nappy Hair* had sold 13,000 copies; four months later, sales had leapt to 90,000.[23] Showing an affinity for the self-esteem age, Herron not only wrote the book to build self-esteem but also in the ensuing debates exhibited no small measure of it herself. "I think it's perfect as I wrote it," she said of *Nappy Hair,* hedging her bets (and perhaps proving a bit disloyal) by admitting that some of the book was the result of compromises with her editors and that she herself did not like the illustrations before she saw them in color.[24] She fondly recalls being called by a stranger, an African American woman who saw Herron adorned in a purple cape, "the caped and napped crusader."[25] Herron writes in *Nappy Hair* about the book's main character that her hair is not just beautiful but inimitable, and raves about how much she loves her own hair.[26] To those who ask, "Why bother teaching children self-esteem when they need to learn math, science, English," she says, "People cannot learn when they hate themselves."[27]

Championed by most as the heroine in the entire mess, Herron has produced a book that is undoubtedly entertaining and harmless in the overall scheme of things. Lesser books have been part of the curriculum for years. And cries for the banning of books and censoring of teachers will never—and should never—be the answer to the issue of contentious material in a free society. But that does not mean books should not be debated and analyzed.

In the perceived need to defend Sherman and Herron from the angry parents—an artificial need, given that the school and most parents backed down immediately as soon as they read the whole book—none of those professing educational enlightenment seems to have read the book carefully enough to detect that the book really does contain a racially based insult of just the kind its supporters said it did not include. Even if one grants that *Nappy Hair* contains no slur against blacks' hair, since it turns that slur into a compliment, the book does insult a particular type of hair. The ultimate irony is that *Nappy Hair* comes right out and insults *non*-"nappy" hair—the kind adorning the heads not only of most whites of European origin but also of many people of Asian, Native American, and Middle Eastern origin.

Drawing a metaphor between African Americans and Afro-type hair, Herron recites how indomitable the girl with the Afro-type hair was and, in turn, the hair itself. Both came all the way from Africa, resisting all the horrors of slavery, surviving, bursting with life through every attempt to shackle and straighten their unruliness. In the entire controversy, no one seemed to notice that Herron went on to write that the wonderful "nappy" hair "danced right on through all the wimp hair" wanting nothing at all to do with it.[28]

Herron says she enjoys reading her book to racially mixed audiences. And a *Courier-Journal* writer calls *Nappy Hair* "one of the few children's books with an African American theme to reach crossover audiences" to this great extent.[29] Even if it is true, as Herron and the educational establishment that rose to support her seem so certain,[30] that black youngsters still suffer from debilitatingly low levels of self-esteem, is it acceptable to build the self-esteem of one group of children by directly insulting many others? That Herron's insult, which one assumes was accidental or an unthoughtful attempt at humor, went undetected and unchallenged suggests the degree to which the self-esteem crusade has permeated American life. Hardly confined to one racial or ethnic group, this crusade is universal. Assuming their own ministrations to be universally positive, the self-esteem promoters and their audience collude in an atmosphere in which unlimited self-celebration, even at the expense of common respect for others, is permitted.

What is worse, this self-centeredness is promulgated in the name of social justice. Self-affirmation is equated with freedom, and freedom to elevate one's own group and one's self, even to the detriment of others, is equated with fairness and justice. In the self-esteem mentality—a mentality that, in the case of multicultural education, parades itself as the fulfillment of the civil rights revolution—personal liberation has become the goal. This version of liberation, however, has lost its old emphasis on equality with others, the sharing of universal rights, duties, and privileges, or real justice that presupposes a transcendent standard to which we all aspire and which we all honor as an ideal. Instead, this is the drastically shrunken definition of personal freedom imparted by the New Age therapy movements: the freedom to be me, the freedom to love myself unconditionally, the freedom to create my identity and revel in it, the freedom to let my hair down, the freedom to be as self-absorbed as I want to be.

THE SELF-AFFIRMATION MARKET

Herron is just one of many writers who have carried the extremes of self-affirmation from the periphery of the original motivational tapes, encounter and group therapy groups, and early talk shows, to the mainstream culture, where an adolescent preoccupation with self was once roundly lampooned. This popularization of the human potential movement's philosophy has occurred not only in multicultural education, of course, but throughout American society. Yet some strains of multicultural education have at least in some measure been complicitous in the human potential movement's worst incursions, because they have helped foster special exemptions to traditional mores regarding reserve and humility. Much as writers like Herron might think they are striking a blow for equality by turning an old insult on its head, they are also turning the civil rights movement on its head by embracing the new double standards of the therapeutic world in which we all must continually affirm ourselves without any regard to the antisocial, divisive ramifications of this self-boosterism.

After all is said and done, *Nappy Hair* is best seen as one in the pantheon of consumer products that feed off this self-affirmation frenzy. In the one arena of "nappy hair," for instance, a Dallas journalist named Linda Jones goes modestly by the nickname Mosetta because she is considered "a female Moses who's leading black women out of hair bondage." Jones's modus operandi is unlimited celebration of "non-chemically treated or 'nappy' hair" through "informal hair grooming parties," a bimonthly newsletter called *Nappy News,* production of a mini-documentary about these parties called *A Nappy Hair Affair,* and a compact disc of poetry called *Love and Nappiness,* which aims at "the promotion of a positive self-concept of people of the African diaspora." Beyond Jones's individual efforts, there are Web sites and conventions for "'nappy' hair advocates," such as the World Natural Hair and Beauty Show held in Georgia in May 2000.[31]

Perhaps deserving the award for the most nonsensical comment about the whole *Nappy Hair* controversy was a comment by Cheryl Willis Hudson, head of the independent black-owned publisher Just Us Books, that the problem is that there are not enough books about black Americans in the curriculum: "If there are [sic] more books that portray African Americans and children of color in all kinds of situations, there would be less controversy about one particular book."[32]

Quite to the contrary, there has been a true renaissance in African American writing at all levels, and multicultural books and guides to these offerings have become plentiful. And it has been argued that the multicultural paradigm is fast becoming the dominant way in which readings are organized and presented for use in the curriculum. One guide, Barbara Thrash Murphy's *Black Authors and Illustrators of Books for Children and Young Adults* (1999), presents biographical sketches and lists of the publications of over 150 authors.[33] Rebecca L. Thomas's *Connecting Cultures: A Guide to Multicultural Literature for Children* (1996), which includes many groups in addition to African Americans, gives an annotated list of 1,637 books and a more than 200-page list of titles by subject.[34] And there are numerous others.

MULTICULTURAL ALTERNATIVES TO SELF-ESTEEM LITERATURE

In any society, but certainly in one as culturally diverse and committed to pluralism as ours, the publication of good books on African Americans (or any other cultural or ethnic group), interracial issues, or multicultural themes is desirable and welcome. In a nation grappling with the still very recent phenomena of integration and equality, children's books can help set the stage for acceptance of others. Many of the books aimed at children of preschool and elementary school age that treat racial, interracial, or multicultural themes are, in a word, outstanding. Sometimes explicitly didactic and sometimes not, these picture books exhibit a remarkable variety of approaches, adding to the rich body of children's literature that aims to instruct, humanize, entertain, and expand the imaginations and horizons of our children.

Just a few examples can hint at the tremendous treasures available for broadening children's perspectives on cultural difference. Sheila Hamanaka's *All the Colors of the Earth,* the illustrations for which are charming oil paintings on canvas also by the upstate New York author, depicts children of all complexions and hair types, without falling into self-esteem boosterism. Celebrating and appreciating physical differences reminding us of our belonging to the natural world, Hamanaka explains that children have all different complexions, from "The roaring browns of bears and soaring eagles" to "The tinkling pinks of tiny seashells by the rumbling sea."[35] The book's tone is one of grateful reverence and joy for the variegated beauty of humankind. Marguerite W. Davol's *Black, White, Just Right!* also deliberately forsakes celebration of one ethnic group over another, even as it explicitly affirms the normality and desirability of the traits of a young girl with a black mother and white father. Affirmative enough to assuage the qualms of any parent or educator worried about African American children's self-esteem, the book also forsakes the crudest elements of the self-esteem crusade, such as the notion that one's self-image should be based mainly on physical traits having to do with ethnicity. The girl in *Black, White, Just Right!* defines herself through her hobbies, habits, and active nature as well as her place in and love for her family—all of which affirm she is "just right." Charmingly illustrated by Irene Trivas in gouache, the book would undoubtedly be a great addition to any collection of children's books.[36] Another excellent book that celebrates and affirms the physical variations of humankind is the lush *Whoever You Are,* by the best-selling author Mem Fox, which features stunning multicolored illustrations by the New Orleans painter Leslie Staub in oil on gessoed paper, with gem-studded, gilded frames around the illustrations that were originally made of hand-carved wood and plaster and also with hand-lettered type. The text tells of children whose skin, homes, schools, lands, and languages "may be different from yours," but whose hearts, smiles, joys, love, pains, and blood are "the same . . . all over the world."[37]

Other books deal more explicitly with the history of racial wrongs, but some do so with a tone that is both gently didactic and aimed at reconciliation. *Dear Willie Rudd,* by Libba Moore Gray, with its mood-setting oil painting illustrations by Peter M. Fiore, intertwines a white woman's fond memories of the black housekeeper who helped raise her with her sorrowful realization of the pain and discrimination her housekeeper must have endured under segregation.[38]

Sister Anne's Hands, written by Marybeth Lorbiecki and illustrated in dreamlike pastels by K. Wendy Popp, while a bit more heavy-handed, is another story along these interracial lines. Still other books implicitly address the theme of ethnicity and self-respect, depicting people of color who discover parts of themselves and inner resources they did not know they had. Rather than locating pride in physical traits, Amy Hest's *Jamaica Louise James* and Phil Mendez's *The Black Snowman* stress concrete accomplishments and acts of heroism, respectively, as sources for self-respect. For example, *The Black Snowman* even invokes African heritage as *Nappy Hair* does, but it calls on this heritage as a source for strength in the face of adversity and as a resource for acts of courage in the present, not as a source of pride in itself. [39]

Even better are the books that depict African Americans with realism and engagement and with a light touch that gives an implicit message of self-respect. *In My Momma's Kitchen,* written by the award-winning author Jerdine Nolen and illustrated with lovely oil paintings by Colin Bootman, is one of the best recent children's books on any theme. Describing all of the various kinds of activities that take place in the kitchen, from the receiving of important family news to collective weekly cooking parties, the book conveys a sense of a young girl's identity and self-worth through membership in a loving family and participation in its traditions. These traditions are subtly and implicitly tied to the heritage of the book's African American characters, but the tale has a heartwarming message of belonging and gratitude for all children (and, indeed, adults). Other outstanding books in this vein are Elizabeth Fitzgerald Howard's enchanting *Chita's Christmas Tree* and *Mac and Marie and the Train Toss Surprise,* both of which are exquisitely illustrated, the former by Floyd Cooper and the latter by Gail Gordon Carter. Both capture the magic and hope of childhood in terms that have universal resonance and are invaluable additions to any child's library. [40]

Other children's stories that forsake false generalizations and depict the variations of character, behavior, and belief among African Americans include Alice Faye Duncan's entertaining *Miss Viola and*

Uncle Ed Lee, which has original, old-fashioned, watercolors by Catherine Stock, and tells touchingly of a budding friendship between a very neat, virtuous woman and a very lazy, messy man, both neighbors of the little boy narrating the story—all of whose characters are black.[41] Don Freeman's outstanding *A Pocket for Corduroy,* part of his wonderful Corduroy series, relates the adventures of a little stuffed bear and his "best friend," Lisa, who appears to be African American, Latina, or of mixed race. Its bold, vibrant illustrations by the author show Lisa and Corduroy in an integrated setting, going about their lives in a natural fashion.[42] Works that depict African American life in all its human complexity certainly work against stereotypes and ignorance as well as, if not better than, most books that take up themes of race head-on. It might be argued that the use of books for young children that take a heavy-handed approach to racial themes in some ways emanates from a stereotypical view of African Americans—one that projects an obsessive concern with racial matters and an impoverished sense of self-worth onto a whole group of people. Drilling into children at a very early an age a hypersensitivity toward race matters might actually perpetuate some of the tensions of the past instead of allowing us to move on—led in part by the children themselves, who do not automatically share the catalog of prejudices of earlier generations. As most parents know, messages are often best taught subtly and indirectly, rather than with a tone of self-righteousness that tends to go hand in hand with simplification.

"ILLIBERAL" MULTICULTURALISM AND THE DECLINE OF STANDARDS

Sandra Stotsky has recently written a bold and helpful invective against what she sees as a wrong-headed strain of multicultural education, entitled *Losing Our Language: How Multicultural Classroom Instruction Is Undermining Our Children's Ability to Read, Write, and Reason.*

Dismissed by at least one key theorist in the field of multicultural education, Christine E. Sleeter, as one of the many conservatives who recklessly attack the entire movement of multicultural education as ideological, while considering their own view to be "apolitical,"[43] Stotsky has, in fact, devoted much research and sustained thought to the issue. Concentrating her attention on the "basal readers," or the textbooks used in schools to teach English and reading skills (mainly for grades 4 to 6), Stotsky notes with alarm that many of the books promoted by the multicultural movement in education since the 1960s distinctly do not measure up to the standards for rigorous and effective instruction. Driven by revelations about low academic performance among many African American and Hispanic students, educational reformers sought measures that would enhance students' "self-image" and "in turn improve their academic performance." Initially, multicultural curricula stressed "the positive contributions of minority groups in this country" and "a balanced range of social groups from around the world," she writes. Citing Shelby Steele and the Harvard University Afro-American studies professor Anthony Appiah, Stotsky argues that the new emphasis—what Appiah calls "illiberal" multiculturalism—conveys predetermined notions of ethnic group identity as a way of building self-esteem and derides so-called Western values and whites, rather than fostering black students' academic skills. Indeed, she writes soberingly, after a period of improvement, black reading scores declined in the 1990s.[44]

After an analysis of the textbooks, Stotsky concludes that the current readers reflect a long-term decline in rigor that began well before the "illiberal" phase of the multicultural movement but has lately been aggravated by it. She looks at such factors as "vocabulary level, complexity of sentence structure, and level of paragraph development" and concludes that the current readers have traits "that may help to account for the low reading level of many American students today." Because of the pressures to include multicultural content, which keeps expanding to represent every possible cultural group throughout the world, the vocabulary emphasizes non-English terms and proper nouns—even incorporating numerous letters from other alphabets, while sacrificing the English vocabulary and complexity of prose that is vital for "understanding mature literary and academic English prose." Texts are increasingly chosen, Stotsky writes, for "the purpose of shaping children's feelings in specific ways," and often lose sight of what is appropriate intellectual fare for advancing reading ability at a particular grade level.[45] To support her view that this represents a significant crisis in our educational system, she cites a body of research from the past one hundred years that repeatedly confirms that "children's language development is the engine that drives intellectual growth":

> Thought and language interact at the level of the word. As students acquire the words denoting the concrete information and abstract ideas embedded in the language of the subjects they study, these words become the essential building blocks for conceptual growth, academic achievement, and critical thinking.

Stotsky thinks that the injection of heavy-handed moralizing into the curriculum has led to anti-intellectualism and incoherence, which have had disastrous consequences for literacy among all students. The readers from the 1970s to the present show a drastic decline in vocabulary alone, as well as a decrease in the rate at which new words are introduced at each grade level. Ironically, a major reason that academic performance has declined among blacks might be the very curricula designed—condescendingly, in Stotsky's view—"to foster the group identity and group esteem of low achieving students."[46]

The Language of Children's Books

Indeed, Stotsky's analysis forces us to take stock of another aspect of Carolivia Herron's *Nappy Hair* that did not enter into the public discussion of the book: its language. The controversy centered on the use of the word "nappy," and the educational and media establishment came out largely in support of the author's decision to use it. Yet the rest of the book's words are worth at least some further thought, particularly the generous sprinkling of contractions, incomplete sentences, deliberate misspellings, and slang. The book's call-and-response rhythms are lively and fun to read, and one can imagine how a reader's exaggerated southern drawl might entertain children further—an accent both Sherman and Herron apparently used when reading the book aloud. But pronunciation and spelling are different matters. While an adult reading the book might pronounce the word "child" in the book "chile," as Herron does, is it really desirable to spell it c-h-i-l-e?[47] The use of the vernacular has a long tradition as a valid and effective technique in literature (particularly in quoted dialogue) and in entertainment, but its proliferation in forms explicitly associated with African Americans—from children's literature to rap music—and its widespread appearance as part of a deliberate cultural crusade should come under scrutiny. The language in *Nappy Hair* includes a heavy dose of dialect or slang, such as "hisself" for "himself" or "outta" for "out of." Some strings of words have punctuation that makes them appear to be complete sentences, but they lack crucial elements. It is questionable whether this kind of language is appropriate in a book designed for children who are trying to master reading.

Stotsky was troubled by the vocabulary in the fourth- through sixth-grade readers she reviewed, which included a surprising "number of selections featuring non-standard English" in the form of so-called black, small-town, or deaf dialect. She points out that alleged black dialect is often inconsistently depicted within a text: final letters of words, as in "*demandin'*," are sometimes but not always dropped; apostrophes in place of the dropped letters are added sometimes but not always; in third-person singular verbs, as in she "sings," the final "s" is dropped sometimes but not always; and the "uninflected form of the verb *to be*," as in "he be free" is used sometimes but not always. She worries about this inconsistency, since there is "no one form of black dialect" and "in fact no one correct way to transcribe it." Yet she also wonders about the use of dialect in general, since "it is likely to exert a negative influence on the development of language and writing skills in the very children who most need exposure to well-written English." She argues that "dialect in literature is appropriate only for stories studied as literature." Another side effect of the use of so-called black dialect that alarms Stotsky is that it may teach "many children that most blacks speak in dialect, which is certainly not the case."[48] Thus, the very goal of enhancing tolerance and understanding and abandoning old generalizations about a whole group could actually be countered by the overuse of such formulations. One cannot help wondering whether this technique is a form of condescension that is ultimately damaging to children's educational attainment. In addition, apropos of Stotsky's scathing critique of most contemporary readers, which do not include significantly challenging vocabulary for the grade level for which they are designed, it is startling to note as well that the level of the pupils to which Sherman was reading *Nappy Hair* was third grade. The level of the prose, vocabulary, and presentation of the picture book would certainly seem to be designed for a lower level.

SELF-ESTEEM VERSUS THE CIVIC SENSE

Stotsky also worries that the emphasis in current curricula and pedagogy on students' feelings makes room for further anti-intellectualism in the form of the particularly simplistic ministrations of teachers who engage in what the writer Frances FitzGerald has called "incessant moralism" and "manipulativeness."[49] On the one hand, they aim to validate the self-esteem of African Americans through an uncritical presentation of all blacks; on the other, they convey "a blanket indictment of whites or the larger society." Stotsky argues that reading selections, and the teachers' guides that accompany them, often use a simplistic, ahistorical model of all blacks (and other groups) as the victims and all whites as the victimizers. Besides having historical inaccuracies that trivialize the tremendous achievements of those who endured or achieved despite outright oppression, this approach denies any substantial change over time. This heavy-handed tack can have severe "anti-civic" consequences, Stotsky contends, both by denying white children any knowledge of the parts of the nation's past that could be legitimate sources of respect and by instilling in black children an inaccurate, imbalanced, and even hostile view of the nation.[50]

Looking to the larger population, Orlando Patterson has in his *Ordeal of Integration* pursued the negative consequences of ignorance about basic facts regarding the nation's racial makeup. He cites the common misconception held by many blacks and whites that the nation is made up of a much larger percentage of blacks than is the case. Both groups thought blacks made up about 25 percent of the population and whites made up about 45–50 percent, when in reality blacks make up 13 percent and whites about 75–80 percent. Patterson says such "misinformation" perpetuates inflated feelings of grievance: "If the average Afro-American goes around thinking that Euro-Americans are a minority of only 45 percent of the population, the fact that Euro-Americans appear to dominate all the major institutions of the nation must be a source of constant rage." He notes, "Those misperceptions, by themselves, explain a good deal of the confusion and resentment over 'race' in the nation."[51] In this climate, one can only imagine, then, the disastrous consequences of qualitative misconceptions coming from depictions of all whites as inherently racist or all blacks as victims. The linguist John H. McWhorter argues that many blacks indeed have adopted victimization as a given and, in turn, embrace anti-intellectualism as part of a separate racial identity. This development has tragic effects for individuals' capacity to imagine and create their own futures.[52]

If carried out with a commitment to instilling high standards and purveying knowledge and adding to, rather than replacing traditional skills and knowledge, the goal of a more inclusive curriculum and classroom can only be seen as consistent with our best traditions of egalitarianism and cultural pluralism. This was the original emphasis of multicultural education as it took root in the 1970s. Yet critics charge that a different strain of multicultural education has substituted superficial celebrations of and emphasis on cultural difference for real study and reflection, furthering the slippage in educational achievement and social unity visible in the nation at large. These critics lament the declining mastery of works and ideas considered part of the traditional canon, falling standards, and a loss of a common core of knowledge that helps Americans build a sense of ourselves as a people.

The strain of multicultural education that seems the most prone to have this less than salutary effect is precisely the one that gives theoretical underpinnings and academic legitimacy to the self-esteem crusade. With origins earlier than those of the multicultural movement as such, this educational movement can be traced back to the early twentieth-century influence of John Dewey and progressive education, but it received a tremendous boost from the political and cultural climate of the 1960s. Calling itself "critical pedagogy," the movement attempts to fuse radical politics and educational style and content. Adherents often make finer distinctions on the basis of whether they emphasize race, class, or gender, distinguishing between multicultural education, critical pedagogy, or feminist pedagogy. But most share the basic precepts of critical pedagogy, making it a helpful term for the larger educational philosophy of this strain of multicultural education.

Early architects of multicultural theory included James Banks, professor of education and director of the Center for Multicultural Education at the University of Washington in Seattle and prolific author on multicultural education, and G. Gay. They were joined by Christine Sleeter, who is a professor of teacher education at the University of Wisconsin-Parkside, author of *Keepers of the American*

Dream, and editor of numerous collections of essays on multicultural education. Peter McLaren, professor in the Graduate School of Education and Information at the University of California at Los Angeles, is also acknowledged as a leader in the field. But perhaps the best-known figure to expound upon the theories of this self-designated vanguard in multicultural theory is the writer bell hooks, widely acknowledged as one of the most prominent black intellectuals of our age. She has taught and written prolifically on the subject and is in great demand as a speaker throughout the world.

CRITICAL PEDAGOGY

Like her comrades in the so-called vanguard of critical pedagogy, which they also refer to as "equity pedagogy" or "radical pedagogy," hooks wholeheartedly believes that her ideas represent a radical departure from mainstream culture. She is a self-invented revolutionary. Commenting on her own life course, from her early years in a segregated small-town black world to her study and teaching in predominantly white, elite colleges and universities, she says that a constant impulse in her life was for "crossing boundaries" or "borders," which challenges the "coercive hierarchical domination" and "cultural fascism" she thinks is omnipresent in contemporary America. She calls her own work "inspired by revolutionary political visions," part of a larger movement "to decolonize minds and imaginations." Through "cultural criticism" and "education for critical consciousness," hooks is dedicated to "the open mind," which is "the heartbeat of cultural revolution": "The fierce willingness to repudiate domination in a holistic manner is the starting point for progressive cultural revolution."[53]

Despite this revolutionary posture, hooks's ideas could not possibly fit better with the cultural movements described throughout this book—movements for social engineering that started on the periphery of American life but increasingly became more mainstream. Her social criticism, which dissects specific figures, films, or other cultural expressions in order to show how they represent continued inequality is often insightful and entertaining. However, her theories about the process, content, and cultural role of education reveal the deep affinity that exists between this radical vanguard of the multicultural education movement and the therapeutic culture. The terms of critical pedagogy, in fact, bear an uncanny resemblance to the human potential movement, the self-esteem crusade, and the combination of therapy and politics inherent in New Age therapies. Bell hooks is best understood as one of a whole cadre of experts on race whose work makes the most sense when seen as part of the movement to engineer not only behavior, but thought and feeling as well.

OPPRESSION PEDAGOGY

Hooks, like other theorists of the multicultural education movement, is, by her own admission, profoundly indebted to the work of the educator Paulo Freire. Freire, the Brazilian author of the famous *Pedagogy of the Oppressed,* has probably been the most significant influence on late twentieth-century American educational philosophy. His ideas left a deep and lasting impression on the generations that came to political consciousness in the 1960s, fitting as he did the spirit and hopes for radical change prevalent not only among Americans inspired by the civil rights, antiwar, and student protest movements but among the student movements in many other countries. Exiled for twenty years from Brazil after the military coup of 1964, Freire spent time in Chile and then the United States, which gave him the authentic radical credentials that made him even more alluring to those who romanticized rebellion for its own sake. He articulated a theory of literacy education for illiterate peasants that would bring about their political awareness and foster their participation in a larger movement toward liberation from colonization.

In the context of movements for participatory democracy, the struggle for equal rights of blacks and other minorities, students, women, gays, and workers, and other challenges to received authority, Freire seemed to many Americans an attractive revolutionary thinker. His ideas about education fit the tenor of the times and seemed directly applicable to their own aspirations. Easily grasped, Freire's pedagogy appeared to address the question of how the promise of egalitarianism would be fulfilled. Probably most important, Freire's theory described a role for those who were sympathetic with the revolutionary struggles of the oppressed. A new radical conception of educational philosophy gave a much needed pseudo-intellectual tenor to the counterculture's mandate to question all authority. Converts could fuse New Left politics and the counterculture's lifestyle revolt, within the safe confines of employment as teachers or professors.

Freire aimed his pedagogy above all at the "liberation" of what he called the "oppressed" individual. His vagueness about the nature of this oppression is undoubtedly what makes his theories seem so universally applicable, even outside of directly coercive or forceful regimes. He was writing in the context of the aftermath of colonialism, and his concerns were with a colonial subject who had become passive or immobilized and thus politically powerless. The role of the educator "for liberation," in Freire's view, was not to teach or lead an individual so much as to foster an awareness of his or her situation, which Freire called *conscientização,* or conscientization. According to Freire's translator's note, this term means "learning to perceive social, political, and economic contradictions, and to take action against the oppressive elements of reality."[54]

Freire thought education was about liberation—liberation from forces he consistently left imprecise. His premise was that all of social organization rested on the division between the oppressors and the oppressed. Coming out of his Brazilian context, he was especially preoccupied with what he thought were the ways that colonization affected the mind of the oppressed and the oppressors alike. The oppressed, he believed, lost the ability to think independently and to determine their own destiny. The oppressors, in turn, became alienated from their better natures as human beings.

The overarching political and social struggle, in Freire's conceptualization, is a battle against the "dehumanization" of colonial oppression. Dehumanization, as he defined it, "is a *distortion* of the vocation of becoming more fully human." Revolution is its natural offspring: "sooner or later being less human leads the oppressed to struggle against those who made them so." The oppressed are destined to become the "restorers of the humanity" of both the oppressed and the oppressors; this restoration is, in fact, the "great humanistic task of the oppressed." Freire's entire philosophy rests on this goal of humanization, which comes only through the "struggle for freedom," the "restoration of true generosity," and the "creation of a world in which it will be easier to love."[55]

EDUCATION AS CONSCIOUSNESS-RAISING

Freire considered education vital for this process of humanizing liberation. Paternalistic reforms originating with the oppressor class to help the oppressed will not suffice. To Freire, they are just "false generosity" or "false charity" designed to "soften," but not to end, injustice. Instead, the oppressed need to help themselves: "real generosity" should aim instead to allow the oppressed themselves to work to "transform the world." What keeps the oppressed from doing that entirely on their own is their internalization of the dominant oppressor mentality. The oppressed have accepted the oppressors' "model of humanity," Freire writes—a model that rests on the belief that "to be men is to be oppressors." Thus, when the oppressed "directly or indirectly participate in revolution," they often merely want "to make it their private revolution," for they have accepted the ethos of individualist gain. When moving from peasant to "overseer," the formerly oppressed individual becomes a "tyrant." Freire's explanation for this is that the oppressed have not become conscious of themselves and their position, since their minds have been colonized by the oppressor. Their whole being is suffused with a false consciousness. What is more, the oppressed are either prone to play the part of the social inferior or adopt the new role of the oppressor out of a "fear of freedom."[56]

In order to become free of the constraints of this all-pervasive logic of oppression, the oppressed "must first critically recognize" the causes of their oppression, must "objectivize" the oppressor as a force "'outside' themselves," and "struggle to be more fully human" by working "to transform the situation." Only the oppressed can bring about a humanizing change in the social structure, since oppressors have lost their humanity. Yet the oppressed are held back from full "engagement in the struggle for their liberation" because they suffer from a dual existence created by oppression. They are alienated from their true selves because they are also "hosts" of the oppressor. "The pedagogy of the oppressed" allows for the "critical discovery that both they and their oppressors are manifestations of dehumanization." Only "liberating pedagogy" offers the "midwifery" necessary for the birth of a new, humanized individual. "The man or woman who emerges is a new person," writes Freire. Yet it is not enough to understand the "oppressor-oppressed contradiction": one must go on to participate in the struggle against it.[57] In turn, it is not enough that former oppressors feel the "anguish" and acknowledge the realities of their power over the oppressed. They must join the collective struggle, risking "an act of love."[58]

The educational process suited to this liberation is one aimed at changing the reality of oppression by altering the world view of the oppressed, who must "unveil the world of oppression." Freire calls education that relies on rote memorization the "banking system," which merely seeks to get students to absorb information uncritically. As an operative of the oppressive society, the teacher merely gives a "motionless, static, compartmentalized, and predictable" version of reality to his or her students, without relating it to their own experiences. Instead, "libertarian education" must focus on the "reconciliation" of the "teacher-student contradiction": both should be "simultaneously teachers *and* students." Authority, in this case, resides not in the teacher or in knowledge or truth but in the process of liberation. The subject matter should be "problems" from the "real world" upon which students and teachers both reflect in order to see that, because reality was formed historically, it can be altered. It should concentrate on the "expulsion of the myths" of "the old order." Because Freire describes oppression not only as exploitation or harm but as interference with the "pursuit of self-affirmation," he can construe this dialogue in the classroom as a kind of revolutionary action. This sort of education "affirms men and women as beings in the process of *becoming,*" Freire concludes.[59]

It is to this "solidarity" with the oppressed and "critical intervention" into reality that Freire's followers in the "critical pedagogy" movement devote themselves. Bell hooks, who gives high praise to Freire, writes that "education for critical consciousness" is "essential to the decolonization process."[60] Freire's emphasis on humanization, the "emergence" of consciousness, and the search for identity through unveiling the forces of oppression places this pedagogy firmly within the mainstream American therapeutic culture. Hooks's own adaptations of Freire's views could scarcely be more illustrative in this regard.

"HOLISTIC PEDAGOGY" FOR THE NEW AGE: THE TWILIGHT OF RADICALISM

In her *Teaching to Transgress: Education as the Practice of Freedom,* bell hooks describes her views of "progressive, holistic," and "engaged pedagogy" to be a direct application of Freire's ideas of "critical awareness and engagement" through teaching as "an act of resistance." She makes it clear that she believes this kind of teaching involves dialogue and not lecture, destabilization of the traditional assumption of authority residing in the teacher and the subject matter, untraditional techniques, and continuous challenging of the forces of "domination."[61]

Hooks embraces the priority Freire places on "praxis," or "action and reflection upon the world in order to change it," and draws a connection between this reform ethos and the quest for personal growth or "self-actualization." On this point, she draws on the ideas of the Vietnamese Buddhist monk Thich Nhat Hanh, whose "holistic approach to learning and spiritual practice" convinced her of the need for teachers to see students "as whole human beings with complex lives and experiences." She writes that this "holistic" pedagogy, in which students and professors alike see each other "as 'whole' human beings" and teachers "share in the intellectual and spiritual growth" of students, goes even beyond "conventional critical or feminist pedagogy" because of its emphasis on personal growth not only for students but for teachers as well. For hooks, "holistic" pedagogy

> emphasizes well-being. That means that teachers must be actively committed to a process of self-actualization that promotes their own well-being if they are to teach in a manner that empowers students. Thich Nhat Hanh emphasized that "the practice of a healer, therapist, teacher or any helping professional should be directed toward his [sic] or herself first, because if the helper is unhappy, he or she cannot help many people."

Hooks sees teachers as having a kind of psychiatric and spiritual role. Exactly echoing the emphasis of the encounter group and its offshoot therapies, she writes that teachers have a responsibility as healers to "be self-actualized individuals."[62]

Hooks's mode of writing weaves together her theories of education and her own personal experiences, forcing her most significant claims to stand on the shaky ground of her early personal rebellions rather than on a clear-sighted logical argument. To agree with hooks that the emphasis on self-actualization for teachers is important, we must follow her own experiences with educators who were "smart in book knowledge" but "unfit for social interaction" because they were interested only in students' minds, not in the rest of their identities. Rather than see the classes she found dull and alienating as merely the result of lackluster teaching, she traces the problem to a basic desire among the old-fashioned teachers to "exercise power and authority" and interfere with the students' "struggle for self-actualization." Her own "estrangement" from this educational system, she insists, came because she "did not conform—would not be an unquestioning, passive student." Rather than a typical phase of graduate student ennui or angst, hooks's disenchantment was revealed, when she discovered Freire, to be the result of teaching that merely buttressed oppression. Even the "pedagogical practices" of "white male professors who claimed to follow Freire's model"— presumably those who introduced Freire's work to her—"were mired in structures of domination."[63]

What hooks wants is more teaching that aims at the "empowerment" of both students and teachers. This results only from taking collective "risks" in the classroom, or the act of becoming "vulnerable." The preferred mode here is precisely that of the New Age therapies: total self-disclosure on everyone's part. Teachers are expected to "share" along with their students:

> When professors bring narratives of their experiences into classroom discussions it eliminates the possibility that we can function as all-knowing, silent interrogators. It is often productive if professors take the first risk, linking confessional narratives to academic discussions so as to show how experience can illuminate and enhance our discussion of academic material.

Hooks's stress on confession, self-actualization, emotional risk taking, and holistic personal growth gives the notion of "teaching for liberation" all of the connotations of the personal growth crusade, which she sees as intrinsically connected to political rebellion.[64]

Considering hooks's affinity for the most mainstream, dominant ethos of our time, it should come as no surprise that she is the author of not only an academic treatise cum self-help book for black women, *Sisters of the Yam: Black Women and Self-recovery*, published in 1993,[65] which adopts the terms of the recovery movement wholesale, but also an esteem-building children's book. Yes, you guessed it: the children's book is entitled *Happy to Be Nappy*, a story about how wonderful it is to have "nappy hair."[66] Appearing two years after Herron's *Nappy Hair*, this is a harmless but rather inane book with no point or plot except the promotion of pride based on a physical feature, and similarly dashed-off illustrations to match. The work perfectly symbolizes the extent to which hooks's so-called transgressions mesh with the imperatives of the therapeutic ethos, which has been for many self-help and self-esteem experts as lucrative as the proverbial pot that would not stop. But hooks must already know that.

As a society we have perpetuated a kind of cultural lag, refusing to let go of codes and scripts for social behavior that carve out particular roles for blacks and whites—erecting in some places a differential code of etiquette of sorts. Whereas the civil rights movement sought to end any association between race and social etiquette or conduct, to universalize expectations and treatment, and to do away with double standards, newly emergent codes of racial difference are now one of the obstacles that still stand in the way of our addressing and moving beyond the race complex we have inherited. Of course, the problem of bridging equality and difference has become a major preoccupation of our time, not just on racial issues. We cannot seem to get a handle on the question, perhaps because we are not content, like earlier generations, to stop at philosophical resolutions. But our inability to address this issue is making us exaggerate the importance of our differences and even creating artificial group differences where such generalizations do not hold.

On the one hand, race advocates feed a kind of racial-problems industry that focuses unduly on crime, low test scores, and welfare entitlement among blacks out of the larger context of violence, substance abuse, low educational quality and achievement, and an abdication of responsibility and sense of entitlement among Americans more generally. On the other hand, race advocates feed a kind of racial-solutions industry that often perpetuates a ritual of overcompensation for the racist past that encourages disingenuous behavior by whites and exempts blacks from standards of expression and behavior to which others are expected to adhere (until such behavior comprises violations of the law, at which point much can change). The racial-solutions industry prescribes differential behavior, often legitimizing in blacks the self-aggrandizing, antisocial behavior that results from their special exemption, and prompting a hypersensitivity to "difference" and false admissions of racism in whites. In its benign appearance, this looks like enlightenment, antiracism, and progress, but it is actually an insidious reincarnation of double standards and differentiation.[1]

Tragically, it is not the revolutionary spirit of civil rights egalitarianism but a reactionary turn that has eventually come subtly to prevail in our time. As the civil rights movement ebbed in the mid-1960s, so did the certainty that racial differences should not be of fundamental importance. In fact, it is precisely the racialist wing of the black liberation movement, together with its white sympathizers, that has come to dominate at least a good share of the mainstream racial ideology. As instituted in movements such as multicultural education, diversity training, and cross-cultural counseling, this ideology, seen as the most radical, avant-garde thought on race by its proponents, emphasizes coming to grips with difference, not moving beyond differential thinking. Touted as new and even prescient, it amounts to reaction.

Contrary to what the narrow debate over affirmative action would tell us, the only alternative to differential or racialist thinking is not "colorblindness," which ridiculously denies the aesthetic and sensory nature of the human condition and neglects our unfortunate historical inheritance. A better alternative would entail more careful judgment, finer distinctions, a repudiation of the stale terms and rituals that have taken us nowhere, and a sense of proportion about where differences really come into play and even exist. Moreover, the alternative to hypersensitivity to group differences does not have to be insensitivity or soul-baring authenticity and "radical honesty,"[2] which have been integral to the sensitivity tangent. Sensitivity to other people as individuals should be part of any democratic concept of civility and eti-

quette, but that must always be buttressed by a radical egalitarianism, which is precisely not case sensitive. Certainly it was this universalism that was the genius of the civil rights movement.

The pitfalls of the experts' way of thinking are legion. Race experts adhere to a narrow paradigm for understanding the self. Because race pop psychology interprets every problem as having to do with race and claims legitimacy from its attenuated association with civil rights, blacks and whites often fail to see that they, in accepting the racialized perspective, frequently share the same sources of frustration. Pop psychology helps middle-class blacks entering the corporate world, for instance, to interpret the anxieties they experience as solely caused by the racially integrated environment, obscuring the connection of these anxieties to the egregious imbalance of power and wealth the modern corporation embodies.

The concentration on race alone often keeps blacks, whites, and others from pinpointing other sources of frustration that involve the broader contours of American life. Population growth and the overcrowding of urban or suburban areas, the decline of general civility, the bureaucratization and growing impersonality of modern life, overreliance on technology, the rationalization of life, and environmental ravages are among these larger trends. The idea of a racial self narrows the sphere of experience to one determined above all by race relations. The various pressures for emotional truncation in an environment characterized by extreme individualism have led to competition  in the seemingly intangible realm of emotional expression or style. This competition in turn surfaces in attempts to impose or describe new expectations for interracial conduct, as in the effort to claim possession of the extremes of emotional expression for blacks. The consequence of this shrinkage of possibility for both social life and the self—our willingness to accept the dictates of a racialized consciousness—paradoxically furthers the narrowing of emotional outlets and buttresses a double standard of behavior. When racial matters are dealt with primarily in the realm of pop psychology, they fall outside a

231

moral realm in which people are directly responsible for their actions according to shared standards.

Ultimately, the new race therapies have set the underlying terms for the public discussion of race, ensuring that the rituals and rhetoric of race will renew old tensions. The race experts teach that racism is alive and well and that the psychological devastation of racial discrimination is as complete as ever, despite studies in racial attitudes and black self-esteem that conclude that this is not so.[3] What is more, experts employ the simplifications of the therapeutic sensibility, which has no conception of guilt or evil and thus no way to understand or combat real racial wrongs. By not discussing the policies, techniques, and theories of the race experts, we fail to submit them to collective debate and referendum. We have been lulled into acquiescence by the experts' claims of expertise, by what appears to be their rather innocuous commitment to "valuing diversity," and by the way they align themselves with the rituals and rhetoric with which we have become all too familiar.

We are playing with fire. When racial oppression and racism are cast only in terms of incorrect attitudes or estranged emotions, solid ground for condemning them imperceptibly slips away. The resulting confusion potentially allows for a resurgence of racism—either by blacks or by whites—all under the guise of self-expression. If that self-expression ever goes beyond the pale into clear racism, the logic to tackle it is hard to retrieve. After all, racists might have only been expressing themselves, which is the first step toward recovery, even if recovery itself seems always to be receding over the horizon.

The civil rights revolutionaries did not turn to these experts for advice on how to live in peace with our neighbors and loved ones. They assumed that we had the potential to master that ourselves. Let us prove them right.

Prologue

1. Orlando Patterson, *The Ordeal of Integration: Progress and Resentment in America's "Racial" Crisis* (Washington, D.C.: Civitas, 1997), 1–2.

2. See Glenn C. Loury, *One by One from the Inside Out: Essays and Reviews on Race and Responsibility in America* (New York: Free Press, 1995).

3. Patterson, *Ordeal of Integration* and *Rituals of Blood: Consequences of Slavery in Two American Centuries* (New York: Civitas, 1998); Jim Sleeper, *Liberal Racism* (New York: Viking, 1997); and, e.g., Cornel West, *Race Matters* (Boston: Beacon, 1993) and *Keeping Faith: Philosophy and Race in America* (New York: Routledge, 1993).

Chapter 1: The New Racial Etiquette

1. Shelby Steele, *The Content of Our Character: A New Vision of Race in America* (New York: St. Martin's, 1990), 1–2.

2. Ibid., 2–3.

3. Ibid., 17.

4. Ibid., 1–2.

5. *Jerry Maguire,* dir. Cameron Crowe, 138 min., Tri Star/Gracie Films, 1996.

6. Ibid.

7. Orlando Patterson writes that since "nearly all respectable geneticists have abandoned the idea of different human races," we would be better off using the notion of ethnicity rather than race: "My question is, why do we need the term *race* at all?" This is a compelling line of thought. Patterson carries this idea out in his own work by placing the term in quotation marks and referring to blacks as Afro-Americans and whites as Euro-Americans. See his *Ordeal of Integration: Progress and Resentment in America's "Racial" Crisis* (Washington, D.C.: Civitas, 1997), x–xi, 72–73. This makes good sense. But even those sympathetic with the effort to do away with old mental habits

that reinforce the notion that races do exist might worry that each new nomenclature diverts us from rather than focuses us on the deeper issues remaining.

8. On this theme, Stanley Crouch gives a stirring rendering of the pluralistic view of the writer Albert Murray, who asserted that *"American culture"* is *"patently and irrevocably composite . . . incontestably mulatto."* Murray quoted in Crouch, *Always in Pursuit: Fresh Perspectives, 1995–1997* (New York: Pantheon, 1998), 141. See also Henry Louis Gates Jr., "King of Cats," *New Yorker*, April 8, 1996, 70–81, for a thoughtful analysis of Murray's perspective, which he shows was contrarian and bold in the 1960s.

9. Adolph Reed Jr. "Black Athletes on Parade," *Progressive* 61 (July 1997): 18–19. On Reverend Sharpton, see, e.g., Jim Sleeper, *The Closest of Strangers: Liberalism and the Politics of Race in New York* (New York: Norton, 1990), and Stephan Thernstrom and Abigail Thernstrom, *America in Black and White: One Nation, Indivisible* (New York: Simon and Schuster, 1997), 498, 510–11.

10. The ritualized nature of race relations prior to the watershed of the civil rights movement has already been well established. Drawing on theoretical insights from anthropology and psychology, historians like John Blassingame, Lawrence Levine, Elizabeth Fox-Genovese, and Eugene Genovese sought to articulate the significance of the master-slave relationship by examining unspoken assumptions and expectations, roles and patterns of behavior, and the function of institutions like religion and festivals. In his *Southern Honor: Ethics and Behavior in the Old South* (1982) and *Honor and Violence in the Old South* (1986), Bertram Wyatt-Brown illustrated the larger "moral code" of white southerners—a world view based on a belief in the "rule of honor"—in which slavery was embedded. The explosion of scholarship on slavery since the 1960s built on earlier efforts to unearth the workings of its distinctive social and cultural apparatus, efforts dating back to direct observations by the system's contemporaries, such as Frederick Douglass. Similarly, contemporaries of Jim Crow such as Ida B. Wells and, later, Jessie Daniel Ames detailed the peculiar, ritualized nature of racial oppression in their separate battles against lynching by questioning its stated rationale—the protection of white womanhood. In the 1930s, the black sociologist Bertram Doyle spelled out in minute detail the expectations for interracial social interaction in his *Etiquette of Race Relations in the South* (1937), as did John Dollard in his *Caste and Class in a Southern Town* (1937). Subsequent scholarship analyzed these rules and rituals, placing them firmly in their context—the power relations of white supremacy: Wilbur Cash's *Mind of the South* (1941), C. Vann Woodward's *The Strange Career of Jim Crow* (1974), I. A. Newby's *Jim Crow's Defense* (1965), George Fredrickson's *Black Image in the White Mind* (1971), and

Jacquelyn Dowd Hall's biography of Ames, *Revolt against Chivalry* (1979). In the mid–1960s, works like Calvin Hernton's *Sex and Racism in America* (1965) popularized some of this body of ideas, outlining what they saw as the various inherited roles for black and white men and women, in the unique American race-sex complex. More recent taboos and rituals have been greatly illuminated by social critics such as Shelby Steele, Glenn Loury, Michael Meyers, Stanley Crouch, Orlando Patterson, Stephan and Abigail Thernstrom, and others. Some of the most astute and sustained examinations of the racial etiquette of liberalism come in the work of the journalist Jim Sleeper; see, e.g., his *Liberal Racism* (New York: Viking, 1997).

11. Martin Luther King Jr., "The Dream," in Thomas R. West and James Mooney, eds., *To Redeem a Nation: A History and Anthology of the Civil Rights Movement* (St. James, N.Y.: Brandywine, 1993), 83–85; Martin Luther King Jr., *Where Do We Go from Here: Chaos or Community?* (Boston: Beacon, 1967).

12. *Guess Who's Coming to Dinner*, dir. Stanley Kramer, 108 min., Columbia, 1967. The story and screenplay were written by William Rose.

13. Tom Wolfe, *Radical Chic and Mau-mauing the Flak Catchers* (New York: Noonday, 1970), 9. "Radical Chic" originally appeared in *New York* magazine in June 1970 in different form.

14. Norman Mailer, "The White Negro: Superficial Reflections on the Hipster," originally published in *Dissent* in 1957, in Mailer, *The Time of Our Time* (New York: Random House, 1998), 226.

15. Wolfe, *Radical Chic*, 32–33.

16. *Six Degrees of Separation*, dir. Fred Schepisi, 111 min., MGM, 1993. This is an adaptation by John Guare of his play of the same title.

17. Lore Segal, *Her First American, a Novel* (New York: New Press, 1985), 39–40.

18. Bill Cosby, foreword to Sheila Rush and Chris Clark, *How to Get Along with Black People: A Handbook for White Folks, and Some Black Folks Too* (New York: Third Press, 1971), 6.

19. Rush and Clark, *How to Get Along with Black People*, 52.

20. Ibid., 48–49.

21. Ibid., 53.

22. Ibid., 11–30.

23. Amoja Three-Rivers, "Cultural Etiquette: A Guide," excerpted in *Ms.*, Sept.–Oct. 1991, 42–43.

24. Amoja Three-Rivers, *Cultural Etiquette: A Guide for the Well-Intentioned* (Distributed by Market Wimmin, Indian Valley, Va., 1990), 7. This is an interesting contrast to the scene in *Guess Who's Coming to Dinner* when Poitier's character points

out to Tracy's that blacks might seem to dance better than whites for cultural reasons; "they are dancing *our* dances," he laughs.

25. Three-Rivers, *Cultural Etiquette*, 18.
26. Ibid., 7.
27. Ibid., 16–17.
28. Dick Gregory, *Nigger: An Autobiography* (New York: Dutton, 1964).
29. Karla F. C. Holloway, *Codes of Conduct: Race, Ethics, and the Color of Our Character* (New Brunswick, N.J.: Rutgers University Press, 1995), 69.
30. Ibid., 76.
31. Ibid., 80.
32. Ibid., 31-34.
33. Bell hooks quoted in Holloway, *Codes of Conduct,* 35. The quotation is from bell hooks, *Black Looks: Race and Representation* (Boston: South End Press, 1992).
34. Holloway, *Codes of Conduct,* 30–31. Holloway quotes Lorene Cary, who wrote in *Black Ice* of her mother's "turning it out" (New York: Vintage, 1991).
35. James Baldwin, *The Fire Next Time* (New York: Dell, 1963), 140–41.
36. Ibid., 139.
37. Ibid.
38. Ishmael Reed quoted in William M. Banks, *Black Intellectuals: Race and Responsibility in American Life* (New York: Norton, 1996), 137.
39. Imamu Amiri Baraka (LeRoi Jones), "Black Dada Nihilismus," from *The Dead Lecturer* (New York: Grove Press, 1963), quoted in Eldridge Cleaver, *Soul on Ice* (New York: McGraw-Hill, 1968), 14, 15.
40. Cleaver, *Soul on Ice,* 14.
41. Ibid., 14–15.
42. Ibid., 15.
43. Ibid., 150, 205, 207.
44. Ibid., 202.
45. Ibid., 203.
46. Ibid., 203.
47. Ibid., 103.
48. Ibid., 98.
49. Ralph Wiley, *Why Black People Tend to Shout: Cold Facts and Wry Views from a Black Man's World* (New York: Penguin, 1991), 1.
50. Ibid.
51. Ibid., 33.
52. Ibid., 84-85.
53. Ibid., 85.

54. Karen Grigsby Bates and Karen Elyse Hudson, *Basic Black: Home Training for Modern Times* (New York: Doubleday, 1996), vix.

55. Ibid., 10.

56. Ibid., 11-12.

57. Ibid., 12.

58. For a brief introduction to the civility debate, see "The Civility Wars," *Utne Reader* (March–April 1997): 15–16; Judith Martin, *Miss Manners Rescues Civilization from Sexual Harassment, Frivolous Lawsuits, Dissing, and Other Lapses in Civility* (New York: Crown, 1996); Stephen L. Carter, *Civility: Manners, Morals, and the Etiquette of Democracy* (New York: Perseus, 1998); Rochelle Gurstein, "The Tender Democrat," *New Republic,* Oct. 5, 1998, 44–45; Jean Bethke Elshtain, *Democracy on Trial* (New York: Basic Books, 1994).

59. Norbert Elias, *The Civilizing Process,* vol. 1, *The History of Manners* (New York: Pantheon, 1978).

60. John F. Kasson, *Rudeness and Civility: Manners in Nineteenth-Century Urban America* (New York: Hill and Wang, 1990).

61. Carol Zisowitz Stearns and Peter N. Stearns, *Anger: The Struggle for Emotional Control in America's History* (Chicago: University of Chicago Press, 1986), 157.

62. Arlie R. Hochschild, *The Managed Heart: Commercialization of Human Feeling* (Berkeley: University of California Press, 1983), 6.

63. Norine Dresser, *Multicultural Manners: New Rules of Etiquette for a Changing Society* (New York: Wiley, 1996), 4.

64. Steele, *Content of Our Character,* 17.

65. Ibid., 19.

66. Ibid., 2–3.

Chapter 2: Radical Chic and the Rise of a Politics of Therapy

1. "Civil Rights Blues," originally published in 1979, was reprinted in Stanley Crouch, *Notes of a Hanging Judge: Essays and Reviews, 1979–1989* (New York: Oxford University Press, 1990), 22.

2. Ibid., 22-27.

3. Ibid.

4. Harold Cruse, *The Crisis of the Negro Intellectual* (New York: William Morrow,

1967), 421; Christopher Lasch, "Black Power: Cultural Nationalism as Politics," in his *The Agony of the American Left* (New York: Knopf, 1969), 127–28.

5. Cruse, *Crisis of the Negro Intellectual*, 421.

6. Lasch, "Black Power," 127–28.

7. Crouch, "Civil Rights Blues," 27.

8. Michael Walzer, "The Obligations of Oppressed Minorities," in his *Obligations: Essays on Disobedience, War, and Citizenship* (Cambridge: Harvard University Press, 1970), 59.

9. Crouch, "Civil Rights Blues," 22; Lasch, "Black Power," 125; Cruse, *The Crisis of the Negro Intellectual*, 421.

10. Philip Rieff, *The Triumph of the Therapeutic: Uses of Faith after Freud* (New York: Harper & Row, 1966), 3–4, 12–17.

11. Ibid., 63n.

12. Ibid., 63n., 23.

13. Richard Sennett, *The Fall of Public Man* (New York: Alfred A. Knopf, 1977), 29–30.

14. Ibid., 29–30, 17, 338. See also Christopher Lasch, *The Culture of Narcissism: American Life in an Age of Diminishing Expecations* (New York: Norton, 1978), for a sustained examination of these themes; Jean Bethke Elshtain, *Augustine and the Limits of Politics* (Notre Dame: University of Notre Dame Press, 1997); and Robert N. Bellah et al., *Habits of the Heart: Individualism and Commitment in American Life* (Berkeley: University of California Press, 1985).

15. Virginia Foster Durr to James Dombrowski, July 10, 1968, Virginia Foster Durr Papers, Schlesinger Library, Radcliffe College, Cambridge, Mass.

16. Virginia Foster Durr to Clark and Mairi Foreman, Aug. 12, 1968, Virginia Foster Durr Papers, Schlesinger Library.

17. Clayborne Carson, *In Struggle: SNCC and the Black Awakening of the 1960s* (Cambridge: Harvard University Press, 1981), 240–41.

18. Stokely Carmichael and Charles V. Hamilton, *Black Power: The Politics of Liberation in America* (New York: Random House, 1967), 83–84.

19. Cruse, *Crisis of the Negro Intellectual*, 409.

20. Charles J. Levy, *Voluntary Servitude: Whites in the Negro Movement* (New York: Appleton-Century-Crofts, 1968), v.

21. Ibid., 3–125.

22. Ibid., 3–8.

23. Ibid., 7–10.

24. Ibid., 23, 27.

25. Ibid., 31–64.

26. Ibid., 71–125.

27. Louis E. Lomax, *The Negro Revolt* (New York: Harper, 1962), 198, 203.

28. Kenneth Clark, "Delusions of the White Liberal," *New York Times Magazine,* April 4, 1965, 137.

29. Inge Powell Bell, *CORE and the Strategy of Non-Violence* (New York: Random House, 1968), 65–71.

30. Alphonso Pinkney, *The Committed: White Activists in the Civil Rights Movement* (New Haven, Conn.: College and University Press, 1968), 24.

31. Ibid., 52–53.

32. Norman Mailer, "The White Negro: Superficial Reflections on the Hipster," originally published in *Dissent* in 1957, in Mailer, *The Time of Our Time* (New York: Random House, 1998), 212–14.

33. Ibid., 219.

34. Ibid., 219–220, 222, 226.

35. Levy, *Voluntary Servitude*, 10.

36. Eldridge Cleaver, *Soul on Ice* (New York: McGraw-Hill, 1968), 128–37, 176–204.

37. Chicago Office of SNCC, *We Want Black Power* (leaflet, 1967), reprinted in August Meier, Elliott Rudwick, and Francis L. Broderick, eds., *Black Protest Thought in the Twentieth Century,* 2nd ed. (New York: Bobbs-Merrill, 1971), 486–89.

38. Editorials, *Crisis,* Nov. 1967, reprinted in Meier et al., eds., *Black Protest Thought,* 601.

39. Charles V. Hamilton, "An Advocate of Black Power Defines It," *New York Times Magazine,* April 14, 1968, reprinted in Meier et al., eds., *Black Protest Thought,* 561.

40. Huey Newton in Meier et al., eds., *Black Protest Thought,* 495–502.

41. In "Black Power," Lasch's promotion of collectivist organizing as part of cultural rehabilitation rested on his differentiation between "the narrow sense of the word culture"—musical expression and such, and its broadest rendering as "a design for living"—an institutional, moral, and practical matter (125).

42. Tom Wolfe, *Radical Chic and Mau-mauing the Flak Catchers* (New York: Noonday, 1970), 40.

43. Ibid., 58.

44. Cathy Tumber, "Empowerment for What?" (article in author's possession), 2–3, 8–9; Nathan Wright Jr. quoted on 8–9.

CHAPTER 3: THE ENCOUNTER GROUP

1. Frantz Fanon, *The Wretched of the Earth* (New York: Grove, 1963); see the critique of this embrace of Fanon by Martin Luther King Jr., in his *Where Do We Go from Here: Chaos or Community?* (Boston: Beacon, 1967), 65–66. Henry Louis

Gates Jr. writes that in the black radical milieu at the end of the 1960s "violence (or, anyway, talk of violence) had acquired a Fanonist glamour." Gates, "King of Cats," *New Yorker,* April 8, 1996, 72.

2. Alfred J. Marrow, *The Practical Theorist: The Life and Work of Kurt Lewin* (New York: Basic Books, 1969), 210–14.

3. Ibid., 210-11.

4. Ibid., 211.

5. Ibid., 212.

6. Ibid., 211–13.

7. Warren Bennis quoted in Marrow, *Practical Theorist,* 210.

8. Leland Bradford, quoted in Marrow, *Practical Theorist,* 214.

9. Carl Rogers quoted in Marrow, *Practical Theorist,* 213-14.

10. Howard, *Please Touch: A Guided Tour of the Human Potential Movement* (New York: McGraw-Hill, 1970), 258–67.

11. Carl Rogers quoted in "Human Potential: The Revolution in Feeling," *Time,* Nov. 9, 1970, 54.

12. George B. Leonard, *Education and Ecstasy* (New York: Delacorte, 1968), 193.

13. Quoted on the jacket cover of Leonard, *Education and Ecstasy.*

14. Jane Howard, "Inhibitions Thrown to the Gentle Winds," *Life,* July 12, 1968, 57.

15. Ibid.

16. Howard, *Please Touch,* 3–4.

17. Rogers, "Human Potential: The Revolution in Feeling," *Time,* Nov. 9, 1970, 54.

18. Howard, *Please Touch,* 5.

19. George Steiner quoted in Howard, "Inhibitions," 64.

20. Christopher Lasch, *The Culture of Narcissism: American Life in an Age of Diminishing Expectations* (New York: Norton, 1979). See also Lasch's afterword in a later paperback edition (New York: Norton, 1991), 240–42.

21. Two works that do make this important connection in the course of showing the larger therapeutic turn in American life are Ellen Herman, *The Romance of American Psychology: Political Culture in the Age of Experts* (Berkeley: University of California Press, 1995), esp. chaps. 7 and 8; and James L. Nolan Jr., *The Therapeutic State: Justifying Government at Century's End* (New York: New York University Press, 1998), esp. chap. 6. See also Phillip M. Richards, "Henry Louis Gates, Sterling Brown, and the Professional Languages of African American Literary Criticism," in Elizabeth Fox-Genovese and Elisabeth Lasch-Quinn, eds., *Reconstructing History: The Emergence of a New Historical Society* (New York: Routledge, 1999), 119–38, for a literary analysis of this theme.

22. *Bob and Carol and Ted and Alice,* directed and written by Paul Mazursky, 104 min., Columbia, 1969.

23. Morton Hunt, *The Story of Psychology* (New York: Doubleday, 1993), 592.

24. Ibid., 564.

25. Ibid.

26. Ibid.

27. Ibid., 579.

28. Albert Ellis, quoted in Hunt, *Story of Psychology,* 583.

29. Aaron Beck quoted in Hunt, *Story of Psychology,* 584–85.

30. Hunt, *Story of Psychology,* 590.

31. Ibid., 591–92.

32. Caroline B. D. Smith, "Price M. Cobbs," in *Contemporary Black Biography: Profiles from the International Black Community,* vol. 9, ed. L. Mpho Mabunda (New York: Gale Research, 1995), 57.

33. William H. Grier and Price M. Cobbs, *Black Rage* (New York: Basic Books, 1968), 198.

34. Explanations for particular contemporary disorders, they believe, lie in an omnipresent racism little changed since the time of slavery. Furthermore, slavery appears in the book as a monolithic explanatory apparatus, without a sense of the tremendous variation in its practice over the two centuries of its existence or by region, farm size, or other factors. The importance of such variation for how slavery affected the lives of African Americans has since been spelled out by scholars like Ira Berlin. See Berlin, "Time, Space, and the Evolution of Afro-American Society," in Thomas R. Frazier, ed., *The Underside of American History*, 5th ed., vol. 1, *To 1877* (San Diego: Harcourt Brace Jovanovich, 1987), 83–112, and Berlin, *Many Thousands Gone: The First Two Centuries of Slavery in North America* (Cambridge: Harvard University Press, 2000).

35. Grier and Cobbs, *Black Rage,* 112–13.

36. Ibid.

37. Daryl Michael Scott, *Contempt and Pity: Social Policy and the Image of the Damaged Black Psyche, 1880–1996* (Chapel Hill: University of North Carolina Press, 1997).

38. Grier and Cobbs, *Black Rage,* 66–67.

39. Ibid.

40. Ibid., 68.

41. Ibid., 72–73.

42. Ibid., 180.

43. Ibid., 156–57.

44. Ibid., 157–58.

45. Ibid., 178–79. While Grier and Cobbs say that only that emotional or mental disorder above and beyond the disorders one can rationally expect blacks to

possess deserves to be treated therapeutically, by which they seem to mean clinically, their view amounts to a therapeutic view of blacks.

46. Ibid., 179.

47. Ibid., 179–80.

48. Walter Truett Anderson, *The Upstart Spring: Esalen and the American Awakening* (Reading, Mass.: Addison-Wesley, 1983), 161.

49. Ibid., 161–62.

50. Ibid.

51. Ibid., 162.

52. Leonard, *Education and Ecstasy,* 197.

53. Charles M. Christian, *Black Saga* (Washington, D.C.: Civitas, 1995), 435.

54. Esalen's brochure for the interracial encounter, quoted in Leonard, *Education and Ecstasy,* 197–98.

55. Leonard, *Education and Ecstasy,* 198.

56. Ibid., 198–99.

57. Price M. Cobbs, "Ethnotherapy in Groups," in Lawrence N. Solomon and Betty Berzon, eds., *New Perspectives on Encounter Groups* (San Francisco: Jossey-Bass, 1972), 390.

58. Leonard, *Education and Ecstasy,* 199.

59. Ibid.

60. Ibid., 200.

61. Ibid.

62. Ibid., 201–2.

63. Ibid., 202; Anderson, *Upstart Spring,* 163.

64. Leonard, *Education and Ecstasy,* 203–5.

65. Ibid., 205.

66. Ibid., 205–6.

67. Ibid., 206–8.

68. Anderson, *Upstart Spring,* 164.

69. Leonard, *Education and Ecstasy,* 208–9.

70. Anderson, *Upstart Spring,* 164.

71. Ibid., 164, 195.

72. Ibid., 195–96.

73. Ibid., 197.

74. Ibid., 196–97.

75. Ibid., 197.

76. Ibid., 197–98.

77. Ibid.

78. Ibid., 198–99. According to Anderson, Cobbs and Brown remained friendly

with Murphy, but thought he "just never understood" the race issue. For his part, Murphy "searched long and hard within himself, but could never find the secret prejudice that was supposed to lurk there" (198).

79. Cobbs, "Ethnotherapy in Groups," 383.
80. Ibid., 389.
81. Ibid.
82. Ibid., 383.
83. Ibid., 394.
84. Ibid., 393–94.
85. Ibid., 398.
86. Ibid., 396.
87. Ibid.
88. Cobbs quoted in Betty Berzon, F. T. Pollard, and D. Mermin, "Encountertapes for Black/White Groups: A New Approach to Race Relations," *Interpersonaldevelopment* 2 (1971–72): 74.
89. Robert E. Steele and Kermit B. Nash, "Sensitivity Training and the Black Community," *American Journal of Orthopsychiatry* 42, (April 1972): 424.
90. Ibid., 429.
91. Ibid., 425.
92. Ibid., 426–29.
93. Ibid., 429.
94. Ibid., 428.
95. Ibid., 428, 426–27.
96. Ibid., 427.
97. Betty Berzon and Lawrence N. Solomon, "The Self-Directed Therapeutic Group: Three Studies," *Journal of Counseling Psychology* 13 (1966): 491.
98. Ibid., 493.
99. Ibid.
100. Ibid., 494.
101. Ibid., 495.
102. Betty Berzon, "Tape Programs for Self-directed Groups," *Rehabilitation Record* 3 (Nov.–Dec. 1968): 36–37.
103. Berzon, Pollard, and Mermin, "Encountertapes," 73–90.
104. Rochelle Gurstein, *The Repeal of Reticence: A History of America's Cultural and Legal Struggles over Free Speech, Obscenity, Sexual Liberation, and Modern Art* (New York: Hill and Wang, 1996).
105. Nolan, *Therapeutic State*, 2-17.
106. Richard Sennett, *The Fall of Public Man* (New York: Knopf, 1977), 337–40.

CHAPTER 4: RACIAL IDENTITY THEORY

1. Robert Williams, "A History of the Association of Black Psychologists: Early Formation and Development," *Journal of Black Psychology* 1, no.1 (Aug. 1974): 9–10.

2. This figure was given in the Association of Black Psychologists Web site: www.abpsi.org.

3. Williams, "History of the Association of Black Psychologists," 7–15; quotation on 14.

4. William David Smith, "Editorial," *Journal of Black Psychology*, 1, no.1 (Aug. 1974): 5–6.

5. Reginald L. Jones, ed., *Black Psychology* (New York: Harper & Row, 1972), xii.

6. Orlando Patterson, *The Ordeal of Integration: Progress and Resentment in America's "Racial" Crisis* (Washington, D.C.: Civitas, 1997), 83–111.

7. Alvin F. Poussaint, "A Negro Psychiatrist Explains the Negro Psyche," *New York Times Magazine,* Aug. 20, 1967, 52–53.

8. Ibid., 58.

9. See Deborah Gray White's discussion of black women's views on this issue, e.g., in *Too Heavy a Load: Black Women in Defense of Themselves, 1894-1994* (New York: Norton, 1999), 176–211.

10. Michelle Wallace, *Black Macho and the Myth of the Superwoman* (New York: Dial, 1979).

11. Orlando Patterson, *Rituals of Blood: Consequences of Slavery in Two American Centuries* (Washington, D.C.: Civitas, 1998).

12. Daryl Michael Scott, *Contempt and Pity: Social Policy and the Image of the Damaged Black Psyche, 1880–1996* (Chapel Hill: University of North Carolina Press, 1997), 161–83, quotation on 183.

13. Reginald L. Jones, ed., *Black Psychology* (New York: Harper & Row, 1972), 409.

14. William S. Hall, William E. Cross Jr., and Roy Freedle, "Stages in the Development of Black Awareness: An Exploratory Investigation," in Jones, ed., *Black Psychology*, 158–60.

15. Ibid., 159.

16. Ibid., 159–60.

17. Ibid., 160.

18. Judith H. Katz, *White Awareness: Handbook for Anti-racism Training* (Norman: University of Oklahoma Press, 1978).

19. Beverly Daniel Tatum, *"Why Are All the Black Kids Sitting Together in the Cafeteria?"*

and Other Conversations about Race (1997; rev. ed., New York: Basic Books, 1999), xiv.

20. Ibid., xv–xvi.
21. Ibid., xvii.
22. Ibid., 76–77.
23. Ibid., 60.
24. Ibid., 59–60.
25. Ibid., 95-101.
26. Janet E. Helms, "Toward a Model of White Identity Development," in Janet E. Helms, ed., Black and White Racial Identity: Theory, Research, and Practice (Westport, Conn: Greenwood, 1990), 49–66.
27. Ibid.
28. Ibid.
29. Tatum, "Why Are All the Black Kids Sitting Together in the Cafeteria?" 95–113.
30. See, e.g., the multipart series, "How Race Is Lived in America," New York Times, June–July 2000.

CHAPTER 5: REVOLT AGAINST REPRESSION

1. Harvey Jackins, Guidebook to Re-evaluation Counseling (Seattle: Rational Island Publishers, 1975), 1–4.
2. Ibid., 3–5, 40.
3. Ibid., 1, 6; Harvey Jackins, Zest Is Best: Poems (Seattle: Rational Island Publishers, 1973).
4. Jackins, Guidebook, 6.
5. Ibid., 55; "Guidelines for the Re-evaluation Counseling Communities" (Adopted by the International Reference Person's Workshop at Buck Creek, Wash., July 13–19, 1975), 1, 11. These guidelines are included in Jackins, Guidebook, but have separate pagination.
6. Jackins, Guidebook, 49–50.
7. Ibid., 23–25.
8. Ibid., 27.
9. Ibid., 25–30.
10. Ibid., 9–21, 30–38.
11. "Guidelines," in ibid., 10.
12. Ibid., 3.

13. Ibid., 9.
14. Ibid., 34.
15. Ibid.
16. Ibid., 34–35.
17. Ibid., 35–36.
18. *Fundamentals of Co-counseling Manual (Elementary Counselors Manual) for Beginning Classes in Re-evaluation Counseling*, 3d rev. ed. (Seattle: Rational Island Publishers, 1982), 30–31.
19. Jackins, *Guidebook*, 1–4.
20. *Fundamentals*, 31.
21. Ibid., 30–31.
22. Ibid.
23. Chip Berlet and Matthew N. Lyons, *Too Close for Comfort: Right-Wing Populism, Scapegoating, and Fascist Potentials in U. S. Political Traditions* (Boston: South End Press, 1996), reprinted as *Right-Wing Populism in America: Too Close for Comfort* (New York: Guilford Publications, 2000).
24. Matthew Lyons, "Sex, Lies, and Co-counseling," 8. Available as a monograph from Political Research Associates, 1310 Broadway, Suite 201, Somerville, MA 02144, 617-666-5300. Also published in the *Activist Men's Journal* 6, no. 2 (Aug. 1993).
25. Ibid., 10–11. See R. D. Rosen, *Psychobabble: Fast Talk and Quick Cure in the Era of Feeling* (New York: Atheneum, 1977).
26. For a memorable evocation of the ultimate consequences of this transparency under authoritarian regimes, see the works of Milan Kundera, e.g., his *Book of Laughter and Forgetting*, trans. Michael Henry Heim (New York: Knopf, 1981).
27. Some of the most thoughtful recent history and social commentary has highlighted this matter. See, e.g., Rochelle Gurstein, *The Repeal of Reticence: A History of America's Cultural and Legal Struggles over Free Speech, Obscenity, Sexual Liberation, and Modern Art* (New York: Hill and Wang, 1996); Jeffrey Rosen, *The Unwanted Gaze: The Destruction of Privacy in America* (New York: Random House, 2000); and James Davison Hunter, *The Death of Character: Moral Education in an Age without Good or Evil* (New York: Basic Books, 2000).
28. Jackins, "The Key Concepts and Insights of Re-evaluation Counseling to Date—Part I: Report to the 1981 World Conference," in *Fundamentals*, 43, 45.
29. Harvey Jackins, "The Art of Listening: Talk to the Merced County (CA, USA) Mental Health Association" (Nov. 7, 1981), in *Fundamentals*, 50.
30. Jackins, *Guidebook*, 15.
31. Jackins, "Key Concepts," 46.

32. Peter N. Stearns, *Battleground of Desire: The Struggle for Self-control in Modern America* (New York: New York University Press, 1999), 291–320; Wendy Kaminer, *I'm Dysfunctional, You're Dysfunctional: The Recovery Movement and Other Self-help Fashions* (Reading, Mass.: Addison-Wesley, 1992), 9–10.

33. Jackins, "Key Concepts," 47.

34. Jackins, *Fundamentals,* p. 39.

35. See, e.g., Jackins, *Guidebook,* 13.

36. Ibid., 57, 58, 16.

37. Cherie R. Brown and George J. Mazza, "Anti-racism, Healing and Community Activism," *Humanistic Psychologist* 24 (1996): 396, 391; Cherie R. Brown, "Four Principles toward a Politics of Meaning," *Tikkun,* July–Aug. 1996, 45. I am indebted to the political scientist Heidi Swarts for bringing the diversity work of this organization to my attention.

38. White House homepage, www.Whitehouse.net.

39. Cherie R. Brown and George J. Mazza, *Healing into Action: A Leadership Guide for Creating Diverse Communities* (Washington, D.C.: National Coalition Building Institute, 1997), v. In "Anti-racism, Healing, and Community Activism," 395, Brown and Mazza write, "Emotional healing work in NCBI is built on the insights and methods of peer counseling as developed by Re-Evaluation Counseling."

40. Brown, "Four Principles," 44.

41. Ibid., 44–45.

42. Ibid., 45.

43. Ibid.

44. Michael Lerner's "Note" at end of Brown, "Four Principles," 45.

45. Brown, "Four Principles," 45.

46. Cherie R. Brown and George J. Mazza, "Peer Training Strategies for Welcoming Diversity," *New Directions for Student Services,* no. 56 (Winter 1991): 42–43.

47. Harvey Jackins, *The Human Side of Human Beings: The Theory of Re-evaluation Counseling* (1965; reprint, Seattle: Rational Island Publishers, 1978), 45–46.

48. Brown and Mazza, "Peer Training," 43.

49. Ibid.

50. Ibid., 44.

51. Ibid., 47.

52. Jackins, *Human Side,* 77.

53. Brown and Mazza, "Peer Training," 47.

54. Ibid.

55. Jackins, *Fundamentals,* 32.

56. Brown and Mazza, "Peer Training," 49.

57. Ibid., 45.

58. Sari Horwitz, "With Frank Words: A Lesson in Prejudice," *Washington Post,* Dec. 5, 1994, A1, A10.

59. Alan Wolfe, *One Nation after All: What Middle-Class Americans Really Think About God, Country, Family, Racism, Welfare, Immigration, Homosexuality, Work, the Right, the Left, and Each Other* (New York: Viking, 1998).

60. Brown and Mazza, *Healing into Action,* 3.

61. Cathy Tumber, "Empowerment for What?" (article in author's possession).

CHAPTER 6: A WORLD OF ENDLESS SLIGHTS

1. Mary P. Rowe, "Fostering Diversity: Some Major Hurdles Remain," *Change,* March–April, 35.

2. Ibid., 36. See Derek T. Dingle, "Peak Performance," *Black Enterprise,* May 1989, 68, for another discussion of problems such as retention of minority employees.

3. Andrew Ferguson, "Chasing Rainbows," *Washingtonian,* April 1994, 38.

4. Cross quoted in Kevin D. Thompson, "Back to School," *Black Enterprise,* Nov. 1990, 57.

5. Frederick R. Lynch, *The Diversity Machine: The Drive to Change the "White Male Workplace"* (New York: Free Press, 1997), 1–7. Lynch, Ferguson, and others also link the approach of the diversity training movement with the spirit and techniques of the human potential movement; Lynch, *Diversity Machine,* and Ferguson, "Chasing Rainbows."

6. Timothy Egan, "Teaching Tolerance in Workplaces: A Seattle Program Illustrates Limits," *New York Times,* Oct. 8, 1993, A18.

7. Lynch, *Diversity Machine.*

8. Ferguson, "Chasing Rainbows," 36.

9. Lynch, *Diversity Machine,* 2; Ferguson, "Chasing Rainbows," 36.

10. Heather MacDonald, "The Diversity Industry," *New Republic,* July 5, 1993, 23.

11. William B. Johnston and Arnold H. Packer, *Workforce 2000: Work and Workers for the 21st Century* (Indianapolis: Hudson Institute, 1987), 75–95.

12. Lynch, *Diversity Machine,* 9; MacDonald, "Diversity Industry," 23; Ferguson, "Chasing Rainbows," 36.

13. See *Communicating across Cultures,* video produced by Copeland Griggs Produc-

tions in association with Price M. Cobbs, Pacific Management Systems, 1992, just one in a seven-part series developed by Leonard Copeland and Lewis Griggs, entitled *Valuing Diversity*. See Lynch's detailed analysis of the series in his *Diversity Machine*, 51–58; R. Roosevelt Thomas Jr., "From Affirmative Action to Affirming Diversity," *Harvard Business Review*, 90, no. 2 (March–April 1990), 107–17.

14. Lynch, *Diversity Machine*, 9–18, 52–62, quotation on 18.

15. Thomas, "From Affirmative Action to Affirming Diversity," 114.

16. *Blue Eyed*, video written and directed by Bertram Verhaag in cooperation with Jane Elliott, produced by DENKmal, 1996. Available through California Newsreel.

17. Nora Lester, *Blue Eyed: A Guide to Use in Organizations* (training manual for use with *Blue Eyed* video), written with the contribution of Jane Elliott. Available from California Newsreel.

18. Ibid., 3.

19. Ibid., 2.

20. Ibid., 5.

21. Ibid., 6.

22. Ibid.

23. Audrey Edwards, "The Enlightened Manager: How to Treat All Your Employees Fairly," *Working Woman*, Jan. 1991, 46.

24. Edwards, "Enlightened Manager," 46.

25. Ibid., 51.

26. *Managing Diversity*, video directed by Denise Dexter, written by Larry Tuch, produced by Melanie Mihal, and narrated by Brock Peters, CRM Films, 1990.

27. See Stuart Ewen, *Captains of Consciousness: Advertising and the Social Roots of the Consumer Culture* (New York: McGraw-Hill, 1977).

28. Lewis Brown Griggs and Lente-Louise Louw, eds., *Valuing Diversity: New Tools for a New Reality* (New York: McGraw-Hill, 1995); quotations are from chap. 4, "Diversity Issues in the Workplace," by Frances E. Kendall.

29. Griggs and Louw, *Valuing Diversity*, 82.

30. *Diverse Teams at Work: Capitalizing on the Power of Diversity* video produced by Advanced American Communications, Inc., directed and written by Donald R. Ham and produced by Robert Peters and Roy Winnick, CorVision Media, 1995; based on Lee Gardenswartz and Anita Rowe, *Diverse Teams at Work: Capitalizing on the Power of Diversity* (Chicago: Irwin Professional Publishers, 1994).

31. Thompson, "Back to School," 56.

32. Ibid.

33. Allan R. Cohen et al., *A Tale of "O": On Being Different: A Training Tool for Managing Diversity* (Cambridge, Mass.: Goodmeasure, 1993), "User's Manual," 2.

34. Rosabeth Moss Kanter, *Men and Women of the Corporation* (New York: Basic Books, 1977).

35. Cohen et al., *A Tale of 'O,'* "User's Manual," 23.

36. Ibid.

37. Ibid., 24.

38. "A Tale of 'O,' " script in *A Tale of "O,"* "User's Manual," 35.

39. *Let's Talk Diversity!* Video directed and produced by Dan Thompson, written by Richard Leatherman, Human Resource Development Press, 1993, ITC, Inc. Part of "Workforce Diversity: A Video Based Training Workshop," by Carol-Susan DeVaney, Jodi Elizabeth Smith, and Richard Leatherman. Available from HR Press.

40. Floyd Dickens Jr. and Jacqueline B. Dickens, *The Black Manager: Making It in the Corporate World*, rev. ed. (New York: AMACOM, 1991), 293–95.

41. Ibid., 294.

42. Hellen Hemphill and Ray Haines, *Discrimination, Harassment, and the Failure of Diversity Training* (Westport, Conn.: Quorum Books, 1997), 1–4, 14, 50–52. For another perspective on the problems of diversity training see Gerri Hirshey, "You Will Feel Their Pain," *Gentlemen's Quarterly* 65 (March 1995): 212–17.

43. Hemphill and Haines, *Discrimination*, 72, 76.

44. Ibid., 4, 77.

Chapter 7: In Perpetual Recovery

1. Lynette Clemetson, with Evan Helper, "Caught in the Cross-fire," *Newsweek*, Dec. 14, 1998, 38–39.

2. Carolivia Herron, *Nappy Hair* (New York: Knopf, 1997).

3. Clemetson, "Caught in the Cross-fire," 38–39.

4. Liz Leyden, "Story Hour Didn't Have a Happy Ending: New York Teacher Runs Into a Racial Divide with Black Author's 'Nappy Hair,' " *Washington Post*, Dec. 3, 1998, A3.

5. "New York City Teacher Rejects Racial Insensitivity Charge, Mulls Return to Class," *Boston Globe*, Nov. 26, 1998, A21.

6. Joanne Wasserman, "Teacher's Painful Test: 'Nappy Hair' Controversy Still Hurts—So Does Leaving," *New York Daily News*, Dec. 5, 1998, 23.

7. John Marzulli and Joanne Wasserman, with Nancie L. Katz, "Teacher Won't Press Charges in Book Flap," *New York Daily News,* Dec. 3, 1998, 31.

8. "Score One for the Mob," *New York Daily News,* Dec. 2, 1998, 48.

9. Lynette Holloway, "School Officials Support Teacher on Book That Parents Call Racially Insensitive," *New York Times,* Nov. 25, 1998, B10.

10. Ibid.

11. Craig Landrum, "A Hairy Situation," letter to the editor, *Newsweek,* Jan. 18, 1999, 18.

12. Clemetson, "Caught in the Cross-fire," 38–39.

13. Editorial, *Omaha World-Herald,* Dec. 17, 1998.

14. Melinda K. Sutton, "A Hairy Situation," letter to the editor, *Newsweek,* Jan. 18, 1999, 18.

15. Quoted in Holloway, "School Officials Support Teacher," B10.

16. Jill Nelson, "Stumbling upon a Race Secret," *New York Times,* Nov. 28, 1998, A15.

17. Ibid.

18. Quoted in Nanette Asimov, "Fighting Words," *San Francisco Chronicle,* Dec. 9, 1998, A21.

19. Lynette Holloway, "Unswayed by Debate on Children's Book," *New York Times,* Dec. 10, 1998, B3.

20. Ibid.

21. John Leo, "Good Hair, Bad Cake," *U.S. News and World Report,* Dec. 14, 1998, 16.

22. Jeff Jacoby, "Where Racism Really Is," *New Orleans Times-Picayune,* Dec. 28, 1998, B5.

23. Tanika White, "Author Helps Build Bridges," *Kansas City Star,* April 29, 1999, B1; Larry Muhammad, "A Love Note to Kids with Kinks," *Louisville Courier-Journal,* April 4, 2000, 1C. By April 2000, Muhammad writes, it had sold over 100,000 copies.

24. "Author Defends 'Nappy Hair,'" *Boston Globe,* Dec. 10, 1998, A32.

25. Larry Muhammad, "Love Note," 1C.

26. Herron, *Nappy Hair.*

27. Muhammed, "Love Note," 1C.

28. Herron, *Nappy Hair.*

29. Muhammad, "Love Note," 1C.

30. A more insightful view on these matters can be found in Marguerite A. Wright, *I'm Chocolate, You're Vanilla: Raising Healthy Black and Biracial Children in a Race-Conscious World: A Guide for Parents and Teachers* (San Francisco: Jossey-Bass, 1998), a work that contradicts much that is assumed about black children and self-esteem and is dedicated to helping parents raise happy, well-adjusted children.

31. Ginger McFarland, "Natural Way to Hair Happiness," *Atlanta Journal and Constitution*, May 21, 2000, 8M.

32. Lisa Meyer, "'Nappy Hair' Still Touchy Class Subject," *Los Angeles Times*, March 25, 1999, A5.

33. See Diane Ravitch, *Left Back: A Century of Failed School Reforms* (New York: Simon and Schuster, 2000); and James Davison Hunter, *The Death of Character: Moral Education in a Age without Good or Evil* (New York: BasicBooks, 2000), for excellent analyses of the problems with recent trends in education. Barbara Thrash Murphy, *Black Authors and Illustrators of Books for Children and Young Adults* (New York: Garland, 1999.)

34. Rebecca L. Thomas, *Connecting Cultures: A Guide to Multicultural Literature for Children* (New Providence, N.J.: R. R. Bowker, 1996).

35. Sheila Hamanaka, *All the Colors of the Earth* (New York: Morrow Junior Books, 1994).

36. Marguerite W. Davol, *Black, White, Just Right!*, with illustrations by Irene Trivas, (Morton Grove, Ill.: Albert Whitman, 1993).

37. Mem Fox, *Whoever You Are*, with illustrations by Leslie Staub (San Diego: Harcourt Brace, 1997).

38. Libba Moore Gray, with illustrations by Peter M. Fiore, *Dear Willie Rudd* (New York: Simon and Schuster, 1993).

39. Marybeth Lorbiecki, with illustrations by K. Wendy Popp, *Sister Anne's Hands* (New York: Dial, 1998); Amy Hest, with illustrations by Sheila W. Samton, *Jamaica Louise James* (Cambridge: Candlewick Press, 1996); Phil Mendez, with illustrations by Carole Byard, *The Black Snowman* (New York: Scholastic, 1989).

40. Jerdine Nolen, with illustrations by Colin Bootman, *In My Momma's Kitchen* (New York: Lothrop, Lee, and Shepard Books, 1999); Elizabeth Fitzgerald Howard, with illustrations by Floyd Cooper, *Chita's Christmas Tree* (New York: Simon and Schuster, 1989); and Elizabeth Fitzgerald Howard, with illustrations by Gail Gordon Carter, *Mac and Marie and the Train Toss Surprise* (New York: Four Winds Press, 1993).

41. Alice Faye Duncan, with illustrations by Catherine Stock, *Miss Viola and Uncle Ed Lee* (New York: Simon and Schuster, 1999).

42. Don Freeman, *A Pocket for Corduroy* (New York: Viking, 1978).

43. Christine E. Sleeter, *Multicultural Education as Social Activism* (Albany: State University of New York Press, 1996), 60.

44. Sandra Stotsky, *Losing Our Language: How Multicultural Classroom Instruction Is Undermining Our Children's Ability to Read, Write, and Reason* (New York: Free Press, 1999), xi.

45. Ibid.
46. Ibid., 5, 12–13, 41.
47. White, "Author Helps Build Bridges," B1.
48. Stotsky, *Losing Our Language,* 163–65.
49. Frances FitzGerald quoted in Stotsky, *Losing Our Language,* 125.
50. Stotsky, *Losing Our Language,* 125, 133–36.
51. Orlando Patterson, *The Ordeal of Integration: Progress and Resentment in America's "Racial" Crisis* (Washington, D.C.: Civitas, 1997), 56-59.
52. John H. McWhorter, *Losing the Race: Self-sabotage in Black America* (New York: Free Press, 2000).
53. Bell hooks, *Outlaw Culture: Resisting Representations* (New York: Routledge, 1994), 1-7.
54. Paulo Freire, *Pedagogy of the Oppressed* (1970; reprint, New York: Continuum, 1999), 17.
55. Ibid., 22–31.
56. Ibid., 26–28.
57. Ibid., 29–31.
58. Ibid., 31–32.
59. Ibid., 36–37, 52, 53, 61–62.
60. Hooks, *Outlaw Culture,* 5.
61. Bell hooks, *Teaching to Transgress: Education as the Practice of Freedom* (New York: Routledge, 1994), 10–16.
62. Ibid., 10–16, 21.
63. Ibid., 15–18.
64. Ibid., 16–21.
65. Bell hooks, *Sisters of the Yam: Black Women and Self-recovery* (Boston: South End Press, 1993).
66. Bell hooks, *Happy to Be Nappy,* with illustrations by Chris Raschka (New York: Hyperion, 1999).

EPILOGUE

1. Jim Sleeper has astutely analyzed these trends particularly as they affect politics, law, and the media, in *Liberal Racism* (New York: Viking, 1997).
2. This refers to Brad Blanton, *Radical Honesty: How to Transform Your Life by Telling the Truth* (Stanley, Va.: Sparrowhawk Publications, 1994), a book completely in

tune with the therapeutic sensibility despite its claims to present a contrarian perspective.

3. See Marguerite A. Wright, *I'm Chocolate, You're Vanilla: Raising Healthy Blacks and Biracial Children in a Race-Conscious World: A Guide for Parents and Teachers* (San Francisco: Jossey-Bass, 1998), for a much more sound and helpful discussion of the question of self-esteem and racial identity that offers a view strikingly different from those of theorists presented in chapter 4; Orlando Patterson, *The Ordeal of Integration: Progress and Resentment in America's "Racial" Crisis* (Washington, D.C.: Civitas, 1997), 193–98; Stephan Thernstrom and Abigail Thernstrom, *America in Black and White: One Nation, Indivisible* (New York: Simon & Schuster, 1997), 498–501; and the multi-part series, "How Race Is Lived in America," *New York Times,* June–July 2000.